Taste *of* Home®

ALL NEW
Church Supper
RECIPES

W9-BMP-467

TASTE OF HOME BOOKS • RDA ENTHUSIAST BRANDS, LLC • MILWAUKEE, WI

Taste of Home

Reader's digest

A TASTE OF HOME/READER'S DIGEST BOOK
©2015 RDA Enthusiast Brands, LLC, 1610 N. 2nd St., Suite 102, Milwaukee WI 53212-3906. All rights reserved.
Taste of Home and Reader's Digest are registered trademarks of The Reader's Digest Association, Inc.

EDITORIAL

Editor-in-Chief: Catherine Cassidy
Creative Director: Howard Greenberg
Editorial Operations Director: Kerri Balliet

Managing Editor, Print & Digital Books: Mark Hagen
Associate Creative Director: Edwin Robles Jr.

Editors: Jan Briggs, Michelle Rozumalski, Amy Glander
Art Directors: Raeann Sundholm, Maggie Conners
Layout Designer: Nancy Novak
Editorial Production Manager: Dena Ahlers
Copy Chief: Deb Warlaumont Mulvey
Copy Editors: Joanne Weintraub, Dulcie Shoener, Kaitlin Stainbrook
Content Operations Manager: Colleen King
Content Operations Assistant: Shannon Stroud
Executive Assistant: Marie Brannon

Chief Food Editor: Karen Berner
Food Editors: James Schend; Peggy Woodward, RD
Recipe Editors: Mary King; Jenni Sharp, RD; Irene Yeh

Test Kitchen & Food Styling Manager: Sarah Thompson
Test Cooks: Nicholas Iverson (lead), Matthew Hass, Lauren Knoelke
Food Stylists: Kathryn Conrad (senior), Leah Rekau, Shannon Roum
Prep Cooks: Megumi Garcia, Melissa Hansen, Bethany Van Jacobson, Sara Wirtz

Photography Director: Stephanie Marchese
Photographers: Dan Roberts, Jim Wieland
Photographer/Set Stylist: Grace Natoli Sheldon
Set Stylists: Stacey Genaw, Melissa Haberman, Dee Dee Jacq
Photo Studio Assistant: Ester Robards

Editorial Business Manager: Kristy Martin
Editorial Business Associate: Samantha Lea Stoeger

BUSINESS

Vice President, Chief Sales Officer: Mark S. Josephson
General Manager, Taste of Home Cooking School: Erin Puariea

THE READER'S DIGEST ASSOCIATION, INC.

President and Chief Executive Officer: Bonnie Kintzer
Chief Financial Officer: Colette Chestnut
Vice President, Chief Operating Officer, North America: Howard Halligan
Vice President, Enthusiast Brands, Books & Retail: Harold Clarke
Chief Marketing Officer: Leslie Dukker Doty
Vice President, North American Human Resources: Phyllis E. Gebhardt, SPHR
Vice President, Brand Marketing: Beth Gorry
Vice President, Global Communications: Susan Russ
Vice President, Chief Technology Officer: Aneel Tejwaney
Vice President, Consumer Marketing Planning: Jim Woods

International Standard Book Number: 978-1-61765-412-1
Library of Congress Control Number: 2014957265

Cover Photographer: Jim Wieland
Set Stylist: Stephanie Marchese
Food Stylist: Kathryn Conrad

Pictured on front cover: Italian Fresh Vegetable Salad, page 68; Bacon Macaroni & Cheese, page 61; Connie's Tortellini Salad, page 63; Herb & Sun-Dried Tomato Muffins, page 66; and Buffalo Chicken Lasagna, page 173.

Pictured on page 1: Chicken Riggies, page 107.

Pictured on back cover: White and Blue Cheesecake, page 208; Picnic Chicken with Yogurt Dip, page 111; and Squash Medley, page 61.

Printed in China.
7 9 10 8

Scripture quotations are from New Revised Standard Version Bible, ©1989, Division of Christian Education of the National Council of the Churches of Christ in the United States of America. Used by permission. All rights reserved.

LIKE US
facebook.com/tasteofhome

TWEET US
@tasteofhome

FOLLOW US
pinterest.com/taste_of_home

SHOP WITH US
shoptasteofhome.com

SHARE A RECIPE
tasteofhome.com/submit

CONTENTS

ROSEMARY ROASTED LAMB, 207

LEMON CHICKEN & RICE SOUP, 151

PEPPER SAUSAGE PIZZA, 125

OVERNIGHT BRUNCH CASSEROLE, 160

MARINATED CHEESE, 37

Dig in to the Goodness of **359** Potluck **Favorites!**

CHURCH SUPPER CLAM CHOWDER, 239

MAC 'N' CHEESE FOR A BUNCH, 238

Not sure what to take to the potluck? Let *Church Supper Recipes* answer your prayers today!

With the all-new **Taste of Home Church Supper Recipes,** the perfect covered-dish contribution is always at your fingertips! Whether attending an after-service social, church picnic, school potluck or charity bake sale, you're sure to impress with any of the 359 crowd-pleasing delights found here.

> 66 **Day by day, as they spent much time together in the temple, they broke bread at home and ate their food with glad and generous hearts, praising God and having the goodwill of the people.** 99
>
> **ACTS 2:46–47**

TEXAS TACO PLATTER, 43

You'll find ideal dishes for family reunions, classroom treats, block parties and other events that call for large-yield recipes. In fact, nearly all of the specialties in this brand-new collection serve a dozen hungry guests—if not several more!

From slow-cooked classics and hearty casseroles to gigantic sub sandwiches and enormous salads, this colorful collection includes everything you need for a successful event. You'll even find appetizers and side dishes to round out group-dinner menus, in addition to more than 40 sweet treats that are sure to have folks asking for your secret!

Two bonus chapters make contributing to a church supper even easier. See the section "Seasonal Fare" for adorable baked goods as well as savory staples that celebrate any holiday or season of the year. Similarly, the chapter "Feeding a Crowd" offers stick-to-your-ribs recipes that feed 20 or more!

Best of all, the finger-licking dishes found here come from real home cooks. These are the tried-and-true recipes they prepare for potlucks, and now they're sharing them with you. After all, some of the best cooks sit next to you every Sunday, so dig in, and enjoy the goodness of **Church Supper Recipes!**

You'll also find **two At-a-Glance icons** to help you make the most of your time in the kitchen:

FAST FIX ▶

These recipes come together in just 30 minutes or less.

FREEZE IT ▶

Store these convenient dishes in the freezer for last-minute needs.

MAPLE STICKY BUNS, 23

ORANGE FRITTERS, PAGE 27

HAM & GRUYERE
MINI QUICHES, PAGE 21

BUTTERMILK
PANCAKES, PAGE 22

BREAKFAST &
BRUNCH

BRIE & SAUSAGE
BRUNCH BAKE, PAGE 8

❝ Jesus said to them, 'Come and have breakfast.' Now none of the disciples dared to ask him, 'Who are you?' because they knew it was the Lord. ❞

JOHN 21:12

FAST FIX

Fruit Salad with Vanilla

Peach pie filling is the secret ingredient in this crowd-pleasing salad. Make it throughout the year using whatever fruits are in season.
—**NANCY DODSON** SPRINGFIELD, IL

START TO FINISH: 20 MIN.
MAKES: 10 SERVINGS

- 1 **pound fresh strawberries, quartered**
- 1½ **cups seedless red and/or green grapes, halved**
- 2 **medium bananas, sliced**
- 2 **kiwifruit, peeled, sliced and quartered**
- 1 **cup cubed fresh pineapple**
- 1 **can (21 ounces) peach pie filling**
- 3 **teaspoons vanilla extract**

In a large bowl, mix strawberries, grapes, bananas, kiwi and pineapple. Fold in pie filling and vanilla. Chill until serving.

Brie & Sausage Brunch Bake

I've made this for holidays, as well as for a weekend at a friend's cabin, and I always get requests for the recipe. It's make-ahead convenient, reheats well and even tastes great the next day.
—**BECKY HICKS** FOREST LAKE, MN

PREP: 30 MIN. + CHILLING
BAKE: 50 MIN. + STANDING
MAKES: 12 SERVINGS

- 1 **pound bulk Italian sausage**
- 1 **small onion, chopped**
- 8 **cups cubed day-old sourdough bread**
- ½ **cup chopped roasted sweet red peppers**
- ½ **pound Brie cheese, rind removed, cubed**
- ⅔ **cup grated Parmesan cheese**
- 2 **tablespoons minced fresh basil or 2 teaspoons dried basil**
- 8 **eggs**
- 2 **cups heavy whipping cream**
- 1 **tablespoon Dijon mustard**
- 1 **teaspoon pepper**
- ½ **teaspoon salt**
- ¾ **cup shredded part-skim mozzarella cheese**
- 3 **green onions, sliced**

1. In a large skillet, cook sausage and onion over medium heat until meat is no longer pink; drain.

2. Place bread cubes in a greased 13x9-in. baking dish. Layer with sausage mixture, red peppers, Brie and Parmesan cheeses and basil. In a large bowl, whisk the eggs, cream, mustard, pepper and salt; pour over top. Cover and refrigerate overnight.

3. Remove from the refrigerator 30 minutes before baking. Preheat oven to 350°. Bake, uncovered, 45-50 minutes or until a knife inserted near the center comes out clean.

4. Sprinkle with mozzarella cheese. Bake 4-6 minutes or until cheese is melted. Let stand 10 minutes before cutting. Sprinkle with green onions.

BRIE & SAUSAGE BRUNCH BAKE

CLASSIC FRUIT KOLACHES

of raspberry and/or apricot filling into each indentation. Bake 15-20 minutes or until golden brown. Remove from pans to wire racks to cool.

4. Combine the confectioners' sugar, butter, vanilla, salt and enough milk to achieve desired consistency. Drizzle over rolls.

NOTE *This recipe was tested with Solo brand cake and pastry filling. Look for it in the baking aisle.*

Overnight Yeast Waffles

Starting the day with an appealing, hearty breakfast is certainly a step in the right direction when you're trying to follow a healthy eating plan. I even freeze these wonderful waffles for a quick breakfast on busy mornings.

—MARY BALCOMB FLORENCE, OR

PREP: 15 MIN. + CHILLING
COOK: 5 MIN./BATCH
MAKES: 10 SERVINGS

- 1 **package (¼ ounce) active dry yeast**
- ½ **cup warm water (110° to 115°)**
- 1 **teaspoon sugar**
- 2 **cups warm milk (110° to 115°)**
- ½ **cup butter, melted**
- 2 **eggs, lightly beaten**
- 2 **cups all-purpose flour**
- 1 **teaspoon salt**

1. In a large bowl, dissolve yeast in warm water. Add sugar; let stand 5 minutes. Add the milk, butter and eggs; mix well. Combine flour and salt; stir into milk mixture. Cover and refrigerate overnight.

2. Stir batter. Bake waffles in a preheated waffle iron according to manufacturer's directions until golden brown.

Classic Fruit Kolaches

We love baking these melt-in-your-mouth goodies. For extra fun, use Christmas cookie cutters instead of a biscuit cutter.

—GLEN & SUE ELLEN BORKHOLDER STURGIS, MI

PREP: 35 MIN. + RISING
BAKE: 15 MIN./BATCH
MAKES: 2½ DOZEN

- 6 **to 7 cups all-purpose flour**
- ¼ **cup sugar**
- 2 **packages (¼ ounce each) active dry yeast**
- 2 **teaspoons salt**
- 2 **cups 2% milk**
- ½ **cup butter, cubed**
- ½ **cup water**
- 6 **egg yolks**
- ¼ **cup butter, melted**
- 1 **can (12 ounces) raspberry and/or apricot cake and pastry filling**

ICING

- 3 **cups confectioners' sugar**
- ¼ **cup butter, softened**
- 2 **teaspoons vanilla extract**
- ½ **teaspoon salt**
- 4 **to 6 tablespoons 2% milk**

1. In a large bowl, mix 3 cups flour, sugar, yeast and salt. In a large saucepan, heat milk, cubed butter and water to 120°-130°. Add to dry ingredients; beat just until moistened. Add egg yolks; beat until smooth. Stir in enough remaining flour to form a soft dough (dough will be sticky). Do not knead. Cover and let rise until doubled, about 45 minutes.

2. Turn dough onto a floured surface; roll to ½-in. thickness. Cut with a floured 2½-in. biscuit cutter. Place 2 in. apart on lightly greased baking sheets. Brush with melted butter. Cover and let rise in a warm place until doubled, about 30 minutes.

3. Preheat oven to 350°. Using the back of a spoon, make an indentation in the center of each roll. Spoon a heaping teaspoonful

Mustard Ham Strata

I had this at a bed-and-breakfast years ago. They were kind enough to give me the recipe and I've made it many times since.
—**DOLORES ZORNOW** POYNETTE, WI

PREP: 15 MIN. + CHILLING • **BAKE:** 45 MIN.
MAKES: 12 SERVINGS

- 12 slices day-old bread, crusts removed and cubed
- 1½ cups cubed fully cooked ham
- 1 cup chopped green pepper
- ¾ cup shredded cheddar cheese
- ¾ cup shredded Monterey Jack cheese
- ⅓ cup chopped onion
- 7 eggs
- 3 cups whole milk
- 3 teaspoons ground mustard
- 1 teaspoon salt

1. In a 13x9-in. baking dish coated with cooking spray, layer bread cubes, ham, green pepper, cheeses and onion. In a large bowl, combine eggs, milk, mustard and salt. Pour over the top. Cover and refrigerate overnight.

2. Remove from the refrigerator 30 minutes before baking. Preheat oven to 325°.

3. Bake, uncovered, 45-50 minutes or until a knife inserted near the center comes out clean. Let stand 5 minutes before cutting.

Raspberry-Cream Cheese Ladder Loaves

My friend Debbie created this delicious breakfast item. You also can sprinkle the bread with granulated sugar before baking if desired.
—**CHAR OUELLETTE** COLTON, OR

PREP: 45 MIN. + RISING • **BAKE:** 15 MIN. + COOLING
MAKES: 2 LOAVES (8 SLICES EACH)

- 3¾ to 4¼ cups all-purpose flour
- ¼ cup sugar
- 1 package (¼ ounce) quick-rise yeast
- 1¼ teaspoons salt
- 1 teaspoon baking powder
- ½ cup buttermilk
- ½ cup sour cream
- ¼ cup butter, cubed
- ¼ cup water
- 1 egg
- ½ teaspoon almond extract

FILLING

- 1 package (8 ounces) cream cheese, softened
- ¼ cup sugar
- 3 tablespoons all-purpose flour
- 1 egg yolk
- ⅓ cup seedless raspberry jam

1. In a large bowl, combine 2 cups flour, sugar, yeast, salt and baking powder. In a small saucepan, heat buttermilk, sour cream, butter and water to 120°-130°; add to dry ingredients. Beat on medium speed 2 minutes. Add egg, extract and ½ cup flour; beat 2 minutes longer. Stir in enough remaining flour to form a soft dough.

2. Turn dough onto a floured surface; knead until smooth and elastic, about 6-8 minutes. Cover and let rest 10 minutes.

3. Meanwhile, in a small bowl, beat the cream cheese, sugar, flour and egg yolk until smooth; set aside.

4. Divide dough in half. Roll each piece into a 12x10-in. rectangle; place on greased baking sheets. Spread cheese mixture down the center of each rectangle. Stir jam; spoon over cheese mixture.

5. On each long side, cut ¾-in.-wide strips about 2½ in. into center. Starting at one end, fold alternating strips at an angle across filling; pinch ends to seal. Cover and let rise until doubled, about 1 hour.

6. Preheat oven to 350°. Bake 15-19 minutes or until golden brown. Cool on wire racks. Store leftovers in the refrigerator.

**RASPBERRY-CREAM
CHEESE LADDER LOAVES**

ISLAND BREEZES
COFFEE CAKE

Island Breezes Coffee Cake

Invite sunshine to brunch with a delightful make-ahead bread. You won't believe how simple it is.

—DEBRA GOFORTH NEWPORT, TN

PREP: 20 MIN. + CHILLING • **BAKE:** 35 MIN. + COOLING
MAKES: 12 SERVINGS

- ⅔ cup packed brown sugar
- ½ cup flaked coconut, toasted
- 1 package (3.4 ounces) cook-and-serve coconut cream pudding mix
- 20 frozen bread dough dinner rolls
- 1 can (20 ounces) pineapple tidbits, drained
- 1 jar (3 ounces) macadamia nuts, coarsely chopped
- ½ cup butter, cubed

1. In a small bowl, mix brown sugar, coconut and pudding mix. Place 10 rolls in a greased 10-in. fluted tube pan; layer with half of the sugar mixture, 1 cup pineapple tidbits, ⅓ cup macadamia nuts and ¼ cup butter. Repeat layers. Cover with plastic wrap and refrigerate overnight.

2. Remove pan from refrigerator about 1¾ hours before serving; let rise in a warm place until dough reaches top of pan, about 1 hour.

3. Preheat oven to 350°. Remove plastic wrap. Bake coffee cake 35-40 minutes or until golden brown. (Cover loosely with foil if top browns too quickly.) Cool 10 minutes before inverting coffee cake onto a serving plate; serve warm.

NOTE *To toast coconut, spread in a 15x10x1-in. baking pan. Bake at 350° for 5-10 minutes or until golden brown, stirring frequently.*

Colorful Brunch Frittata

A friend called and asked me for a special recipe that could be served at his daughter's wedding brunch. I created this frittata for the occasion. It's loaded with colorful veggies and looks beautiful on a buffet.
—KRISTIN ARNETT ELKHORN, WI

PREP: 15 MIN. • **BAKE:** 55 MIN. + STANDING
MAKES: 12-15 SERVINGS

- 1 pound fresh asparagus, trimmed and cut into 1-inch pieces
- ½ pound sliced fresh mushrooms
- 1 medium sweet red pepper, diced
- 1 medium sweet yellow pepper, diced
- 1 small onion, chopped
- 3 green onions, chopped
- 3 tablespoons olive oil
- 2 garlic cloves, minced
- 3 plum tomatoes, seeded and chopped
- 14 eggs, lightly beaten
- 2 cups half-and-half cream
- 2 cups (8 ounces) shredded Colby-Monterey Jack cheese
- 3 tablespoons minced fresh parsley
- 3 tablespoons minced fresh basil
- ½ teaspoon salt
- ¼ teaspoon pepper
- ½ cup shredded Parmesan cheese

1. Preheat oven to 350°. In a large skillet, saute the asparagus, mushrooms, peppers and onions in oil until tender. Add garlic; cook 1 minute longer. Add tomatoes; set aside.

2. In a large bowl, whisk eggs, cream, Colby-Monterey Jack cheese, parsley, basil, salt and pepper; stir into vegetable mixture.

3. Pour into a greased 13x9-in. baking dish. Bake, uncovered, 45 minutes.

4. Sprinkle with Parmesan cheese. Bake 10-15 minutes longer or until a knife inserted near the center comes out clean. Let stand 10 minutes before cutting.

TOP TIP

Egg Dates

According to the American Egg Board, eggs can be used up to five weeks after the date printed on the carton. The date on the carton is actually the last day the eggs can be sold.

Egg Scramble

Perfect for a special-occasion breakfasts, this easy egg scramble is warm and hearty, with potatoes, ham, cheese and sweet red and green peppers.
—VICKI HOLLOWAY JOELTON, TN

PREP: 15 MIN. • **COOK:** 20 MIN. • **MAKES:** 10 SERVINGS

- 1½ cups diced peeled potatoes
- ½ cup chopped sweet red pepper
- ½ cup chopped green pepper
- ½ cup chopped onion
- 2 teaspoons canola oil, divided
- 2 cups cubed fully cooked ham
- 16 eggs
- ⅔ cup sour cream
- ½ cup 2% milk
- 1 teaspoon onion salt
- ½ teaspoon garlic salt
- ¼ teaspoon pepper
- 2 cups (8 ounces) shredded cheddar cheese, divided

1. Place potatoes in a small saucepan and cover with water. Bring to a boil. Reduce heat; cover and simmer 10-15 minutes or until tender. Drain.

2. In a large skillet, saute half of the peppers and onion in 1 teaspoon oil until tender. Add half of the ham and potatoes; saute 2-3 minutes longer.

3. Meanwhile, in a blender, combine the eggs, sour cream, milk, onion salt, garlic salt and pepper. Cover and process until smooth.

4. Pour half over vegetable mixture; cook and stir over medium heat until eggs are completely set. Sprinkle with 1 cup cheese. Repeat with remaining ingredients.

COLORFUL BRUNCH FRITTATA

FREEZE IT

Breakfast Sausage Patties

Buttermilk is the secret ingredient that keeps these pork patties moist, while a blend of seasonings create a wonderful taste.

—**HARVEY KEENEY** MANDAN, ND

PREP: 30 MIN. • **COOK:** 10 MIN./BATCH
MAKES: 20 PATTIES

- ¾ cup buttermilk
- 2¼ teaspoons kosher salt
- 1½ teaspoons rubbed sage
- 1½ teaspoons brown sugar
- 1½ teaspoons pepper
- ¾ teaspoon dried marjoram
- ¾ teaspoon dried savory
- ¾ teaspoon cayenne pepper
- ¼ teaspoon ground nutmeg
- 2½ pounds ground pork

1. In a large bowl, combine the buttermilk and seasonings. Add pork; mix lightly but thoroughly. Shape into twenty 3-in. patties.
2. In a large skillet coated with cooking spray, cook patties in batches over medium heat 5-6 minutes on each side or until a thermometer reads 160°. Remove to paper towels to drain.
FREEZE OPTION *Wrap each cooked, cooled patty in plastic wrap; transfer to a resealable plastic freezer bag and freeze up to 3 months. To use, preheat oven to 350°. Unwrap patties and place on a baking sheet coated with cooking spray. Bake 15 minutes on each side or until heated through.*

Hash Brown & Chicken Brunch Casserole

My husband and I love to have a hot breakfast, but find it difficult with two kids. This dish is excellent to prepare the night before and bake the next day for your family.

—**JENNIFER BERRY** LEXINGTON, OH

PREP: 20 MIN. + CHILLING
BAKE: 1¼ HOURS
MAKES: 12 SERVINGS

- 15 eggs, beaten
- 1 package (28 ounces) frozen O'Brien potatoes
- 1 rotisserie chicken, skin removed, shredded
- 1½ cups 2% milk
- 1 can (10 ounces) diced tomatoes and green chilies, undrained
- 2 cups (8 ounces) shredded cheddar cheese, divided
- 5 green onions, chopped
- 3 tablespoons minced fresh cilantro
- 1 teaspoon ground cumin
- 1½ teaspoons salt
- ½ teaspoon pepper

1. In a very large bowl, combine eggs, potatoes, chicken, milk, tomatoes, 1 cup cheese, green onions, cilantro and seasonings until blended. Transfer to a greased 13x9-in. baking dish; sprinkle with remaining cheese. Refrigerate, covered, several hours or overnight.
2. Preheat oven to 350°. Remove the casserole from refrigerator while the oven heats. Bake, uncovered, 1¼ to 1½ hours or until golden brown and a knife inserted near the center comes out clean. Let stand 5-10 minutes before serving.

HASH BROWN & CHICKEN BRUNCH CASSEROLE

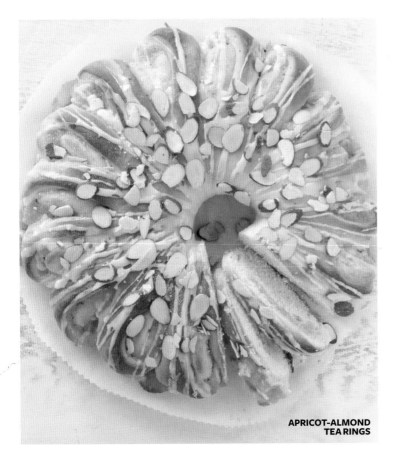

**APRICOT-ALMOND
TEA RINGS**

Apricot-Almond Tea Rings

Apricots and almonds find the perfect pairing in this luscious iced ring. It's a great breakfast treat to serve at coffee date with friends.

—ANN HILLMEYER SANDIA PARK, NM

PREP: 45 MIN. + RISING
BAKE: 20 MIN. + COOLING
MAKES: 2 RINGS (8 SLICES EACH)

- 2 **packages (¼ ounce each)
  active dry yeast**
- ¼ **cup warm water (110° to 115°)**
- 1¼ **cups warm 2% milk
  (110° to 115°)**
- ½ **cup butter, softened**
- ⅓ **cup sugar**
- ½ **teaspoon salt**
- ½ **cup mashed potato flakes**
- 2 **eggs**
- 3½ **to 4 cups all-purpose flour**

FILLING
- 1½ **cups apricot preserves**
- ⅔ **cup sugar**
- 5 **ounces almond paste**
- ⅓ **cup butter, softened**

ICING
- 1⅓ **cups confectioners' sugar**
- ½ **teaspoon vanilla extract**
- 2 **to 3 tablespoons 2% milk**
- ⅓ **cup sliced almonds, toasted**

1. In a large bowl, dissolve yeast in warm water. In another bowl, mix milk, butter, sugar, salt, potato flakes and eggs. Let stand 1 minute. Add milk mixture and 3 cups flour to yeast mixture; beat until smooth. Add enough of the remaining flour to form a soft dough.

2. Turn onto a floured surface; knead until smooth and elastic, about 6-8 minutes. Place in a greased bowl, turning once to grease the top. Cover and let rise in a warm place until doubled, about 1 hour.

3. Place the preserves, sugar, almond paste and butter in a food processor; cover and process until blended. Punch the dough down. Divide in half. On a lightly floured surface, roll each portion into 14x7-in. rectangle. Spread filling evenly to within ½ in. of edges. Roll up jelly-roll style, starting with a long side; pinch the seams to seal.

4. Place rolls, seam side down, on two parchment paper-lined baking sheets. Pinch ends together to form two rings. With scissors, cut from outside edge to two-thirds of the way toward center of rings at 1-in. intervals. Separate strips slightly; twist to allow filling to show. Let rise until doubled about 35-40 minutes.

5. Preheat oven to 375°. Bake for 18-22 minutes or until lightly browned. Remove from pans to wire racks to cool. Combine the confectioners' sugar, vanilla and enough milk to achieve a drizzling consistency. Drizzle over warm tea rings and sprinkle with almonds.

TOP TIP

Storing Yeast

Unopened packages of dry yeast should be stored in a cool, dark place and used by the "best if used by" date on the package. Open packages or bulk dry yeast should be stored in an airtight container in the refrigerator for about 6 weeks or frozen up to 6 months.

COLORFUL BACON & EGG BAKE

1. In a large skillet, cook bacon over medium heat until crisp. Using a slotted spoon, remove to paper towels; drain, reserving 1 tablespoon drippings. In same skillet, saute sweet peppers in drippings until tender; transfer to a large bowl. Stir in bacon, bread and cheese.

2. In another large bowl, combine eggs, milk, chilies, chili powder and cumin. Pour over the bread mixture; gently stir to combine. Transfer to a greased 13x9-in. baking dish. Cover and refrigerate overnight.

3. Preheat oven to 350°. Remove the casserole from refrigerator while the oven heats. Bake, uncovered, 50-55 minutes or until a knife inserted near the center comes out clean. Let stand 5 minutes before serving. If desired, serve with salsa and sour cream.

FREEZE OPTION *After assembling the unbaked casserole, cover and freeze up to 3 months. To use, completely thaw in the refrigerator overnight. Remove from the refrigerator 30 minutes before baking. Preheat oven to 350°. Bake, uncovered, 50-60 minutes or until a knife inserted near the center comes out clean. Let stand 5 minutes before serving. Serve as directed.*

FREEZE IT | **FAST FIX**

Whole Wheat Pancakes

These light, fluffy pancakes seem like a treat. Whole wheat flour and toasted wheat germ make them so filling.
—**LINE WALTER** WAYNE, PA

START TO FINISH: 25 MIN. • **MAKES:** 20 PANCAKES

- 2 cups whole wheat flour
- ½ cup toasted wheat germ
- 1 teaspoon baking soda
- ½ teaspoon salt
- 2 eggs, lightly beaten
- 3 cups buttermilk
- 1 tablespoon canola oil

1. In a large bowl, combine the flour, wheat germ, baking soda and salt. In another bowl, whisk the eggs, buttermilk and oil. Stir into dry ingredients just until blended.

2. Pour batter by ¼ cupfuls onto a hot griddle coated with cooking spray; turn when bubbles form on top. Cook until the second side is golden brown.

FREEZE OPTION *Freeze cooled pancakes between layers of waxed paper in a resealable plastic freezer bag. To use, place pancakes on an ungreased baking sheet, cover with foil and reheat in a preheated 375° oven 6-10 minutes. Or, place a stack of three pancakes on a microwave-safe plate and microwave on high for 45-90 second or until heated through.*

FREEZE IT

Colorful Bacon & Egg Bake

Whip this tasty breakfast casserole up the night before to make the morning meal a snap. We used peppers, bacon and cheese to lend home-style appeal.
—*TASTE OF HOME* TEST KITCHEN

PREP: 20 MIN. + CHILLING • **BAKE:** 50 MIN. • **MAKES:** 12 SERVINGS

- 1 pound bacon strips, diced
- ½ cup julienned sweet orange pepper
- ½ cup julienned sweet red pepper
- 6 cups cubed day-old bread
- 1½ cups shredded Mexican cheese blend
- 9 eggs, lightly beaten
- 2 cups milk
- 1 can (4 ounces) chopped green chilies
- 1½ teaspoons chili powder
- 1 teaspoon ground cumin
  Salsa and sour cream, optional

Banana Mocha-Chip Muffins

Two of my favorite things—chocolate and coffee—are combined in these moist muffins. The banana is just an added bonus.

—MELISSA WILLIAMS TAYLORVILLE, IL

PREP: 20 MIN. • **BAKE:** 20 MIN. • **MAKES:** 2 DOZEN

- 5 teaspoons instant coffee granules
- 5 teaspoons hot water
- ¾ cup butter, softened
- 1¼ cups sugar
- 1 egg
- 1⅓ cups mashed ripe bananas
- 1 teaspoon vanilla extract
- 2¼ cups all-purpose flour
- 1½ teaspoons baking powder
- ½ teaspoon baking soda
- ½ teaspoon salt
- 1½ cups semisweet chocolate chips

1. Preheat oven to 350°. In a small bowl, dissolve coffee granules in hot water. In a large bowl, cream butter and sugar until light and fluffy. Add egg; beat well. Beat in bananas, vanilla and coffee mixture. Combine flour, baking powder, baking soda and salt; add to creamed mixture just until moistened. Fold in chocolate chips.

2. Fill paper-lined muffin cups two-thirds full. Bake 18-20 minutes or until a toothpick inserted in muffin comes out clean. Cool 5 minutes before removing from pans to wire racks. Serve warm.

Cherry Syrup

My mom and grandma have been making this fruity syrup to serve with fluffy waffles and pancakes ever since I was a little girl. Now I make it for my sons!

—SANDRA HARRINGTON NIPOMO, CA

START TO FINISH: 30 MIN. • **MAKES:** 3 CUPS

- 1 package (12 ounces) frozen pitted dark sweet cherries, thawed
- 1 cup water
- 2½ cups sugar
- 2 tablespoons butter
- ½ teaspoon almond extract
  Dash ground cinnamon

1. Bring the cherries and water to a boil in a small saucepan. Reduce heat; simmer, uncovered, for 20 minutes.

2. Add the sugar and butter; cook and stir until sugar is dissolved. Remove from heat; stir in extract and cinnamon.

3. Cool leftovers; transfer to airtight containers. Store in the refrigerator up to 2 weeks.

BANANA
MOCHA-CHIP MUFFINS

CHERRY
SYRUP

Lemon-Raspberry Streusel Cake

Buttery almond streusel tops the luscious, raspberry-studded lemon cream in these very special bars.
—**JEANNE HOLT** MENDOTA HEIGHTS, MN

PREP: 25 MIN. • **BAKE:** 35 MIN. + COOLING • **MAKES:** 24 SERVINGS

- ⅓ **cup shortening**
- ⅓ **cup butter, softened**
- 1¼ **cups sugar**
- 3 **eggs**
- ½ **teaspoon almond extract**
- 2¼ **cups all-purpose flour**
- 1¼ **teaspoons baking powder**
- ½ **teaspoon salt**
- 1 **package (8 ounces) cream cheese, softened**
- ½ **cup lemon curd**
- ½ **cup seedless raspberry jam**
- 1 **cup fresh raspberries**

STREUSEL
- ⅔ **cup all-purpose flour**
- ⅓ **cup sugar**
- ⅓ **cup sliced almonds, finely chopped**
- ¼ **cup cold butter**

ICING
- 1 **cup confectioners' sugar**
- 4 **teaspoons lemon juice**

1. Preheat oven to 350°. In a large bowl, cream shortening, butter and sugar until light and fluffy. Beat in eggs and extract. Combine flour, baking powder and salt; gradually add to creamed mixture and mix well. Set aside 1 cup batter.

2. Spread remaining batter into a greased 13x9-in. baking pan. Combine cream cheese and lemon curd; spoon over batter. In a small bowl, beat jam; stir in raspberries. Drop by tablespoonfuls over lemon mixture. Drop reserved batter by tablespoonfuls over top.

3. For streusel, in a small bowl, combine flour, sugar and almonds. Cut in butter until crumbly. Sprinkle over batter.

4. Bake 35-40 minutes or until a toothpick inserted in the center comes out clean. Cool on a wire rack.

5. Combine icing ingredients; drizzle over cake.

FREEZE IT FAST FIX

Sweet Potato Muffins

This is my own recipe, and I make it often. My five grandchildren think the muffins are a delicious treat.
—**CHRISTINE JOHNSON** RICETOWN, KY

START TO FINISH: 25 MIN. • **MAKES:** 2 DOZEN

- 2 **cups self-rising flour**
- 2 **cups sugar**
- 2 **teaspoons ground cinnamon**
- 1 **egg**
- 2 **cups cold mashed sweet potatoes (without added butter or milk)**
- 1 **cup canola oil**

GLAZE
- 1 **cup confectioners' sugar**
- 2 **tablespoons plus 1½ teaspoons 2% milk**
- 1½ **teaspoons butter, melted**
- 1 **teaspoon vanilla extract**
- ½ **teaspoon ground cinnamon**

1. Preheat oven to 375°. In a small bowl, combine flour, sugar and cinnamon. In another bowl, whisk egg, sweet potatoes and oil. Stir into dry ingredients just until moistened.

2. Fill greased muffin cups two-thirds full. Bake 15-18 minutes or until a toothpick inserted in muffin comes out clean. Cool 5 minutes before removing from pans to wire racks.

3. In a small bowl, combine glaze ingredients; drizzle over warm muffins.

FREEZE OPTION *Freeze unglazed cooled muffins in resealable plastic freezer bags. To use, thaw at room temperature or, if desired, microwave each muffin on high 20-30 seconds or until heated through.*

NOTE *As a substitute for each cup of self-rising flour, place 1½ teaspoons baking powder and ½ teaspoon salt in a measuring cup. Add all-purpose flour to measure 1 cup.*

SWEET POTATO MUFFINS

Cream Cheese Cranberry Muffins

Moist and packed with colorful berries, these marvelous muffins are a seasonal specialty. They are light and tasty, and they freeze very well without the drizzle.

—LEONARD KESZLER BISMARCK, ND

PREP: 15 MIN. • **BAKE:** 20 MIN.
MAKES: 2 DOZEN

- 1 **cup butter, softened**
- 1 **package (8 ounces) cream cheese, softened**
- 1½ **cups sugar**
- 4 **eggs**
- 1½ **teaspoons vanilla extract**
- 2 **cups all-purpose flour**
- 1½ **teaspoons baking powder**
- ½ **teaspoon salt**
- 2 **cups fresh or frozen cranberries**
- ½ **cup chopped pecans**

DRIZZLE
- 2 **cups confectioners' sugar**
- 3 **tablespoons 2% milk**

1. Preheat oven to 350°. In a large bowl, cream butter, cream cheese and sugar until light and fluffy. Add the eggs, one at a time, beating well after each addition. Beat in vanilla. Combine flour, baking powder and salt; stir into the creamed mixture just until moistened. Fold in the cranberries and pecans.
2. Fill greased or paper-lined muffin cups three-fourths full. Bake 20-25 minutes or until a toothpick inserted in the muffins comes out clean. Cool 5 minutes before removing from the pans to wire racks.
3. Combine confectioners' sugar and milk; drizzle over muffins.

CREAM CHEESE
CRANBERRY MUFFINS

FREEZE IT
Ham & Gruyere Mini Quiches

By making this in muffin cups, each person gets their own quiche. I have also doubled the recipe and used jumbo muffin cups; I just bake about 10 minutes longer.
—**GENA STOUT** RAVENDEN, AR

PREP: 30 MIN. • **BAKE:** 20 MIN.
MAKES: 10 MINI QUICHES

- 4 **eggs, lightly beaten**
- 1 **cup 2% cottage cheese**
- ¼ **cup 2% milk**
- 2 **tablespoons all-purpose flour**
- ½ **teaspoon baking powder**
- ¼ **teaspoon ground nutmeg**
- ¼ **teaspoon pepper**
- 1½ **cups (6 ounces) shredded Gruyere or Swiss cheese**
- ¾ **cup finely chopped fully cooked ham**
- 3 **tablespoons thinly sliced green onions**

1. Preheat oven to 375°. In a large bowl, combine the first seven ingredients; fold in Gruyere cheese, ham and onions. Fill greased muffin cups three-fourths full.

2. Bake 18-22 minutes or until a knife inserted near the center comes out clean. Cool 5 minutes before removing from pans to wire racks.

FREEZE OPTION *Bake and cool quiches. Transfer quiches to a large resealable plastic freezer bag and freeze up to 3 months. To use, thaw the quiches in the refrigerator overnight. Preheat oven to 350°. Transfer the quiches to a greased baking sheet; bake 10-14 minutes or until heated through.*

Overnight Raisin French Toast

This dish came from a colleague and has become a potluck, brunch and family favorite! My staff used to ask for it every holiday.
—**STEPHANIE WEAVER** SLIGO, PA

PREP: 15 MIN. + CHILLING • **BAKE:** 45 MIN.
MAKES: 12 SERVINGS

- 1 **loaf (1 pound) cinnamon-raisin bread, cubed**
- 1 **package (8 ounces) cream cheese, cubed**
- 8 **eggs, lightly beaten**
- 1½ **cups half-and-half cream**
- ½ **cup sugar**
- ½ **cup maple syrup**
- 2 **tablespoons vanilla extract**
- 1 **tablespoon ground cinnamon**
- ⅛ **teaspoon ground nutmeg**

1. Place half of the bread cubes in a greased 13x9-in. baking dish. Top with the cream cheese and remaining bread.

2. In a large bowl, whisk the remaining ingredients. Pour over the top. Cover and refrigerate overnight.

3. Remove from the refrigerator 30 minutes before baking. Preheat oven to 350°. Cover and bake for 30 minutes. Uncover; bake 15-20 minutes longer or until a knife inserted near the center comes out clean.

HAM & GRUYERE MINI QUICHES

Gingerbread-Spiced Syrup

Here's a wonderful treat you can use in a variety of ways. Stir a tablespoon into coffee, tea or cider. Try drizzling it over pancakes, hot cereal or yogurt. This syrup can even be used as a glaze for chicken or pork chops.
—**DARLENE BRENDEN** SALEM, OR

PREP: 20 MIN. • **COOK:** 30 MIN. + COOLING • **MAKES:** 2 CUPS

- 2 cinnamon sticks (3 inches), broken into pieces
- 16 whole cloves
- 3 tablespoons coarsely chopped fresh gingerroot
- 1 teaspoon whole allspice
- 1 teaspoon whole peppercorns
- 2 cups sugar
- 2 cups water
- 2 tablespoons honey
- 1 teaspoon ground nutmeg

1. Place the first five ingredients on a double thickness of cheesecloth; bring up corners of cloth and tie with string to form a bag.
2. In a large saucepan, combine the sugar, water, honey, nutmeg and spice bag; bring to a boil. Reduce heat; simmer, uncovered, for 30-45 minutes or until syrup reaches desired consistency.
3. Remove from the heat; cool to room temperature. Discard the spice bag; transfer the syrup to an airtight containers. Store in the refrigerator for up to 1 month.

FREEZE IT

Buttermilk Pancakes

You just can't beat a basic buttermilk pancake for a down-home hearty breakfast. Pair it with sausage and fresh fruit for a mouthwatering morning meal.
—**BETTY ABREY** IMPERIAL, SK

PREP: 10 MIN. • **COOK:** 5 MIN./BATCH • **MAKES:** 2½ DOZEN

- 4 cups all-purpose flour
- ¼ cup sugar
- 2 teaspoons baking soda
- 2 teaspoons salt
- 1½ teaspoons baking powder
- 4 eggs
- 4 cups buttermilk

1. In a large bowl, combine the flour, sugar, baking soda, salt and baking powder. In another bowl, whisk the eggs and buttermilk until blended; stir into dry ingredients just until moistened.
2. Pour batter by ¼ cupfuls onto a lightly greased hot griddle; turn when bubbles form on top. Cook until second side is golden brown.
FREEZE OPTION *Freeze cooled pancakes between layers of waxed paper in a resealable plastic freezer bag. To use, preheat oven to 375°. Place pancakes on an ungreased baking sheet, cover with foil and reheat 6-10 minutes. Or, place a stack of three pancakes on a microwave-safe plate and microwave on high 45-90 seconds or until heated through.*

GINGERBREAD-
SPICED SYRUP

BUTTERMILK
PANCAKES

Maple Sticky Buns

My family has a small sugaring operation in our backyard. The rolls makes good use of the maple syrup we make. It's a family tradition to serve these sticky buns on Thanksgiving every year.

—**PRISCILLA ROSSI** EAST BARRE, VERMONT

PREP: 30 MIN. + CHILLING • **BAKE:** 25 MIN. • **MAKES:** 2½ DOZEN

- 2 **packages (¼ ounce each) active dry yeast**
- 2 **cups warm water (110° to 115°)**
- ¼ **cup shortening**
- ½ **cup sugar**
- 1 **egg**
- 2 **teaspoons salt**
- 6 **to 6½ cups all-purpose flour**
- 6 **tablespoons butter, softened**
- ¾ **cup packed brown sugar**
- 1 **tablespoon ground cinnamon**
- ¾ **cup chopped walnuts**
- 1½ **cups maple syrup**
  Additional brown sugar

1. In a large bowl, dissolve yeast in water. Add the shortening, sugar, egg, salt and 5 cups flour. Beat until smooth. Add enough remaining flour to form a soft dough. Cover and refrigerate overnight or up to 24 hours.

2. Punch dough down. Turn onto a floured surface; knead until smooth and elastic, about 6-8 minutes, adding more flour if needed. Divide into thirds. Roll each portion into a 16x10-in. rectangle.

3. On each rectangle, spread 2 tablespoons butter; sprinkle each with ¼ cup brown sugar, 1 teaspoon cinnamon and ¼ cup walnuts. Pour syrup into three greased 9-in. round baking pans. Sprinkle with additional brown sugar.

4. Tightly roll up each rectangle, jelly-roll style, starting with a short side. Slice each roll into 10 pieces; place over syrup. Cover and let rise until doubled, about 30 minutes.

5. Preheat oven to 350°. Bake 25-30 minutes or until golden brown. Cool in pans 5 minutes; invert onto serving plates.

NOTE *11x7-in. baking pans may be substituted for the 9-in. round pans.*

Cherry Coffee Cake

With its pretty layer of cherries and crunchy streusel topping, this coffee cake is great for breakfast. Or you can even serve it for dessert.

—**GAIL BUSS** BEVERLY HILLS, FL

PREP: 25 MIN. • **BAKE:** 35 MIN. + COOLING
MAKES: 12-16 SERVINGS

- 1 package yellow cake mix (regular size), divided
- 1 cup all-purpose flour
- 1 package (¼ ounce) active dry yeast
- ⅔ cup warm water (120° to 130°)
- 2 eggs, lightly beaten
- 1 can (21 ounces) cherry pie filling
- ⅓ cup butter, melted

GLAZE

- 1 cup confectioners' sugar
- 1 tablespoon corn syrup
- 1 to 2 tablespoons water

1. Preheat oven to 350°. In a large bowl, combine 1½ cups cake mix, flour, yeast and water until smooth. Stir in eggs until blended. Transfer to a greased 13x9-in. baking dish. Gently spoon pie filling over top.
2. In a small bowl, mix butter and remaining cake mix; sprinkle over filling.
3. Bake 35-40 minutes or until lightly browned. Cool on a wire rack. In a small bowl, combine confectioners' sugar, corn syrup and enough water to achieve desired consistency. Drizzle over coffee cake.

Eggs Benedict Bake with Bearnaise Sauce

I've made this recipe for my family every Christmas for 10 years—it's a food tradition that my family looks forward to every year. Part of what makes this dish so special is the croissants which make the egg bake extra light and fluffy.

—**SUSAN TRIPLETT**
CITRUS HEIGHTS, CA

PREP: 20 MIN. + CHILLING • **BAKE:** 45 MIN.
MAKES: 12 SERVINGS

- ¾ pound Canadian bacon
- 6 croissants, cut into ½-inch cubes
- 10 eggs
- 2 cups 2% milk
- 3 green onions, chopped
- 1 teaspoon onion powder
- 1 teaspoon ground mustard
- 1 teaspoon dried tarragon
- ½ teaspoon salt
- ½ teaspoon white pepper
- ½ teaspoon paprika
- 1 envelope bearnaise sauce

1. Place half of the Canadian bacon in a greased 13x9-in. baking dish. Layer with croissants and remaining Canadian bacon. In a large bowl, whisk the eggs, milk, green onions, onion powder, mustard, tarragon, salt and pepper until blended; pour over top. Sprinkle with paprika. Refrigerate, covered, several hours or overnight.
2. Preheat oven to 375°. Remove casserole from refrigerator while oven heats. Bake, covered, 30 minutes. Bake, uncovered, 15-20 minutes longer or until a knife inserted near the center comes out clean. Let stand 5-10 minutes before serving.
3. Prepare the sauce according to package directions. Serve with casserole.

EGGS BENEDICT BAKE WITH BEARNAISE SAUCE

EASY BREAKFAST STRATA

Easy Breakfast Strata

We start this breakfast casserole the night before, so it's ready for the oven the next day. Plus, you don't have to deal with the prep and dirty dishes first thing in the morning!

—DEBBIE JOHNSON
CENTERTOWN, MO

PREP: 20 MIN. + CHILLING • **BAKE:** 30 MIN.
MAKES: 12 SERVINGS

- 1 pound bulk pork sausage
- 1 large green pepper, chopped
- 1 medium onion, chopped
- 1 loaf (1 pound) herb or cheese bakery bread, cubed
- 1 cup (4 ounces) shredded cheddar cheese
- 6 eggs
- 2 cups 2% milk
- 1 teaspoon ground mustard

1. In a large skillet, cook the sausage, pepper and onion over medium heat until meat is no longer pink; drain.

2. Place the bread in a greased 13x9-in. baking dish. Top with sausage mixture; sprinkle with cheese. In a large bowl, whisk eggs, milk and mustard. Pour over top. Cover and refrigerate overnight.

3. Remove from the refrigerator 30 minutes before baking. Preheat oven to 350°. Bake the casserole, uncovered, 30-35 minutes or until a knife inserted near the center comes out clean. Let stand for 5 minutes before cutting.

CRUMB-TOPPED
CRANBERRY CAKE

Crumb-Topped Cranberry Cake

Here's a coffee cake that- has something for everyone—
moist yellow cake, cream cheese filling and a cranberry-
coconut topping. Serve it at breakfast, lunch or dinner!
—**DARLENE BRENDEN** SALEM, OR

PREP: 40 MIN. • **BAKE:** 50 MIN. + COOLING • **MAKES:** 12 SERVINGS

- 2 **cups plus 2 tablespoons all-purpose flour**
- ⅔ **cup sugar**
- ½ **teaspoon baking powder**
- ½ **teaspoon baking soda**
- 1 **package (8 ounces) cream cheese, divided**
- 2 **eggs**
- ¾ **cup 2% milk**
- 2 **tablespoons canola oil**
- 1 **teaspoon vanilla extract**
- ½ **cup flaked coconut**
- 1 **cup whole-berry cranberry sauce**

TOPPING

- 6 **tablespoons all-purpose flour**
- 2 **tablespoons sugar**
- 2 **tablespoons cold butter**

1. Preheat oven to 350°. In a large bowl, combine
flour, sugar, baking powder and baking soda; cut in
3 ounces cream cheese until mixture resembles
fine crumbs.

2. In another bowl, whisk 1 egg, milk and oil; stir into
crumb mixture just until moistened. Spread batter into a
greased and floured 9-in. springform pan; set aside.

3. In a small bowl, beat the remaining cream cheese
until fluffy. Beat in the vanilla and remaining egg;
carefully spread over batter. Sprinkle with coconut.
Dollop with cranberry sauce. In a small bowl, combine
flour and sugar; cut in butter until crumbly. Sprinkle
over the top.

4. Bake 50-55 minutes or until golden brown. Cool on
a wire rack 15 minutes. Carefully run a knife around
edge of pan to loosen. Remove sides of pan. Cool
completely. Store in the refrigerator.

ORANGE
FRITTERS

1. In a large bowl, whisk flour, biscuit mix, sugar and baking powder. In another bowl, whisk eggs, orange peel and orange juice until blended. Add to dry ingredients, stirring just until moistened.

2. In an electric skillet or deep fryer, heat oil to 375°. Drop batter by rounded tablespoonfuls, a few at a time, into hot oil. Fry about 1-2 minutes on each side or until golden brown. Drain on paper towels; cool slightly. Dust with confectioners' sugar.

Mashed Potato Doughnuts

As a special treat in winter, my parents would make a double batch of these doughnuts to welcome us six kids home from school. This recipe from my great-aunt has been handed down through the generations.

—**TAMMY EVANS** NEPEAN, ON

PREP: 20 MIN. + CHILLING • **COOK:** 25 MIN.
MAKES: ABOUT 2 DOZEN

- 1 package (¼ ounce) active dry yeast
- 1 cup warm buttermilk (110° to 115°)
- 1½ cups warm mashed potatoes (without added milk and butter)
- 3 eggs
- ⅓ cup butter, melted
- 3 cups sugar, divided
- 4 teaspoons baking powder
- 1½ teaspoons baking soda
- 1 teaspoon salt
- 1 teaspoon ground nutmeg
- 6 cups all-purpose flour
  Oil for deep-fat frying
- ½ teaspoon ground cinnamon

1. In a large bowl, dissolve yeast in warm buttermilk. Add potatoes, eggs and butter. Add 2 cups sugar, baking powder, baking soda, salt, nutmeg and 3 cups flour. Beat until smooth. Stir in enough remaining flour to form a soft dough. Do not knead. Cover and refrigerate 2 hours.

2. Turn onto a floured surface; divide into fourths. Roll each portion to ½-in. thickness. Cut with a floured 3-in. doughnut cutter.

3. In an electric skillet or deep-fat fryer, heat oil to 375°. Fry doughnuts, a few at a time, until golden brown on both sides. Drain on paper towels. Combine remaining sugar and cinnamon; roll doughnuts in cinnamon sugar while warm.

NOTE *Warmed buttermilk will appear curdled.*

Orange Fritters

My daughter made a citrusy version of apple fritters for 4-H demonstrations at our county and state fair. This crowd-size recipe yields 11 dozen but you can easily cut the ingredients in half for a family-size yield.

—**DEBBIE JOHNSON** CENTERTOWN, MO

PREP: 15 MIN. • **COOK:** 5 MIN./BATCH
MAKES: ABOUT 11 DOZEN

- 6 cups all-purpose flour
- 6 cups biscuit/baking mix
- 2 cups sugar
- 2 tablespoons baking powder
- 6 eggs
- 2 to 3 tablespoons grated orange peel
- 4 cups orange juice
  Oil for deep-fat frying
  Confectioners' sugar

COUNTRY SAUSAGE & EGG ROLLS

Country Sausage & Egg Rolls

These savory rolls are always a great choice. They're nice enough to serve company and make an excellent on-the-go breakfast, too.
—**LISA SPEER** PALM BEACH, FL

PREP: 50 MIN. • **BAKE:** 30 MIN. • **MAKES:** 12 SERVINGS

- 1 pound bulk pork sausage
- 1 cup chopped sweet onion
- 1 garlic clove, minced
- ½ teaspoon pepper, divided
- 1 tablespoon butter
- 8 eggs
- 3 tablespoons whole milk
- ¼ teaspoon salt
- ¾ cup shredded sharp cheddar cheese
- 3 green onions, chopped
- 15 sheets phyllo dough, (14x9 inches)
- ⅓ cup butter, melted

1. In a large skillet, cook sausage, sweet onion, garlic and ¼ teaspoon pepper over medium heat until meat is no longer pink; drain. Remove and keep warm.

2. In same skillet, melt butter over medium-high heat. Whisk eggs, milk, salt and remaining pepper; add to skillet. Cook and stir until almost set. Stir in cheese, green onions and sausage mixture. Remove from heat.

3. Preheat oven to 350°. Place one sheet of phyllo dough on a work surface; brush with melted butter. Layer with four more phyllo sheets, brushing with butter after each layer. (Keep remaining phyllo covered with plastic wrap and a damp towel to prevent it from drying out.) Repeat, making three stacks.

4. Cut each stack in half widthwise and in half crosswise, forming four 7x4½-in. rectangles. Spoon ¼ cup egg mixture along a long side of each rectangle; roll up.

5. Place seam side down on an ungreased baking sheet. With a sharp knife, make four shallow slashes across each roll; brush with butter. Bake 30-35 minutes or until golden brown.

Buttermilk Angel Biscuits

When I make these slightly sweet biscuits, I sometimes fold them over a third of the way for a traditional look.
—**CAROL HOLLADAY** DANVILLE, AL

PREP: 30 MIN. + STANDING • **BAKE:** 10 MIN. • **MAKES:** 2 DOZEN

- 2 packages (¼ ounce each) active dry yeast
- ¼ cup warm water (110° to 115°)
- 5¼ to 5½ cups self-rising flour
- ⅓ cup sugar
- 1 teaspoon baking soda
- 1 cup shortening
- 1¾ cups buttermilk

1. In a small bowl, dissolve yeast in warm water. In a large bowl, whisk 5¼ cups flour, sugar and baking soda. Cut in shortening until mixture resembles coarse crumbs. Stir in buttermilk and yeast mixture to form a soft dough (dough will be sticky).

2. Turn dough onto a floured surface; knead gently 8-10 times, adding additional flour if needed. Roll dough to ¾-in. thickness; cut with a floured 2½-in. biscuit cutter. Place 2 in. apart on greased baking sheets. Let stand at room temperature 20 minutes.

3. Preheat oven to 450°. Bake 8-12 minutes or until golden brown. Serve warm.

Baked Oatmeal

My mom liked this recipe because it was quick and easy and made enough to fill up all seven of us hungry kids.
—**KATHY SMITH** BUTLER, IN

PREP: 10 MIN. • **BAKE:** 30 MIN. • **MAKES:** 18 SERVINGS

- 12 cups quick-cooking oats
- 2 cups sugar
- 2 cups packed brown sugar
- 4 teaspoons salt
- 2 teaspoons baking powder
- 4 cups milk
- 2 cups canola oil
- 8 eggs, lightly beaten
  Additional milk

Preheat oven to 350°. In a large bowl, combine the first eight ingredients. Pour into two greased 13x9-in. baking dishes. Bake, uncovered, 30-35 minutes or until set. Serve with additional milk.

SOUR CREAM
COFFEE CAKE

Sour Cream Coffee Cake

This yummy cake is so moist, you won't even need the cup of coffee! Make it for your next get together-your guests will thank you.

—KATHLEEN LARIMER DAYTON, OH

PREP: 40 MIN. • **BAKE:** 45 MIN. + COOLING
MAKES: 16 SERVINGS

⅔ cup chopped pecans
2 tablespoons brown sugar
1½ teaspoons ground cinnamon
BATTER
1 cup butter, softened
2 cups sugar
2 eggs
½ teaspoon vanilla extract
2 cups all-purpose flour
1 teaspoon baking powder
¼ teaspoon baking soda
¼ teaspoon salt
1 cup (8 ounces) sour cream
Confectioners' sugar

1. Preheat oven to 350°. In a small bowl, combine pecans, brown sugar and cinnamon; set aside. In a large bowl, cream butter and sugar until light and fluffy. Add eggs, one at a time, beating well after each addition. Beat in vanilla. Combine flour, baking powder, baking soda and salt; add to creamed mixture alternately with sour cream, beating well after each addition.

2. Pour half of the batter into a greased and floured 10-in. fluted tube pan; sprinkle with half of the pecan mixture. Gently top with the remaining batter and pecan mixture.

3. Bake 45-50 minutes or until a toothpick inserted in center comes out clean. Cool 10 minutes before removing from pan to a wire rack to cool completely. Sprinkle with confectioners' sugar.

MARINATED
CHEESE, PAGE 37

FRUITED
PUNCH,
PAGE 46

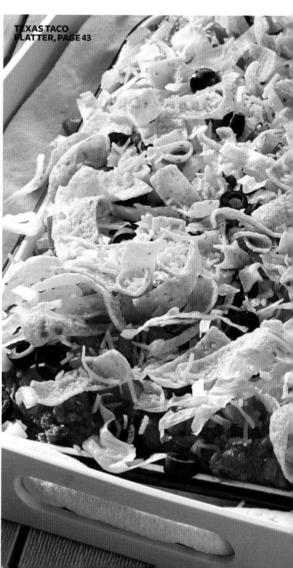

TEXAS TACO
PLATTER, PAGE 43

APPETIZERS &
SNACKS

SKEWERED CHICKEN WITH
PEANUT SAUCE, PAGE 51

" Do not neglect to show
hospitality to strangers,
for by doing that some
have entertained angels
without knowing it. "

HEBREWS 13:2

FAST FIX

Kiddie Crunch Mix

This no-bake snack mix is a real treat for kids, and you can easily increase the amount to fit your needs. Place it in individual plastic bags or pour some into colored ice cream cones and cover with plastic wrap.
—**KARA DE LA VEGA** SANTA ROSA, CA

START TO FINISH: 10 MIN.
MAKES: 6 CUPS

- 1 cup animal crackers
- 1 cup chocolate bear-shaped crackers
- 1 cup miniature pretzels
- 1 cup salted peanuts
- 1 cup M&M's
- 1 cup chocolate-or yogurt-covered raisins

In a bowl, combine all ingredients. Store in an airtight container.

Sausage Phyllo Rolls

My brother shared his recipe for appetizer rolls with me years ago, and they've been a family favorite ever since. The delicate phyllo dough wraps around a hearty sausage filling.
—**KATTY CHIONG** HOFFMAN ESTATES, IL

PREP: 40 MIN. + COOLING • **BAKE:** 10 MIN.
MAKES: ABOUT 4½ DOZEN

- ¾ pound bulk Italian sausage
- 1 small onion, chopped
- 1 celery rib, chopped
- ½ cup chopped fresh mushrooms
- 2 garlic cloves, minced
- ¼ cup chopped walnuts
- ¼ cup dried cranberries or raisins
- ½ teaspoon sugar
- ¼ teaspoon pepper
- ⅛ teaspoon cayenne pepper
- 20 sheets phyllo dough (14x9 inches)
- ½ cup butter, melted
- 1⅓ cups fresh baby spinach
- ¼ cup julienned roasted sweet red peppers
- 1 egg, lightly beaten

1. Preheat oven to 400°. In a large skillet, cook sausage, onion, celery, mushrooms and garlic over medium heat 6-8 minutes or until sausage is no longer pink, breaking up the sausage into crumbles; drain. Stir in walnuts, cranberries, sugar, pepper and cayenne. Remove from the pan; cool completely.

2. Place one sheet of phyllo dough on a work surface; brush lightly with butter. Layer with four additional phyllo sheets, brushing each layer. (Keep the remaining phyllo covered with plastic wrap and a damp towel to prevent it from drying out.)

3. Arrange ⅓ cup spinach, one-fourth of the sausage mixture and 1 tablespoon roasted peppers in a narrow row across bottom of phyllo within 1 in. of edges. Fold bottom edge of phyllo over filling, then roll up. Brush end of phyllo dough with butter and press to seal. Repeat three times. Place rolls on a 15x10x1-in. baking pan, seam side down.

4. Cut rolls diagonally into 1-in. pieces (do not separate). Brush tops with remaining butter; brush again with beaten egg. Bake 10-12 minutes or until golden brown.

SAUSAGE
PHYLLO ROLLS

Peanut Butter Chocolate Pretzels

Chocolate and peanut butter, sweet and salty, crunchy and smooth— what's not to love? A gift of dipped and drizzled pretzels is sure to garner smiles from everyone on your list.
—**MARCIA PORCH** WINTER PARK, FL

PREP: 30 MIN. + STANDING
MAKES: ABOUT 3 DOZEN

- 2 **cups (12 ounces) semisweet chocolate chips**
- 4 **teaspoons canola oil, divided**
- 35 **to 40 pretzels**
- ½ **cup peanut butter chips**

1. In a microwave, melt chocolate chips and 3 teaspoons oil; stir until smooth. Dip pretzels in chocolate; allow excess to drip off. Place on waxed paper-lined baking sheets to set.

2. Melt peanut butter chips and remaining oil; transfer to a small resealable plastic bag. Cut a small hole in a corner of bag; drizzle over pretzels. Allow to set. Store in airtight containers.

DEVILED EGGS
WITH BACON

FAST FIX

Deviled Eggs with Bacon

These deviled eggs went over so well at our summer cookouts, I started making them for holiday dinners as well. Everyone likes the addition of bacon.
—**BARBARA REID** MOUNDS, OK

START TO FINISH: 30 MIN.
MAKES: 2 DOZEN

- 12 **hard-cooked eggs**
- ⅓ **cup mayonnaise**
- 3 **bacon strips, cooked and crumbled**
- 3 **tablespoons finely chopped red onion**
- 3 **tablespoons sweet pickle relish**
- ¼ **teaspoon smoked paprika**

Cut eggs in half lengthwise. Remove yolks; set whites aside. In a small bowl, mash yolks. Add the mayonnaise, bacon, onion and relish; mix well. Stuff into egg whites. Refrigerate until serving. Sprinkle with paprika.

Pork Canapes

People will relish these festive, pretty appetizers. They're relatively simple to do, but look impressive.
—RANEE BULLARD EVANS, GA

PREP: 35 MIN. • **BAKE:** 25 MIN. • **MAKES:** 3 DOZEN

- 1½ teaspoons garlic powder
- 1 teaspoon dried rosemary, crushed
- 1 teaspoon dried thyme
- ¾ teaspoon pepper
- ½ teaspoon salt
- 2 pork tenderloins (¾ pound each)
- 36 slices French bread baguette (½ inch thick)
- ¼ cup olive oil
- ¾ cup garlic-herb spreadable cheese
- 3 tablespoons seedless raspberry or seedless strawberry jam
- 36 fresh thyme sprigs

1. Preheat oven to 425°. In a small bowl, combine the first five ingredients; rub over meat. Place on a rack in a shallow roasting pan. Bake, uncovered, 20-25 minutes or until a thermometer reads 145°. Let stand 10 minutes. Cut each tenderloin into ¼-in. slices.
2. Brush the bread slices with olive oil. Place on an ungreased baking sheet. Bake at 425° 1-2 minutes or until toast is lightly browned. Spread each with the spreadable cheese; top with meat, ¼ teaspoon jam and a thyme sprig.

Shrimp Toast Cups

These treats always disappear quick as a flash. The pretty toast cups lend themselves to other favorite fillings, too.
—AWYNNE THURSTENSON SILOAM SPRINGS, AR

PREP: 30 MIN. • **BAKE:** 15 MIN./BATCH • **MAKES:** 8 DOZEN

- 24 slices white bread, crusts removed
- 1 cup butter, melted
- 2 packages (8 ounces each) cream cheese, softened
- ½ cup mayonnaise
- 3 tablespoons sour cream
- 3 tablespoons prepared horseradish
- 3 cans (6 ounces each) small shrimp, rinsed and drained
- 16 green onions, sliced
  Fresh dill sprigs, optional

1. Preheat oven to 325°. Flatten bread with a rolling pin; cut each slice into four pieces. Place butter in a shallow dish; dip both sides of bread in butter; press into miniature muffin cups. Bake 14 minutes or until golden brown. Remove from pans to wire racks to cool.
2. In a large bowl, beat the cream cheese, mayonnaise, sour cream and horseradish until blended. Just before serving, stir in shrimp and onions; spoon into cups. Garnish with dill if desired. Refrigerate leftovers.

PORK CANAPES

SHRIMP TOAST CUPS

SALSA FOR
A CROWD

Salsa for a Crowd

When planning your next fiesta, look no further than this hearty, pretty salsa. The succulent seasoning includes coriander, cumin, garlic and cilantro, your crowd will definitely say, "Ole!"

—BETSY SAMS JAMESVILLE, NY

START TO FINISH: 30 MIN. • **MAKES:** 56 SERVINGS (¼ CUP EACH)

- 4   **cans (14½ ounces each) diced tomatoes**
- 4   **large tomatoes, chopped**
- 2   **cups frozen corn, thawed**
- 1   **can (15 ounces) black beans, rinsed and drained**
- 1   **medium sweet onion, finely chopped**
- ⅓   **cup lime juice**
- ¼   **cup minced fresh cilantro**
- 2   **tablespoons cider vinegar**
- 2   **tablespoons hot pepper sauce**
- 1   **garlic clove, minced**
- 1   **tablespoon coriander seeds, crushed**
- 1   **tablespoon ground cumin**
- 1   **teaspoon salt**
- 1   **teaspoon coarsely ground pepper**
  Chopped jalapeno pepper, optional
  corn chips or tortilla chips

1. Place two undrained cans of tomatoes in a large bowl; drain the two remaining cans and add tomatoes to the bowl.

2. Stir in the chopped fresh tomatoes, corn, beans, onion, lime juice, cilantro, vinegar, pepper sauce, garlic and seasonings. Stir in jalapeno if desired. Cover and refrigerate until serving. Serve with chips.

NOTE *Wear disposable gloves when cutting hot peppers; the oils can burn skin. Avoid touching your face.*

Hot Bacon Cheddar Spread

This is my go-to recipe when I'm having people over. The warm, luscious dip is always quite popular.

—CARA LANGER OVERLAND PARK, KS

PREP: 30 MIN. • **BAKE:** 15 MIN. • **MAKES:** 3 CUPS

- 1   **package (8 ounces) cream cheese, softened**
- ½   **cup mayonnaise**
- ¼   **teaspoon dried thyme**
- ⅛   **teaspoon pepper**
- 1   **cup (4 ounces) shredded sharp cheddar cheese**
- 3   **green onions, chopped**
- 8   **bacon strips, cooked and crumbled, divided**
- ½   **cup crushed butter-flavored crackers**
  Assorted crackers

1. Preheat oven to 350°. In a large bowl, combine cream cheese, mayonnaise, thyme and pepper. Stir in cheese, green onions and half the bacon. Transfer to a greased 3-cup baking dish.

2. Bake, uncovered, 13-15 minutes or until bubbly. Top with crushed crackers and remaining bacon. Serve with assorted crackers.

Spicy Beef Satay

The fragrant spices and full flavors of North African cuisine make these appetizers a tasty party food.
—**ROXANNE CHAN** ALBANY, CA

PREP: 35 MIN. • **BROIL:** 5 MIN. • **MAKES:** 2 DOZEN (½ CUP SAUCE)

- 1 **cup white wine vinegar**
- ¾ **cup sugar**
- ½ **cup water**
- 1 **tablespoon orange marmalade**
- ¼ **teaspoon grated orange peel**
- ¼ **teaspoon crushed red pepper flakes**
- ½ **cup finely chopped salted roasted almonds**
- 2 **tablespoons minced fresh mint**
- 1 **green onion, finely chopped**
- 1 **tablespoon lemon juice**
- 1 **garlic clove, minced**
- ¼ **teaspoon each ground cinnamon, cumin and coriander**
- 1 **pound lean ground beef (90% lean)**
  Minced fresh parsley

1. In a small saucepan, combine first six ingredients. Bring to a boil. Reduce heat; simmer, uncovered, about 25 minutes or until reduced to ½ cup.
2. Meanwhile, in a large bowl, combine almonds, mint, onion, lemon juice, garlic and spices. Crumble beef over mixture and mix well. Divide into 24 pieces. Shape each piece into a 3x1-in. rectangle; insert a soaked wooden appetizer skewers into each.
3. Broil 6 in. from the heat 2-4 minutes on each side or until a thermometer reads 160°. Arrange on a serving platter. Drizzle with the sauce mixture and sprinkle with parsley.

Sensational Slush

Colorful and refreshing, this sweet-tart slush has become a family favorite. I freeze the mix in 2- and 4-cup containers, so it can be served in small portions for individuals or the whole family. I also freeze crushed strawberries to make preparation simpler.
—**CONNIE FRIESEN** ALTONA, MB

PREP: 25 MIN. + FREEZING • **MAKES:** 20 SERVINGS

- ½ **cup sugar**
- 1 **package (3 ounces) strawberry gelatin**
- 2 **cups boiling water**
- 1 **cup unsweetened pineapple juice**
- 2 **cups sliced fresh strawberries**
- 1 **can (12 ounces) frozen lemonade concentrate, thawed**
- 1 **can (12 ounces) frozen limeade concentrate, thawed**
- 2 **cups cold water**
- 2 **liters lemon-lime soda, chilled**

1. In a large bowl, dissolve the sugar and gelatin in boiling water. In a blender combine pineapple juice and strawberries; cover and process until blended. Add to gelatin mixture. Stir in concentrates and cold water. Cover and freeze 8 hours or overnight.
2. Remove from the freezer 45 minutes before serving. For each serving, combine ½ cup slush mixture with ½ cup lemon-lime soda; stir well.

SPICY BEEF SATAY

Marinated Cheese

This special appetizer always makes it to the parties in our neighborhood and is the first to disappear at the table.
—**LAURIE CASPER** CORAOPOLIS, PA

PREP: 30 MIN. + MARINATING • **MAKES:** ABOUT 2 POUNDS

- 2 **blocks (8 ounces each) white cheddar cheese**
- 2 **packages (8 ounces each) cream cheese, softened**
- ¾ **cup chopped roasted sweet red peppers**
- ½ **cup olive oil**
- ¼ **cup white wine vinegar**
- ¼ **cup balsamic vinegar**
- 3 **tablespoons chopped green onions**
- 3 **tablespoons minced fresh parsley**
- 2 **tablespoons minced fresh basil**
- 1 **tablespoon sugar**
- 3 **garlic cloves, minced**
- ½ **teaspoon salt**
- ½ **teaspoon pepper**
  Toasted sliced French bread or assorted crackers

1. Slice each block of cheddar cheese into twenty ¼-in. slices. Cut each block of cream cheese into 18 slices; sandwich between cheddar slices, using a knife to spread evenly. Create four 6-in.-long blocks of cheese; place in a 13x9-in. dish.

2. In a small bowl, combine the roasted peppers, oil, vinegars, onions, herbs, sugar, garlic, salt and pepper; pour over cheese.

3. Cover and refrigerate overnight, turning once. Drain excess marinade. Serve cheese with bread or crackers.

White Grape Punch

Here's a mix-ahead drink that never sticks around long once I set it out. The refill requests come quickly!
—**DEBRA FRAAKEN** FORT COLLINS, CO

START TO FINISH: 15 MIN. • **MAKES:** 6 QUARTS

- 2 **cans (12 ounces each) frozen apple juice concentrate, thawed**
- 2 **cans (11½ ounces each) frozen white grape juice concentrate**
- 6 **cups cold water**
- 12 **cups lemon-lime soda (about 3 liters), chilled**
  Lemon and lime slices

1. In a large pitcher, mix the juice concentrates and water. Refrigerate until serving.

2. Just before serving, pour mixture into two pitchers or a punch bowl. Stir in soda and top with lemon and lime slices.

FAST FIX

Taco Dip

This dip recipe is one of my favorites. It's so easy to make and always goes over well at the parties and large get-togethers I bring it to.

—**ALETA AMICK** MADISON, WI

START TO FINISH: 25 MIN.
MAKES: ABOUT 6½ CUPS

- 12 ounces cream cheese, softened
- ½ cup sour cream
- 1 teaspoon chili powder
- ½ cup salsa
- 2 cups shredded iceberg lettuce
- 1 cup (4 ounces) shredded cheddar cheese
- 1 cup (4 ounces) shredded Monterey Jack cheese
- ½ cup chopped tomatoes
- 1 can (4¼ ounces) sliced ripe olives, drained, optional
  Tortilla chips

1. In a large bowl, beat first three ingredients until smooth; stir in salsa. Spread cream cheese mixture over a large serving platter. Cover and refrigerate 15 minutes.
2. Layer cream cheese mixture with lettuce, cheddar cheese, Monterey Jack cheese, tomato and olives if desired. Serve with chips.

FAST FIX
Spruced-Up Cheese Spread

A neighbor who's a wonderful cook is the one who gave me the recipe for this zippy cracker spread. It's easy to shape into a Christmas tree for a festive occasion.

—**JUDY GRIMES** BRANDON, MS

START TO FINISH: 20 MIN.
MAKES: 4 CUPS

- 1 jar (4 ounces) diced pimientos, drained, divided
- 1 small onion, grated
- 1 cup mayonnaise
- 1 to 2 tablespoons prepared mustard
- 1 tablespoon Worcestershire sauce
- 1 teaspoon celery seed
- ½ teaspoon paprika
- ¼ teaspoon garlic salt
- 3 cups (12 ounces) finely shredded sharp cheddar cheese
- 2 tablespoons finely chopped pecans
  Minced fresh parsley
  Assorted crackers

1. Set aside 2 tablespoons pimientos for topping. In a large bowl, combine the remaining pimientos and the next seven ingredients. Stir in cheese.
2. Transfer to a serving bowl; sprinkle with pecans, parsley and reserved pimientos. Serve with crackers.

SPRUCED-UP
CHEESE SPREAD

Sage & Prosciutto Pinwheels

I love appetizers for entertaining and I came up with this recipe because I can make them ahead and keep the rolls in the freezer, then slice and bake as needed.

—KATE DAMPIER QUAIL VALLEY, CA

START TO FINISH: 30 MIN.
MAKES: 3 DOZEN

- 1 **package (17.3 ounces) frozen puff pastry, thawed**
- ¼ **cup honey mustard**
- 1 **cup (4 ounces) shredded Gruyere or Swiss cheese**
- 8 **thin slices prosciutto or deli ham, chopped**
- 2 **tablespoons chopped fresh sage**

1. Preheat the oven to 400°. Unfold one pastry sheet. Spread 2 tablespoons mustard to within ½ in. of edges. Sprinkle with ½ cup cheese; top with half each chopped prosciutto and sage. Roll up jelly-roll style. Using a serrated knife, cut roll crosswise into 18 slices.

2. Place cut side down on a greased baking sheet. Repeat with the remaining ingredients. Bake for 12-15 minutes or until golden brown. Serve warm.

FREEZE OPTION *Cover and freeze unbaked rolls on a waxed paper-lined baking sheet until firm. Transfer the rolls to resealable plastic freezer bags; return to freezer. To use, let rolls stand at room temperature for 10 minutes. Cut and bake the pinwheels as directed, increasing time as necessary.*

SAGE & PROSCIUTTO PINWHEELS

Hot Spiced Cider

Next time you're entertaining, stir up a batch of this nicely spiced cider. The wonderful aroma will make your guests feel welcome on a chilly day.
—**KIMBERLY WALLACE** DENNISON, OH

START TO FINISH: 20 MIN. • **MAKES:** 4½ QUARTS

- 1 **gallon apple cider or apple juice**
- 1 **cup orange juice**
- ¼ **cup maple syrup**
- ½ **teaspoon orange extract**
- ½ **teaspoon lemon extract**
- 4 **cinnamon sticks**
- 2 **teaspoons whole cloves**
- 1 **teaspoon whole allspice**

In a Dutch oven, combine the first five ingredients. Place the cinnamon sticks, cloves and allspice on a double thickness of cheesecloth; bring up corners of cloth and tie with string to form a bag. Add to the pan. Cook, uncovered, over medium heat for 10-15 minutes or until flavors are blended (do not boil). Discard the spice bag.

Sour Cream and Beef Turnovers

I always serve these turnovers at family get-togethers. If you like, add a tossed green salad and serve them for dinner. They freeze well, too.
—**ELVA KELLY** PRINCE GEORGE, BC

PREP: 40 MIN. + CHILLING • **BAKE:** 15 MIN./BATCH
MAKES: ABOUT 4½ DOZEN

- 2 **cups all-purpose flour**
- 1 **tablespoon sugar**
- 1 **teaspoon salt**
- ½ **cup shortening**
- 1 **cup (8 ounces) sour cream**
- 1 **egg yolk**

FILLING
- ¾ **pound ground beef**
- 1 **large onion, finely chopped**
- ¼ **cup finely chopped fresh mushrooms**
- ½ **cup sour cream**
- ½ **teaspoon salt**
- ½ **teaspoon dried oregano**
- ¼ **teaspoon pepper**
- 1 **egg**
- 2 **teaspoons water**

1. In a large bowl, combine flour, sugar and salt. Cut in shortening until crumbly. Stir in sour cream and egg yolk just until moistened. Shape into a ball. Cover and refrigerate 2 hours or until easy to handle.
2. Preheat oven to 450°. In a large skillet over medium heat, cook beef, onion and mushrooms until meat is no longer pink. Remove from heat; drain. Stir in sour cream, salt, oregano and pepper.
3. On a floured surface, roll out the dough to ⅛-in. thickness. Cut with a floured 3-in. round cutter. Place a rounded teaspoon of filling on one side of each circle; fold dough over filling. Press edges with a fork to seal. Prick tops with a fork. Reroll scraps; repeat.
4. Place on greased baking sheets. Beat egg with water; brush over turnovers. Bake 12-15 minutes or until lightly browned.
FREEZE OPTION *Cover and freeze unbaked pastries on waxed paper-lined baking sheets until firm. Transfer to resealable plastic freezer bags; return to freezer. To use, bake pastries as directed, increasing time as necessary to heat through.*

SOUR CREAM AND
BEEF TURNOVERS

Sweet Tea Concentrate

Sweet iced tea is a Southern classic and this is a fabulous recipe for your favorite tea lovers.

—NATALIE BREMSON PLANTATION, FL

PREP: 30 MIN. + COOLING
MAKES: 20 SERVINGS
(5 CUPS CONCENTRATE)

- 2 medium lemons
- 4 cups sugar
- 4 cups water
- 1½ cups English breakfast tea leaves or 20 black tea bags
- ⅓ cup lemon juice

EACH SERVING
- 1 cup cold water
  Ice cubes

1. Remove peels from lemons; save fruit for another use.
2. In a large saucepan, bring sugar and water to a boil over medium heat. Reduce the heat; simmer, uncovered, 3-5 minutes or until the sugar is dissolved, stirring occasionally. Remove from the heat; add tea leaves and lemon peels. Cover and steep for 15 minutes. Strain tea, discarding tea leaves and lemon peels; stir in lemon juice. Cool to room temperature.
3. Transfer to a container with a tight-fitting lid. Store in the refrigerator for up to 2 weeks.
TO PREPARE TEA *In a tall glass, mix water with ¼ cup concentrate; add ice.*

Ham 'n' Cheese Biscuit Stacks

These finger sandwiches are pretty enough for the gals and hearty enough for the guys.

—KELLY WILLIAMS FORKED RIVER, NJ

PREP: 1 HOUR • **BAKE:** 10 MIN. + COOLING
MAKES: 40 APPETIZERS

- 2 tubes (12 ounces each) refrigerated buttermilk biscuits
- ¾ cup stone-ground mustard, divided
- ½ cup butter, softened
- ¼ cup chopped green onions
- ¼ cup mayonnaise
- ¼ cup honey
- 10 thick slices deli ham
- 10 slices Swiss cheese
- 2½ cups shredded romaine
- 40 frilled toothpicks
- 20 pitted ripe olives, drained and patted dry
- 20 pimiento-stuffed olives, drained and patted dry

1. Preheat oven to 400°. Cut each biscuit in half, forming half circles. Place 2 in. apart on ungreased baking sheets. Spread each with ½ teaspoon mustard. Bake 8-10 minutes or until golden brown. Remove from pans to wire racks to cool.
2. In a small bowl, combine butter and onions. In another bowl, combine mayonnaise, honey and remaining mustard. Cut each slice of ham into four rectangles; cut each slice of cheese into four triangles.
3. Split each biscuit in half; spread bottom halves with butter mixture. Layer with one ham piece, one cheese piece and 1 tablespoon romaine on each biscuit bottom.
4. Spread mustard mixture over biscuit tops; place over romaine. Thread toothpicks through olives; insert into stacks. Refrigerate leftovers.

HAM 'N' CHEESE BISCUIT STACKS

TEXAS TACO PLATTER

1. In a large skillet or Dutch oven, cook beef and onion over medium heat until meat is no longer pink; drain. Add next seven ingredients; simmer 1½ hours.

2. Add beans and heat though. On a platter, layer the corn chips, rice, meat mixture, cheese, onion, lettuce, tomatoes and olives. Serve with picante sauce if desired.

FAST FIX

Chipotle Avocado Dip

Thanks to the avocado base, this dip provides a bonus of healthy fats and fiber. Try spooning it on tacos.

—BARBARA OLIPHANT
VALLEY CENTER, KS

START TO FINISH: 15 MIN. • **MAKES:** 3 CUPS

- 3 **medium ripe avocados, peeled**
- 1 **cup reduced-fat mayonnaise**
- ¼ **cup finely chopped onion**
- 1 **tablespoon finely chopped banana pepper**
- 1 **tablespoon minced pickled hot cherry peppers**
- 1½ **teaspoons garlic powder**
- 1 **to 1½ teaspoons ground chipotle pepper**
- 1 **teaspoon onion powder**
- 1 **teaspoon seasoned salt**
  Assorted fresh vegetables

In a small bowl, mash avocados. Stir in the mayonnaise, onion, peppers and seasonings. Chill until serving. Serve with vegetables.

NOTE *Wear disposable gloves when cutting hot peppers; the oils can burn skin. Avoid touching your face.*

Texas Taco Platter

When I'm entertaining, this colorful dish is my top menu choice. My friends can't resist the hearty appetizer topped with cheese, lettuce, tomatoes and olives.

—KATHY YOUNG WEATHERFORD, TX

PREP: 20 MIN. • **COOK:** 1½ HOURS
MAKES: 10-12 SERVINGS

- 2 **pounds ground beef**
- 1 **large onion, chopped**
- 1 **can (14½ ounces) diced tomatoes, undrained**
- 1 **can (12 ounces) tomato paste**
- 1 **can (15 ounces) tomato puree**
- 2 **tablespoons chili powder**
- 1 **teaspoon ground cumin**
- ½ **teaspoon garlic powder**
- 2 **teaspoons salt**
- 2 **cans (15 ounces each) Ranch Style beans (pinto beans in seasoned tomato sauce)**
- 1 **package (10½ ounces) corn chips**
- 2 **cups hot cooked rice**

TOPPINGS

- 2 **cups (8 ounces) shredded cheddar cheese**
- 1 **medium onion, chopped**
- 1 **medium head iceberg lettuce, shredded**
- 3 **medium tomatoes, chopped**
- 1 **can (2¼ ounces) sliced ripe olives, drained**
- 1 **cup picante sauce, optional**

1. Preheat oven to 350°. In a large bowl, combine the first 12 ingredients. Add pork; mix lightly but thoroughly. With wet hands, shape mixture into 1-in. balls.

2. Place meatballs on a greased rack in a shallow baking pan. Bake 14-17 minutes or until meatballs are cooked through. Drain on paper towels.

3. Meanwhile, in a large skillet, combine the glaze ingredients. Add meatballs; cook over medium heat 8-10 minutes or until meatballs are glazed and heated through, stirring occasionally.

NOTE *To make soft bread crumbs, tear bread into pieces and place in a food processor or blender. Cover and pulse until crumbs form. One slice of bread yields ½ to ¾ cup crumbs.*

Bacon-Sausage Quiche Tarts

As a teacher, I attend many meetings and also have special celebrations with the rest of the staff. The other teachers a very fond of this treat and often request that I bring it to our functions.

—**JACKIE MILLIKEN** PITTSBORO, NC

PREP: 30 MIN. • **BAKE:** 10 MIN. • **MAKES:** 40 APPETIZERS

- 2 **cans (12 ounces each) refrigerated buttermilk biscuits**
- 6 **uncooked breakfast sausage links, chopped**
- 2 **tablespoons chopped onion**
- 2 **tablespoons chopped fresh mushrooms**
- 2 **tablespoons chopped green pepper**
- 1 **package (8 ounces) cream cheese, softened**
- 2 **tablespoons heavy whipping cream**
- 3 **eggs**
- 1½ **cups (6 ounces) finely shredded cheddar cheese, divided**
- 5 **bacon strips, cooked and crumbled**

1. Preheat oven to 375°. Split each biscuit into two layers; press each into an ungreased miniature muffin cup.

2. In a large skillet, cook sausage, onion, mushrooms and pepper over medium heat until meat is no longer pink and the vegetables are tender; drain.

3. In a large bowl, beat the cream cheese and cream until smooth. Beat in the eggs. Fold in ¾ cup cheddar cheese and the sausage mixture. Spoon 1 tablespoon into each cup. Sprinkle with the bacon and remaining cheese. Bake 10-15 minutes or until golden brown. Serve warm.

Brown Sugar-Glazed Meatballs

I modeled these sweet-spicy pork-and-shrimp meatballs after the filling in Asian wontons. They're a family favorite, whether I serve them alone as an appetizer or over hot cooked rice as a main dish.

—**LILY JULOW** LAWRENCEVILLE, GA

PREP: 35 MIN. • **BAKE:** 15 MIN. • **MAKES:** 3½ DOZEN

- ¾ **pound uncooked small shrimp, peeled, deveined and chopped**
- ½ **cup soft bread crumbs**
- 4 **bacon strips, finely chopped**
- 1 **egg, lightly beaten**
- 1 **tablespoon stone-ground mustard**
- 1½ **teaspoons liquid smoke, optional**
- 1½ **teaspoons smoked paprika**
- 1 **teaspoon salt**
- 1 **garlic clove, minced**
- ¾ **teaspoon dried oregano**
- ½ **to 1 teaspoon hot pepper sauce**
- ½ **teaspoon onion powder**
- 1 **pound ground pork**

GLAZE
- ½ **cup packed brown sugar**
- ¼ **cup cider vinegar**
- 4 **teaspoons stone-ground mustard**

BACON-SAUSAGE
QUICHE TARTS

Fruited Punch

I've been making this for more years than I care to say, but I think this is the best punch ever.

—MARLENE MEIMANN
QUEENSBURY, NY

PREP: 20 MIN. • **COOK:** 10 MIN. + CHILLING
MAKES: 26 SERVINGS (¾ CUP EACH)

- 1½ **cups sugar**
- 1½ **cups water**
- 3 **cups strong brewed tea, chilled**
- 3 **cups orange juice, chilled**
- 3 **cups unsweetened pineapple juice, chilled**
- ½ **cup lemon juice, chilled**
- 3 **cups thinly sliced fresh or frozen strawberries**
- 1 **bottle (2 liters) ginger ale, chilled**

1. In a small saucepan, combine the sugar and water. Bring to a boil over medium heat. Reduce heat; simmer, uncovered, 3-4 minutes or until sugar is dissolved, stirring occasionally. Remove from heat; cool to room temperature. Cover and refrigerate for at least 1 hour.

2. In a punch bowl, combine the tea, juices and sugar mixture. Stir in strawberries. Just before serving, stir in ginger ale.

FRUITED PUNCH

TOP TIP

Storing Tea

Store tea in an airtight container in a cool, dark place away from light. Keep different types of tea separate to keep the flavors from mingling. Properly stored tea will stay fresh for 1½ to 2 years.

**GINGERED SWEET &
SPICY HOT WINGS**

1. In a large resealable plastic bag, combine the first 14 ingredients. Add chicken; seal bag and turn to coat. Refrigerate 8 hours or overnight.
2. Preheat oven to 375°. Drain chicken, discarding marinade. Transfer the chicken to two greased 15x10x1-in. baking pans. Bake 35-45 minutes or until juices run clear.

Miniature Shepherd's Pies

Miniature pies, sweet or savory, are ideal party nibbles. I knew the ever-popular shepherd's pie would be perfect scaled down. I've also made the pies with ground lamb and a teaspoon of dried rosemary.
—**SUZANNE BANFIELD** BASKING RIDGE, NJ

PREP: 40 MIN. • **BAKE:** 15 MIN. • **MAKES:** 4 DOZEN

- ½ pound ground beef
- ⅓ cup finely chopped onion
- ¼ cup finely chopped celery
- 3 tablespoons finely chopped carrot
- 1½ teaspoons all-purpose flour
- 1 teaspoon dried thyme
- ¼ teaspoon salt
- ⅛ teaspoon ground nutmeg
- ⅛ teaspoon pepper
- ⅔ cup beef broth
- ⅓ cup frozen petite peas
- 2 packages (17.3 ounces each) frozen puff pastry, thawed
- 3 cups mashed potatoes

1. Preheat oven to 400°. In a large skillet, cook beef, onion, celery and carrot over medium heat until beef is no longer pink; drain. Stir in flour, thyme, salt, nutmeg and pepper until blended; gradually add broth. Bring to a boil; cook and stir 2 minutes or until sauce is thickened. Stir in peas; heat through. Set aside.
2. Unfold puff pastry. Using a floured 2¼-in. round cutter, cut 12 circles from each sheet (save scraps for another use). Press circles onto the bottoms and up the sides of ungreased miniature muffin cups.
3. Fill each with 1½ teaspoons beef mixture; top or pipe with 1 tablespoon mashed potatoes. Bake for 13-16 minutes or until heated through and potatoes are lightly browned. Serve warm.

Gingered Sweet & Spicy Hot Wings

My hot wings are a foolproof way to curry a little favor with the men in my life. Thanks to tons of sweet (orange marmalade) and hot (Sriracha) flavors bursting through with every bite, these wings are a winner.
—**JENNIFER LOCKLIN** CYPRESS, TX

PREP: 15 MIN. + MARINATING • **BAKE:** 35 MIN.
MAKES: ABOUT 3 DOZEN

- 1 cup orange marmalade
- ½ cup minced fresh cilantro
- ½ cup Sriracha Asian hot chili sauce
- ½ cup reduced-sodium soy sauce
- ¼ cup lime juice
- ¼ cup rice vinegar
- ¼ cup ketchup
- ¼ cup honey
- 4 garlic cloves, minced
- 1 tablespoon minced fresh gingerroot
- 1 tablespoon grated lime peel
- 1 tablespoon sesame oil
- 1 teaspoon salt
- 1 teaspoon pepper
- 4 pounds chicken wingettes and drumettes

Spanakopita Bites

For an easy spanakopita, try this appetizer that is made in a pan, then cut into squares. You'll enjoy the taste of the classic version without all the hassle.
—**BARBARA SMITH** CHIPLEY, FL

PREP: 20 MIN. + FREEZING • **BAKE:** 35 MIN. • **MAKES:** 10½ DOZEN

- 1 **egg, lightly beaten**
- 1 **package (10 ounces) frozen chopped spinach, thawed and squeezed dry**
- 2 **cups (8 ounces) crumbled feta cheese**
- 1 **cup (8 ounces) 4% small-curd cottage cheese**
- ¾ **cup butter, melted**
- 16 **sheets phyllo dough (14x9 inches)**

1. Preheat oven to 350°. In a large bowl, mix egg, spinach and cheeses. Brush a 15x10x1-in. baking pan with some of the butter.

2. Place one sheet of phyllo in prepared pan; brush with butter. Layer with seven additional phyllo sheets, brushing each layer. (Keep remaining phyllo covered with plastic wrap and a damp towel to prevent it from drying out.) Spread top with spinach mixture. Top with remaining phyllo, brushing each sheet with butter.

3. Freeze, covered, 30 minutes. Using a sharp knife, cut into 1-in. squares. Bake 35-45 minutes or until golden brown. Refrigerate leftovers.

TO MAKE AHEAD *Cover and freeze until ready to use. Cut and bake as directed.*

**SWEET &
SALTY CANDY**

**CARAMEL
CORN**

Sweet & Salty Candy

I've been making this candy for the past few years and serving it at Teacher Appreciation lunches and bake sales. It's special because it never fails to win praise from everyone who tries it. For bake sales, I break the candy up and package it in little cellophane bags from the craft store.
—**ANNA GINSBERG** AUSTIN, TX

PREP: 15 MIN. • **BAKE:** 10 MIN. + COOLING
MAKES: ABOUT 1½ POUNDS

- 2 cups miniature pretzels, coarsely crushed
- ½ cup corn chips, coarsely crushed
- ½ cup salted peanuts
- ½ cup butter, cubed
- ½ cup packed brown sugar
- 1½ cups semisweet chocolate chips

1. Preheat oven to 350°. Line a 13x9-in. baking pan with foil and grease the foil; set aside. In a large bowl, combine pretzels, corn chips and peanuts.
2. In a small saucepan, melt butter. Stir in brown sugar until melted. Bring to a boil, stirring frequently. Boil 1 minute, stirring twice. Pour over pretzel mixture; toss to coat. Transfer to prepared pan.
3. Bake 7 minutes. Sprinkle with chocolate chips. Bake 1-2 minutes longer or until chips are softened. Spread over top. Cool on a wire rack 1 hour. Break into pieces. Store in an airtight container.

Caramel Corn

For years, I've taken containers of this yummy snack to our church retreat. Other church members tell us that if we can't attend, we should just send the caramel corn!
—**NANCY BREEN** CANASTOTA, NY

PREP: 10 MIN. • **BAKE:** 1 HOUR • **MAKES:** 12 QUARTS

- 12 quarts plain popped popcorn
- 1 pound peanuts
- 2 cups butter, cubed
- 2 pounds brown sugar
- ½ cup dark corn syrup
- ½ cup molasses

1. Preheat oven to 250°. Place popcorn in two large bowls. Add ½ pound peanuts to each bowl. In a Dutch oven, combine remaining ingredients. Bring to a boil over medium heat; cook and stir 5 minutes.
2. Pour half of the syrup over each bowl of popcorn and stir to coat. Transfer to large roasting or 15x10x1-in. baking pans. Bake 1 hour, stirring every 15 minutes.
3. Remove from oven and break apart while warm. Cool completely. Store in airtight containers.

APPETIZERS & SNACKS

Nutty Berry Trail Mix

This recipe, my son's favorite, earned me an A in my early childhood nutrition course. It lets you take control of what your children snack on!

—**CHERI MAJORS** CLAREMONT, CA

START TO FINISH: 5 MIN.
MAKES: 10 CUPS

- 1 can (15 ounces) mixed nuts
- 2 cups (12 ounces) semisweet chocolate chips
- 1 package (9 ounces) raisins
- 1 package (6 ounces) chopped dried pineapple
- 1 jar (5.85 ounces) sunflower kernels
- 1 package (5 ounces) dried cranberries

In a large bowl, combine all the ingredients; mix well. Store in an airtight container.

No-Bones Chicken Wing Dip

If you love chicken wings, you'll really enjoy the dip. It delivers the great flavor of the chicken wings—without any bones!

—**SHIRLEY GAWLIK** OAKFIELD, NY

PREP: 15 MIN. • **BAKE:** 25 MIN.
MAKES: 6½ CUPS

- 1 package (8 ounces) cream cheese, softened
- 2 cups (16 ounces) sour cream
- 1 cup blue cheese salad dressing
- ½ cup buffalo wing sauce
- 2½ cups shredded cooked chicken
- 2 cups (8 ounces) provolone cheese
- Baby carrots, celery ribs and crackers

1. Preheat oven to 350°. In a large bowl, beat cream cheese, sour cream, salad dressing and buffalo wing sauce until blended. Stir in the chicken and provolone cheese.

2. Transfer to a greased 2-qt. baking dish. Cover and bake for 25-30 minutes or until hot and bubbly. Serve warm with carrots, celery and crackers.

Mini Muffuletta

Everyone likes the bold flavors in these easy sandwich wedges. The recipe is great for parties or taking along to sporting events.

—**GARETH CRANER** MINDEN, NV

PREP: 25 MIN. + CHILLING
MAKES: 3 DOZEN

- 1 jar (10 ounces) pimiento-stuffed olives, drained and chopped
- 2 cans (4¼ ounces each) chopped ripe olives
- 2 tablespoons balsamic vinegar
- 1 tablespoon red wine vinegar
- 1 tablespoon olive oil
- 3 garlic cloves, minced
- 1 teaspoon dried basil
- 1 teaspoon dried oregano
- 6 French rolls, split
- ½ pound thinly sliced hard salami
- ¼ pound sliced provolone cheese
- ½ pound thinly sliced cotto salami
- ¼ pound sliced part-skim mozzarella cheese

1. In a large bowl, mix first eight ingredients; set aside. Hollow out tops and bottoms of rolls, leaving ¾-in. shells (discard removed bread or save for another use).

2. Spread olive mixture over tops and bottoms of rolls. On the roll bottoms, layer with hard salami, provolone cheese, cotto salami and mozzarella cheese. Replace tops.

3. Wrap muffuletta tightly in plastic wrap. Refrigerate overnight. Cut each into six wedges; secure with toothpicks.

NUTTY BERRY TRAIL MIX

SKEWERED CHICKEN
WITH PEANUT SAUCE

Skewered Chicken with Peanut Sauce

Satay-style chicken is always a popular choice. The golden brown chicken is accompanied with a delicious homemade peanut sauce. You'll find that these will be devoured quickly.
—**NANCY STEC** UPPERCO, MD

PREP: 30 MIN. + MARINATING • **GRILL:** 10 MIN
MAKES: 2½ DOZEN

- 3 **pounds boneless skinless chicken breast halves**
- ½ **cup orange juice**
- ½ **cup reduced-sodium soy sauce**
- ¼ **cup lime juice**
- 2 **tablespoons chunky peanut butter**
- 2 **garlic cloves, minced**
- 2 **teaspoons curry powder**
- 1 **teaspoon ground cumin**
- 1 **teaspoon ground ancho chili pepper**

SAUCE

- ¾ **cup coconut milk**
- ½ **cup chunky peanut butter**
- ¼ **cup lemon juice**
- 2 **tablespoons reduced-sodium soy sauce**
- 1 **tablespoon brown sugar**
- 2 **garlic cloves, minced**
- 1 **teaspoon grated fresh gingerroot**
- 1 **teaspoon crushed red pepper flakes**
- ½ **cup heavy whipping cream**
  Minced fresh cilantro

1. Flatten chicken to ¼-in. thickness; cut lengthwise into 1-in.-wide strips. In a small bowl, combine the orange juice, soy sauce, lime juice, peanut butter, garlic, curry powder, cumin and chili pepper.

2. Pour 1 cup mixture into a large resealable plastic bag. Add the chicken; seal bag and turn to coat. Refrigerate for at least 4 hours or overnight. Cover and refrigerate remaining mixture.

3. Drain chicken and discard marinade. Thread chicken onto 30 metal or soaked wooden skewers. Moisten a paper towel with cooking oil; using long-handled tongs, rub on grill rack to coat lightly. Grill chicken, covered, over medium heat or broil 4 in. from heat 3-4 minutes on each side or until no longer pink, basting with reserved juice mixture.

4. In a small saucepan, cook and stir first eight sauce ingredients over medium heat until smooth. Cool slightly. Transfer to a food processor; add cream. Cover and process until smooth. Sprinkle chicken with cilantro. Serve chicken warm with sauce.

FREEZE IT

Mushroom Palmiers

I found this recipe while working at a small-town museum in West Texas. It was the appetizer for a fundraiser a long, long time ago, and it's still a huge hit at parties. Frozen puff pastry helps make it easy and impressive.

—JUDY LOCK PANHANDLE, TX

PREP: 20 MIN. + COOLING
BAKE: 15 MIN./BATCH
MAKES: 4 DOZEN

- 2 tablespoons butter
- ¾ pound fresh mushrooms, finely chopped
- 1 small onion, finely chopped
- 1 teaspoon minced fresh thyme or ¼ teaspoon dried thyme
- ¾ teaspoon lemon juice
- ¾ teaspoon hot pepper sauce
- ¼ teaspoon salt
- 1 package (17.3 ounces) frozen puff pastry, thawed
- 1 egg
- 2 teaspoons water

1. Preheat oven to 400°. In a large skillet, heat butter over medium heat. Add mushrooms and onion; cook and stir until tender. Stir in thyme, lemon juice, hot pepper sauce and salt. Cool completely.

2. Unfold one pastry sheet. Spread half of the mushroom mixture to within ½ in. of edges. Roll up the left and right sides toward the center, jelly-roll style, until rolls meet in the middle. Cut into 24 slices. Repeat with remaining pastry and mushrooms.

3. Place on greased baking sheets. In a small bowl, whisk egg and water; brush over pastries. Bake for 15-20 minutes or until golden brown. Serve warm or at room temperature.

FREEZE OPTION *Freeze cooled appetizers in freezer containers, separating layers with waxed paper. To use, preheat oven to 400°. Reheat appetizers on a greased baking sheet until crisp and heated through.*

BUFFALO WING BITES

Buffalo Wing Bites

The Buffalo wing fans in my family were happy to taste test when I invented these snacks. We love them for every occasion.

—JASEY MCBURNETT
ROCK SPRINGS, WY

PREP: 25 MIN. • **BAKE:** 15 MIN.
MAKES: 2 DOZEN (2 CUPS DRESSING)

- 2 tablespoons grated Parmesan cheese
- 1 envelope ranch salad dressing mix, divided
- 1 cup mayonnaise
- 1 cup 2% milk
- ¼ cup crumbled blue cheese, optional
- 1¼ cups finely chopped cooked chicken breast
- 1¼ cups (5 ounces) shredded cheddar-Monterey Jack cheese
- ¼ cup Buffalo wing sauce
- 1 tube (13.8 ounces) refrigerated pizza crust
- 2 tablespoons butter, melted

1. Preheat oven to 400°. In a small bowl, combine Parmesan cheese and 1 teaspoon dressing mix. In another bowl, mix the mayonnaise, milk and remaining dressing mix. If desired, stir in blue cheese. Refrigerate until serving.

2. In a large bowl, mix chicken, cheddar-Monterey Jack cheese and wing sauce. On a lightly floured surface, unroll pizza crust dough and pat into a 14x12-in. rectangle. Cut into 24 squares.

3. Place 1 rounded tablespoon chicken mixture on the center of each square. Pull the corners together to enclose filling; pinch to seal. Place 1 in. apart on greased baking sheets, seam side down. Brush tops with butter; sprinkle with Parmesan cheese mixture.

4. Bake bites 15-17 minutes or until golden brown. Serve with the dressing.

Raspberry Lemonade Concentrate

Here's a concentrate that allows you to enjoy a refreshing summer beverage any time of year. Sweet raspberries balance the tartness from lemons.

—TASTE OF HOME TEST KITCHEN

PREP: 30 MIN. • **PROCESS:** 10 MIN.
MAKES: 5 PINTS (4 SERVINGS EACH)

- **4 pounds fresh raspberries (about 14 cups)**
- **6 cups sugar**
- **4 cups lemon juice**
  Chilled tonic water or ginger ale
  Ice cubes

1. Place raspberries in a food processor; cover and process until blended. Strain raspberries, reserving juice. Discard seeds. Place juice in a Dutch oven; stir in sugar and lemon juice. Heat over medium-high heat to 190°. Do not boil.

2. Remove from heat; skim off foam. Carefully ladle hot mixture into five hot 1-pint jars, leaving ¼-in. headspace. Wipe the rims; screw on the bands until fingertip tight.

3. Place jars into canner simmering water, ensuring that they are completely covered with water. Bring to a boil; process for 10 minutes. Remove jars and cool.

TO USE CONCENTRATE *Mix 1 pint concentrate with 1 pint tonic water. Serve over ice.*

NOTE *The processing time listed is for altitudes of 1,000 feet or less. Add 1 minute to the processing time for each 1,000 feet of additional altitude.*

Smoky Chicken Spread

The unique "smoky" flavor in this spread comes from smoked almonds. It makes a hearty snack on you favorite crackers. Don't expect many leftovers!

—MARY BETH WAGNER RIO, WI

PREP: 10 MIN. + CHILLING • **MAKES:** 4 CUPS

- **3 cups finely chopped cooked chicken**
- **½ cup finely chopped celery**
- **½ cup coarsely chopped smoked almonds**
- **¾ cup mayonnaise**
- **¼ cup finely chopped onion**
- **1 tablespoon honey**
- **½ teaspoon seasoned salt**
- **⅛ teaspoon pepper**
  Crackers

In a large bowl, combine the first eight ingredients. Cover and chill at least 2 hours. Serve with crackers.

Ranch Snack Mix

This is a wonderful fast-to-fix munchie. The recipe makes a generous 24 cups and doesn't involve any cooking. It's a cinch to make and really keeps its crunch.

—LINDA MURPHY PULASKI, WI

START TO FINISH: 15 MIN. • **MAKES:** 6 QUARTS

- **1 package (12 ounces) miniature pretzels**
- **2 packages (6 ounces each) Bugles**
- **1 can (10 ounces) salted cashews**
- **1 package (6 ounces) miniature cheddar cheese fish-shaped crackers**
- **1 envelope ranch salad dressing mix**
- **¾ cup canola oil**

In two large bowls, combine the pretzels, Bugles, cashews and crackers. Sprinkle with dressing mix; toss gently to combine. Drizzle with oil; toss until well coated. Store in airtight containers.

RANCH SNACK MIX

**HERB & SUN-DRIED
TOMATO MUFFINS, PAGE 66**

**ROASTED VEGETABLE
SALAD, PAGE 71**

**TEX-MEX SUMMER
SQUASH CASSEROLE, PAGE 64**

SALADS &
SIDE DISHES

**SQUASH MEDLEY,
PAGE 61**

66 God said, 'See, I have given
you every plant yielding
seed that is upon the face of
all the earth, and every tree
with seed in its fruit; you
shall have them for food.' 99

GENESIS 1:29

MEXICAN
LAYERED SALAD

FAST FIX
Mexican Layered Salad

I like to make this dish in advance. I add the cheese and chips just before serving. It's a different twist on a layered salad.
—**JOAN HALLFORD** FORT WORTH, TX

START TO FINISH: 20 MIN. • **MAKES:** 10 SERVINGS

- 4 **cups torn romaine**
- 1 **medium red onion, thinly sliced, optional**
- 1 **large cucumber, halved and sliced**
- 3 **medium tomatoes, chopped**
- 2 **medium ripe avocados, sliced or cut into ½-inch chunks**
- 1 **each large green and sweet red pepper, chopped or sliced**
- 1½ **cups mayonnaise**
- ¼ **cup canned chopped green chilies**
- 2 **teaspoons chili powder**
- ½ **teaspoon onion powder**
- ¼ **teaspoon salt**
- ¼ **teaspoon garlic powder**
- 1 **cup crushed tortilla chips**
- ½ **cup shredded cheddar cheese**

In a 2-qt. trifle bowl or glass serving bowl, layer fresh vegetables. In a small bowl, mix mayonnaise, chilies and seasonings; spread over top. Sprinkle with chips and cheese.

FAST FIX
Glazed Snap Peas

I have to have veggies with every meal, and this recipe is perfect for busy days. I love the natural sweet taste from snap peas. It will go well with just about any entree.
—**IDA TUEY** SOUTH LYON, MI

START TO FINISH: 20 MIN. • **MAKES:** 10 SERVINGS

- 2 **packages (24 ounces each) frozen sugar snap peas**
- ¼ **cup honey**
- 2 **tablespoons butter**
- 1 **teaspoon salt**
- ¼ **teaspoon crushed red pepper flakes**
- ¼ **cup real bacon bits**

Cook peas according to package directions; drain. Stir in the honey, butter, salt and pepper flakes. Sprinkle with bacon.

Pickled Mushrooms for a Crowd

Serve tangy pickled mushrooms alongside a steak, as an appetizer with picks, in a salad or as part of an antipasto platter. However you present them, you can't go wrong.
—**JOHN LEVEZOW** EAGAN, MN

PREP: 15 MIN. • **COOK:** 15 MIN. + CHILLING
MAKES: ABOUT 7½ DOZEN (6 CUPS MIXTURE)

- 3 **pounds medium fresh mushrooms**
- 8 **cups water**
- 2 **cups sugar**
- 2 **cups white vinegar**
- 2 **cups dry red wine**
- 3 **tablespoons bitters**
- 1 **teaspoon onion powder**
- 1 **teaspoon garlic salt**
- 1 **teaspoon beef bouillon granules**
- 1 **bay leaf**

1. In a large saucepan, combine mushrooms and water. Bring to a boil; boil 1 minute. Drain; return mushrooms to pan.

2. In a small saucepan, combine the remaining ingredients; bring to a boil, stirring constantly. Pour over mushrooms; cool slightly.

3. Transfer mushroom mixture to glass jars with tight-fitting lids. Cover and refrigerate at least 2 days. Just before serving, discard bay leaf.

PICKLED MUSHROOMS FOR A CROWD

FAST FIX

Special Radicchio-Spinach Salad

When you hear of mint, chipotle pepper and honey blended together, you may wonder how it will taste. Well, plan to be amazed—my spicy-sweet salad is simply delicious.
—**ROXANNE CHAN** ALBANY, CA

START TO FINISH: 20 MIN. • **MAKES:** 12 SERVINGS

- 6 **cups fresh baby spinach**
- 1 **head radicchio, torn**
- 2 **cups fresh raspberries**
- ½ **cup raisins**
- ¼ **cup pine nuts, toasted**
- ¼ **cup thinly sliced red onion**
- ¼ **cup minced fresh mint**
- 3 **tablespoons lime juice**
- 2 **tablespoons olive oil**
- 2 **teaspoons honey**
- 1½ **to 3 teaspoons chopped chipotle pepper in adobo sauce**
- ¼ **teaspoon salt**
- ½ **cup crumbled feta cheese**

In a large salad bowl, combine the first seven ingredients. In a small saucepan, combine the lime juice, oil, honey, chipotle pepper and salt. Cook and stir until blended and heated through. Immediately pour over salad; toss to coat. Sprinkle with cheese.

SPECIAL RADICCHIO-SPINACH SALAD

Pesto Pasta & Potatoes

Although this healthy pasta dish is pretty simple to begin with, it's made even simpler because you can throw the green beans and pasta into one big pot to cook.
—**LAURA FLOWERS** MOSCOW, ID

START TO FINISH: 30 MIN. • **MAKES:** 12 SERVINGS

1½ pounds small red potatoes, halved
12 ounces uncooked whole grain spiral pasta
3 cups cut fresh or frozen green beans
1 jar (6½ ounces) prepared pesto
1 cup grated Parmigiano-Reggiano cheese

1. Place the potatoes in a large saucepan; add water to cover. Bring to a boil. Reduce heat; cook, uncovered, 9-11 minutes or until tender. Drain; place in a large bowl.
2. Meanwhile, cook pasta according to package directions, adding green beans during the last 5 minutes of cooking; drain, reserving ¾ cup pasta water.
3. Add pasta and green beans to potatoes. Stir in pesto, cheese and enough reserved pasta water to coat.

Thyme-Roasted Vegetables

The aroma of the roasting vegetables calls everyone to dinner. Normally it serves 10, but my husband is known to have more than one serving at a time. It's that good.
—**JASMINE ROSE** CRYSTAL LAKE, IL

PREP: 25 MIN. • **BAKE:** 45 MIN.
MAKES: 10 SERVINGS (¾ CUP EACH)

2 pounds red potatoes, cubed (about 9 cups)
3 cups sliced sweet onions (about 1½ large)
3 medium carrots, sliced
½ pound medium fresh mushrooms, halved
1 large sweet red pepper, cut into 1½-inch pieces
1 large sweet yellow pepper, cut into 1½-inch pieces
2 tablespoons butter, melted
2 tablespoons olive oil
1 tablespoon minced fresh thyme or 1 teaspoon dried thyme
1 teaspoon salt
¼ teaspoon pepper

1. Preheat oven to 400°. In a large bowl, combine vegetables. Add remaining ingredients; toss to coat.
2. Transfer to a 15x10x1-in. baking pan. Roast 45-50 minutes or until tender, stirring occasionally.

Company Green Salad

I put this salad partially together in advance and take the remaining ingredients (candied nuts, seeds, rice noodles and dressing) to mix in at the potluck I'm attending. It works perfectly every time.
—**JOAN HALLFORD** FORT WORTH, TX

START TO FINISH: 25 MIN. • **MAKES:** 12 SERVINGS

2 teaspoons butter
¾ cup sliced almonds
1 tablespoon sugar
DRESSING
¼ cup canola oil
3 tablespoons rice vinegar
2 tablespoons brown sugar
SALAD
8 cups torn leaf lettuce
1 medium sweet red pepper, chopped
1 medium sweet yellow pepper, chopped
2 green onions, chopped
1 can (3 ounces) crispy rice noodles
⅓ cup sunflower kernels

1. In a small heavy skillet, melt butter. Add the almonds and cook over medium heat until toasted, about 4 minutes. Sprinkle with sugar. Cook and stir 2-3 minutes or until the sugar is melted. Spread on foil to cool.
2. For dressing, in a small bowl, whisk oil, vinegar and brown sugar. Chill until serving.
3. For salad, in a large bowl, combine the lettuce, peppers and green onions. Add dressing; toss to coat. Sprinkle with rice noodles, sunflower kernels and almonds. Serve immediately.

**COMPANY
GREEN SALAD**

White Cheddar Scalloped Potatoes

I've been tweaking my scalloped potato recipe for more than eight years. After I added the thyme, ham and sour cream, my husband declared, "This is it!"

—**HOPE TOOLE** MUSCLE SHOALS, AL

PREP: 40 MIN. • **BAKE:** 70 MIN.
MAKES: 10 SERVINGS

- ¼ cup butter
- 1 medium onion, finely chopped
- ¼ cup all-purpose flour
- 1 teaspoon salt
- 1 teaspoon dried parsley flakes
- ½ teaspoon dried thyme
- ½ teaspoon pepper
- 3 cups 2% milk
- 1 can (10¾ ounces) condensed cream of mushroom soup, undiluted
- 1 cup (8 ounces) sour cream
- 8 cups thinly sliced peeled potatoes
- 3½ cups cubed fully cooked ham
- 2 cups (8 ounces) shredded sharp white cheddar cheese

1. Preheat oven to 375°. In a large saucepan, heat the butter over medium-high heat. Add onion; cook and stir until tender. Stir in flour and seasonings until blended; gradually whisk in milk. Bring to a boil, stirring constantly; cook and stir 2 minutes or until thickened. Stir in soup. Remove from heat; stir in sour cream.

2. In a greased 13x9-in. baking dish, layer half of each of the following: potatoes, ham, cheese and sauce. Repeat layers.

3. Bake, covered, 30 minutes. Bake, uncovered, 40-50 minutes longer or until potatoes are tender.

WHITE CHEDDAR SCALLOPED POTATOES

Bacon Macaroni & Cheese

Creamy with a hint of beer, this macaroni is one of our favorites for a big family dinner.
—**LAUREN PETERSEN** EVERETT, WA

PREP: 20 MIN. • **BAKE:** 15 MIN. • **MAKES:** 12 SERVINGS

- 1 package (16 ounces) elbow macaroni
- ¼ cup butter
- 2 garlic cloves, minced
- ¼ cup all-purpose flour
- 1 tablespoon ground mustard
- 1 teaspoon salt
- ¾ teaspoon pepper
- 2½ cups 2% milk
- ¾ cup amber beer
- ¼ cup heavy whipping cream
- 3 cups (12 ounces) shredded cheddar cheese, divided
- 2 cups (8 ounces) shredded fontina cheese
- 2 tablespoons grated Parmesan cheese, divided
- 2 tablespoons minced chives
- 5 bacon strips, cooked and crumbled

1. Cook macaroni according to package directions for al dente.
2. Meanwhile, in a Dutch oven, heat butter over medium-high heat. Add garlic; cook and stir for 1 minute. Stir in the flour, mustard, salt and pepper until smooth; gradually whisk in the milk, beer and cream. Bring to a boil; cook and stir for 2 minutes or until thickened.
3. Reduce heat. Stir in 2 cups cheddar cheese, fontina cheese and 1 tablespoon Parmesan cheese until melted. Add chives.
4. Drain macaroni; stir into sauce. Transfer to a greased 3-qt. baking dish. Sprinkle with remaining cheddar and Parmesan cheeses.
5. Bake, uncovered, at 400° for 15-20 minutes or until golden brown and heated through. Top with crumbled bacon. Let stand for 5 minutes before serving.

Caraway Coleslaw with Citrus Mayonnaise

The combination of caraway and orange keeps this slaw from being anything but mediocre. I always get requests to bring a big batch to potlucks.
—**LILY JULOW** LAWRENCEVILLE, GA

PREP: 20 MIN. + CHILLING • **MAKES:** 12 SERVINGS (⅔ CUP EACH)

- 1 medium head cabbage, finely shredded
- 1 tablespoon sugar
- 2 teaspoons salt

DRESSING

- ⅔ cup reduced-fat mayonnaise
- ⅓ cup orange juice
- 3 tablespoons cider vinegar
- 2 tablespoons caraway seeds
- 2 teaspoons grated orange peel
- ¼ teaspoon salt
- ¼ teaspoon pepper

1. Place cabbage in a colander over a plate. Sprinkle with sugar and salt; toss to coat. Let stand 1 hour.
2. In a small bowl, whisk the dressing ingredients until blended. Rinse cabbage and drain well; place in a large bowl. Add dressing; toss to coat. Refrigerate, covered, overnight.

FAST FIX
Squash Medley

This colorful side dish is ideal for a party and a great way to use up your summer bounty of tomatoes and squash.
—**JEN STUTTS** FLORENCE, AL

START TO FINISH: 25 MIN. • **MAKES:** 12 SERVINGS (⅔ CUP EACH)

- 3 medium yellow summer squash, sliced
- 3 medium zucchini, sliced
- 1 medium red onion, chopped
- 2 tablespoons olive oil
- 1½ cups sliced fresh mushrooms
- 1 medium tomato, cut into wedges
- 2 garlic cloves, minced
  - Salt and pepper to taste

In a large skillet, saute squash, zucchini and onion in oil until crisp-tender. Add mushrooms, tomato and garlic, saute 4-5 minutes longer. Season with salt and pepper.

SQUASH MEDLEY

Pierogi Skillet

With sauerkraut, cabbage, onion and egg noodles, this dish has all the flavor of traditional pierogies but without all the work of making the dumplings. Just combine the ingredients in a skillet and let it simmer.

—**BERNICE REMBISZ** HOUSATONIC, MA

PREP: 10 MIN. • **COOK:** 1¼ HOURS • **MAKES:** 12 SERVINGS

- ½ pound sliced bacon, diced
- 1 large onion, chopped
- 1 can (27 ounces) sauerkraut, rinsed and squeezed dry
- 1 small head cabbage, shredded
- ½ teaspoon pepper
- 5 cups uncooked egg noodles
- 6 tablespoons butter
- 1½ teaspoons salt

1. In a large skillet or Dutch oven, cook the bacon over medium heat until almost crisp. Add onion; cook and stir until bacon is crisp and onion is tender. Drain. Add sauerkraut, cabbage and pepper; mix well. Cover and simmer 45 minutes.

2. Meanwhile, cook the noodles according to package directions; drain. Stir the noodles, butter and salt into the cabbage mixture. Cover and simmer 30 minutes.

PIEROGI SKILLET

Colorful Bean Salad

I experimented with all kinds of bean salads before I hit on this one. My husband loves all the different bean varieties, and corn adds to the color and texture.

—**DALE BENOIT** MONSON, MA

PREP: 25 MIN. + CHILLING • **MAKES:** 13 SERVINGS (¾ CUP EACH)

- 2 cups fresh or frozen corn, thawed
- 1 can (16 ounces) kidney beans, rinsed and drained
- 1 can (16 ounces) red beans, rinsed and drained
- 1 can (15½ ounces) white kidney or cannellini beans, rinsed and drained
- 1 can (15¼ ounces) lima beans, rinsed and drained
- 1 can (15 ounces) black beans, rinsed and drained
- 1 can (2¼ ounces) sliced ripe olives, drained
- 1 large green pepper, chopped
- 1 small onion, chopped
- ½ cup chili sauce
- ¼ cup olive oil
- ¼ cup red wine vinegar
- 2 garlic cloves, minced
- 2 teaspoons dried oregano
- ½ teaspoon pepper

1. In a large bowl, combine first nine ingredients. In a small bowl, whisk the chili sauce, oil, vinegar, garlic, oregano and pepper. Pour over bean mixture; toss to coat.

2. Refrigerate at least 1 hour before serving.

FAST FIX ▶

Honey-Thyme Butternut Squash

Instead of potatoes, try whipping up mashed butternut squash with honey, butter and thyme. More than a festive Thanksgiving side, this 30-minute dish will be a new fall favorite for weeknight meals, too.

—**BIANCA NOISEUX** BRISTOL, CT

START TO FINISH: 30 MIN. • **MAKES:** 10 SERVINGS

- 1 large butternut squash (about 5 pounds), peeled and cubed
- ¼ cup butter, cubed
- 3 tablespoons half-and-half cream
- 2 tablespoons honey
- 2 teaspoons dried parsley flakes
- ½ teaspoon salt
- ⅛ teaspoon dried thyme
- ⅛ teaspoon coarsely ground pepper

1. In a large saucepan, bring 1 in. of water to a boil. Add the squash; cover and cook 10-15 minutes or until tender.

2. Drain. Mash squash with the remaining ingredients.

BROCCOLI SAUTE

FAST FIX
Broccoli Saute

When I needed a new recipe for cooking broccoli, I came up with my own. It makes a nice side dish for most entrees.

—JIM MACNEAL WATERLOO, NY

START TO FINISH: 15 MIN. • **MAKES:** 10 SERVINGS

- 1 cup chopped onion
- 1 cup julienned sweet red pepper
- ¼ cup olive oil
- 12 cups fresh broccoli florets
- 1⅓ cups water
- 3 teaspoons minced garlic
- ½ teaspoon salt
- ½ teaspoon pepper

In a Dutch oven, saute onion and red pepper in oil for 2-3 minutes or until crisp-tender. Stir in the broccoli, water, garlic, salt and pepper. Cover and cook over medium heat 5-6 minutes or until the broccoli is crisp-tender.

FAST FIX
Connie's Tortellini Salad

Make this substantial salad for a potluck or for long, leisurely, eat-whenever weekends at the lake.

—CONNIE EATON PITTSBURGH, PA

START TO FINISH: 30 MIN. • **MAKES:** 16 SERVINGS (¾ CUP EACH)

- 1 package (13 ounces) dried cheese tortellini
- 1 medium zucchini, halved and sliced
- 1 cup Italian salad dressing
- 1 pint grape tomatoes
- 1 can (14 ounces) water-packed artichoke hearts, rinsed, drained and quartered
- 1 jar (11.1 ounces) pitted Greek olives, drained
- 1 carton (8 ounces) miniature fresh mozzarella cheese balls, drained

In a large saucepan, cook tortellini according to package directions. Drain; transfer to a large bowl. Immediately add zucchini and dressing; toss to coat. Stir in the remaining ingredients. Serve warm or refrigerate and serve cold.

Tex-Mex Summer Squash Casserole

Mild-flavored yellow squash gets a big boost from flavor-packed chilies, jalapenos and red onion. Use zucchini instead of yellow summer squash if you like.

—TOMMY LOMBARDO EUCLID, OH

PREP: 15 MIN.
BAKE: 40 MIN. + STANDING
MAKES: 10 SERVINGS

- 7 medium yellow summer squash, sliced (about 10 cups)
- 2¼ cups (9 ounces) shredded cheddar cheese, divided
- 1 medium onion, chopped
- 1 can (4 ounces) chopped green chilies
- 1 can (4 ounces) diced jalapeno peppers, drained
- ¼ cup all-purpose flour
- ½ teaspoon salt
- ¾ cup salsa
- 4 green onions, sliced
- ¼ cup chopped red onion

1. Preheat oven to 400°. In a large bowl, combine squash, ¾ cup cheese, onion, chilies and jalapenos. Sprinkle with flour and salt; toss to combine.
2. Transfer to a greased 13x9-in. baking dish. Bake, covered, 30-40 minutes or until squash is tender.
3. Spoon salsa over top; sprinkle with remaining 1½ cups cheese. Bake, uncovered, 10-15 minutes longer or until golden brown. Let stand 10 minutes. Top with green and red onions before serving.

FAST FIX ▶
Sicilian Salad

Loaded with fabulous flavor, this hearty salad comes together in no time. Chop the tomatoes and celery and cube the mozzarella before guests arrive, and you'll have this ready in moments.

—BETH BURGMEIER
EAST DUBUQUE, IL

START TO FINISH: 15 MIN.
MAKES: 10 SERVINGS

- 1 package (9 ounces) iceberg lettuce blend
- 1 jar (16 ounces) pickled banana peppers, drained and sliced
- 1 jar (5¾ ounces) sliced green olives with pimientos, drained
- 3 plum tomatoes, chopped
- 4 celery ribs, chopped
- 1 cup chopped pepperoni
- ½ cup cubed part-skim mozzarella cheese
- ½ cup Italian salad dressing

In a large bowl, combine the first seven ingredients. Drizzle with dressing and toss to coat.

TEX-MEX SUMMER
SQUASH CASSEROLE

Harvest Salad with Cherry Vinaigrette

Mixed greens and plenty of produce make this salad so satisfying, and it's gorgeous to serve for occasions.
—**JAYE BEELER** GRAND RAPIDS, MI

PREP: 10 MIN. • **BAKE:** 50 MIN. + COOLING
MAKES: 10 SERVINGS (1 CUP EACH)

- 3 medium fresh beets (about 1 pound)
- 1 package (5 ounces) spring mix salad greens
- 2 medium apples, thinly sliced
- 1 medium carrot, shredded
- ½ cup grape tomatoes, halved
- ½ cup yellow grape tomatoes or pear tomatoes, halved
- ½ cup garbanzo beans or chickpeas, rinsed and drained
- ½ cup coarsely chopped walnuts, toasted
- 4 thick-sliced bacon strips, cooked and crumbled

CHERRY VINAIGRETTE

- ½ cup tart cherry preserves
- 3 tablespoons olive oil
- 2 tablespoons red wine vinegar
- 2 teaspoons Dijon mustard
- 1 garlic clove, minced
- ¼ teaspoon salt
- ⅛ teaspoon pepper

1. Preheat oven to 400°. Scrub beets and trim tops to 1 in. Wrap in foil; place on a baking sheet. Bake 50-60 minutes or until tender. Remove foil; cool completely. Peel beets and cut into ½-in. pieces.
2. In a large bowl, combine salad greens, apples, carrot, tomatoes, beans, walnuts, bacon and cooled beets. In a small bowl, whisk vinaigrette ingredients until blended. Serve with salad.

HARVEST SALAD WITH CHERRY VINAIGRETTE

HERB & SUN-DRIED TOMATO MUFFINS

Herb & Sun-Dried Tomato Muffins

Mom served these muffins instead of bread or buns. Now I make them to serve with soup or chili. Double the recipe to feed a crowd. These go quickly!
—**ELIZABETH KING** DULUTH, MN

PREP: 15 MIN. • **BAKE:** 20 MIN. • **MAKES:** 1 DOZEN

- 2 **cups all-purpose flour**
- 2 **teaspoons baking powder**
- 1 **teaspoon snipped fresh dill or ¼ teaspoon dill weed**
- 1 **teaspoon minced fresh thyme or ¼ teaspoon dried thyme**
- ½ **teaspoon baking soda**
- ½ **teaspoon salt**
- ½ **teaspoon pepper**
- 1 **egg**
- 1¼ **cups 2% milk**
- ¼ **cup olive oil**
- ½ **cup shredded cheddar cheese**
- ½ **cup oil-packed sun-dried tomatoes, finely chopped**

1. Preheat oven to 375°. In a large bowl, mix first seven ingredients. In another bowl, whisk egg, milk and oil. Add to flour mixture; stir just until moistened. Fold in cheese and tomatoes.
2. Fill greased muffin cups three-fourths full. Bake for 18-20 minutes or until a toothpick inserted in center comes out clean. Cool 5 minutes before removing from pan to a wire rack. Serve warm.

FAST FIX
Chive Smashed Potatoes

No need to peel the potatoes—in fact, this is the only way we make mashed potatoes anymore. Mixing in the flavored cream cheese is a delightful twist.
—**BEVERLY NORRIS** EVANSTON, WY

START TO FINISH: 30 MIN. • **MAKES:** 12 SERVINGS (⅔ CUP EACH)

- 4 **pounds red potatoes, quartered**
- 2 **teaspoons chicken bouillon granules**
- 1 **carton (8 ounces) spreadable chive and onion cream cheese**
- ½ **cup half-and-half cream**
- ¼ **cup butter, cubed**
- 1 **teaspoon salt**
- ¼ **teaspoon pepper**

1. Place potatoes and bouillon in a Dutch oven and cover with 8 cups water. Bring to a boil. Reduce heat; cover and cook for 15-20 minutes or until tender.
2. Drain and return to pan. Mash potatoes with cream cheese, cream, butter, salt and pepper.

MOM'S SPECIAL POTATO SALAD

Mom's Special Potato Salad

A rich and creamy homemade dressing is the perfect base for the potatoes, celery and onion...and any other ingredients you might want to add to this traditional salad. It's always a hit.

—DANIELLE BRANDT RUTHTON, MN

PREP: 30 MIN. • **COOK:** 20 MIN. + CHILLING
MAKES: 18 SERVINGS (¾ CUP EACH)

DRESSING
- 3 eggs
- ½ cup sugar
- ½ cup cider vinegar
- 3 tablespoons heavy whipping cream
- 2 teaspoons butter
- 1 teaspoon ground mustard
  Dash salt
- 2 cups mayonnaise

SALAD
- 6 pounds potatoes, peeled and cubed (about 10 large)
- 5 celery ribs, thinly sliced
- 1 large onion, chopped
  Pepper to taste, optional

1. In a double boiler or metal bowl over simmering water, constantly whisk the eggs, sugar, vinegar, cream, butter, mustard and salt until mixture reaches 160° or is thick enough to coat the back of a metal spoon. Remove from the heat; cool to room temperature. Fold in mayonnaise. Chill until preparing salad.

2. For salad, place potatoes in a large saucepan and cover with water. Bring to a boil. Reduce heat; cover and cook for 10-15 minutes or until tender. Drain and cool to room temperature. In a large bowl, combine the potatoes, celery and onion. Add dressing and, if desired, pepper; stir until blended. Chill until serving.

Baked Vegetable Medley

Good news—you can assemble this dish the night before and then simply bake it the day of the big event. What a time-saver! Add some cooked and cubed chicken for a heartier version.

—LINDA VAIL BALLWIN, MO

PREP: 35 MIN. + CHILLING • **BAKE:** 40 MIN. • **MAKES:** 12 SERVINGS

- 1 medium head cauliflower, broken into florets
- 1 bunch broccoli, cut into florets
- 6 medium carrots, sliced
- 1 pound sliced fresh mushrooms
- 1 bunch green onions, sliced
- ¼ cup butter, cubed
- 1 can (10¾ ounces) condensed cream of chicken soup, undiluted
- ½ cup milk
- ½ cup process cheese sauce

1. Place the cauliflower, broccoli and carrots in a steamer basket; place in a large saucepan over 1 in. of water. Bring to a boil; cover and steam 7-9 minutes or until crisp-tender.

2. Meanwhile, in a large skillet, saute mushrooms and onions in butter until tender.

3. Drain vegetables. In a large bowl, combine soup, milk and cheese sauce. Add vegetables and mushroom mixture; toss to coat. Transfer to a greased 2-qt. baking dish. Cover and refrigerate overnight.

4. Remove from the refrigerator 30 minutes before baking. Preheat oven to 350°. Bake, uncovered, 40-45 minutes or until bubbly.

1. In a large bowl, combine the salad ingredients. In a small bowl, whisk the vinaigrette ingredients.
2. Just before serving, pour ¾ cup vinaigrette over salad; toss to coat. Refrigerate remaining vinaigrette for another use.

Chive & Onion Hash Brown Potatoes

A friend once told me about a potato dish her mother used to make. She remembered that Swiss cheese and butter were standouts. Here's my take on it—my friend actually liked it better than her mom's version.

—**BARB TEMPLIN** NORWOOD, MN

PREP: 15 MIN. • **BAKE:** 45 MIN. + STANDING
MAKES: 12 SERVINGS (¾ CUP EACH)

- 1½ cups half-and-half cream
- 1 container (8 ounces) spreadable chive and onion cream cheese
- 2 tablespoons dried minced onion
- 1 teaspoon salt
- ½ teaspoon pepper
- 2 packages (20 ounces each) refrigerated shredded hash brown potatoes
- 2 cups shredded Swiss cheese
- 3 tablespoons minced fresh chives, divided
- 2 tablespoons butter, cubed

1. Preheat oven to 375°. In a Dutch oven, combine the first five ingredients; cook and stir over medium heat until blended. Stir in potatoes.
2. In a greased 13x9-in. or 3-qt. baking dish, layer a third of the hash brown mixture and ⅔ cup Swiss cheese; sprinkle with 1 tablespoon chives. Repeat layers. Top with remaining hash brown mixture and cheese; dot with butter.
3. Bake, covered, 35 minutes. Bake, uncovered, 10-20 minutes longer or until edges begin to brown and potatoes are heated through. Let stand 10 minutes before serving. Sprinkle with remaining chives.

FAST FIX

Italian Fresh Vegetable Salad

Garden-fresh veggies are a hit at community potlucks. I simply bring the dressing with me in a mason jar to add just before serving.

—**JEANETTE HILDEBRAND** STAFFORD, KS

START TO FINISH: 25 MIN. • **MAKES:** 20 SERVINGS (1 CUP EACH)

SALAD
- 1 bunch romaine, torn
- 4 cups fresh baby spinach
- 2 cups grape tomatoes
- 1 can (14 ounces) water-packed artichoke hearts, rinsed, drained and quartered
- 1 medium zucchini, thinly sliced
- 1 small green pepper, sliced
- 1 small sweet red pepper, sliced
- 1 cup thinly sliced fresh mushrooms
- 1 cup thinly sliced red onion
- 1 cup (4 ounces) shredded part-skim mozzarella cheese
- ½ cup sliced pepperoncini
- 1 can (2¼ ounces) sliced ripe olives, drained

VINAIGRETTE
- ⅔ cup canola oil
- ½ cup red wine vinegar
- ¼ cup minced fresh basil
- 1½ teaspoons garlic powder
- 1½ teaspoons ground mustard
- 1 teaspoon honey
- ½ teaspoon salt

TOP TIP

Easy Onion Options

When there's no time to chop onions, onion powder is one option. Substitute 1 tablespoon of onion powder for one medium chopped onion. For the best onion flavor, however, use frozen chopped onions or dried minced onion. One tablespoon of dried minced onion equals ¼ cup minced raw onion.

**CHIVE & ONION
HASH BROWN POTATOES**

FAST FIX ▶

Green Beans Supreme

Here's a fun alternative to plain green bean casserole. I prepare a well-seasoned cheese sauce that lends a little zip to the familiar side dish.
—**HEATHER CAMPBELL** LAWRENCE, KS

START TO FINISH: 25 MIN. • **MAKES:** 12-16 SERVINGS

- 4 packages (16 ounces each) frozen cut green beans
- ¼ cup finely chopped onion
- ¼ cup butter, cubed
- 2 tablespoons all-purpose flour
- 1 teaspoon salt
- 1 teaspoon paprika
- 1 teaspoon Worcestershire sauce
- ½ teaspoon ground mustard
- 2 cups evaporated milk
- 8 ounces process cheese (Velveeta), shredded

TOPPING
- ¼ cup dry bread crumbs
- 2 teaspoons butter, melted

1. Cook green beans according to package directions. Meanwhile, in a Dutch oven, saute onion in butter until tender. Remove from the heat; whisk in the flour, salt, paprika, Worcestershire sauce and ground mustard until blended.

2. Gradually stir in milk. Bring to a boil; cook and stir for 2 minutes or until thickened and bubbly. Remove from the heat; stir in cheese.

3. Drain beans; gently fold into cheese sauce. Transfer to a large serving bowl. Toss bread crumbs and butter; sprinkle over beans.

Deli-Style Pasta Salad

When I'm having weekend guests, I make this salad the day before they arrive. The flavors blend wonderfully when it's chilled overnight, and it keeps well for several days. It's always welcomed at picnics and potlucks, too.
—**JILL EVELY** WILMORE, KY

PREP: 15 MIN. + CHILLING • **MAKES:** 12 SERVINGS

- 1 package (16 ounces) tricolor spiral pasta
- 2 medium plum tomatoes, seeded and julienned
- 8 ounces sliced salami, julienned
- 8 ounces provolone cheese, julienned
- 1 small red onion, thinly sliced and separated into rings
- 1 jar (5¾ ounces) pimiento-stuffed olives, drained
- 1 can (2¼ ounces) sliced ripe olives, drained
- ¼ cup grated Parmesan cheese
- 1 bottle (8 ounces) Italian salad dressing

1. Cook pasta according to package directions; drain and rinse in cold water.

2. In a large bowl, combine the pasta, tomatoes, salami, provolone cheese, onion, olives and cheese. Add dressing; toss to coat. Cover and refrigerate for several hours or overnight. Serve with a slotted spoon.

FAST FIX ▶

Down Home Succotash

If you grow your own corn, it will be really fresh for this recipe if you make sure everything is ready before you pick the corn. That's the way I like it.
—**MARIAN PLATT** SEQUIM, WA

START TO FINISH: 25 MIN. • **MAKES:** 12-14 SERVINGS

- ¼ pound sliced bacon, chopped
- 2 cups fresh or frozen corn
- ½ pound lima beans
- 1 medium green pepper, chopped
- 1 medium onion, chopped
- 2 medium tomatoes, cut into wedges

1. In a large skillet, cook bacon until crisp. Remove bacon to paper towels and drain all but 1 tablespoon drippings.

2. In the same skillet, add the corn, beans, green pepper and onion. Simmer for 10-15 minutes or until vegetables are almost tender, adding water if necessary. Stir in tomatoes and bacon; cook just until tomatoes are heated through.

DOWN HOME SUCCOTASH

Roasted Vegetable Salad

For even more flavor, mix field greens and crisp, crumbled bacon into this appealing veggie salad. Or whisk a tablespoon of honey into the dressing. Friends will love it.
—**LAURA MCALLISTER** MORGANTON, NC

PREP: 30 MIN. • **BAKE:** 20 MIN. • **MAKES:** 12 SERVINGS (⅔ CUP EACH)

- 1 **pound small red potatoes, quartered**
- 2 **medium ears sweet corn, halved**
- ½ **pound baby portobello mushrooms, halved**
- 1 **medium sweet red pepper, cut into strips**
- 2 **medium leeks (white portion only), cut into 2-inch lengths**
- ¼ **cup plus 2 tablespoons olive oil, divided**
- ½ **teaspoon salt**
- ¼ **teaspoon pepper**
- ½ **pound fresh asparagus, cut into 2-inch lengths**
- 2 **garlic cloves, minced**
- ½ **teaspoon crushed red pepper flakes**
- 2 **cups cubed French bread**
- 10 **cherry tomatoes, halved**
- 1 **cup (4 ounces) crumbled feta cheese**
- 1 **cup thinly sliced fresh basil leaves**

DRESSING
- ⅓ **cup olive oil**
- ¼ **cup red wine vinegar**

1. Preheat oven to 425°. In a large bowl, combine the first five ingredients. Drizzle with ¼ cup oil; sprinkle with salt and pepper and toss to coat. Place in two greased 15x10-in. baking pans. Bake 20-25 minutes or until potatoes are tender.

2. Meanwhile, in a large skillet, saute asparagus in remaining oil until tender. Add garlic and pepper flakes; cook 1 minute longer.

3. Cut corn from cobs; place in a large bowl. Stir in the bread, tomatoes, cheese, basil, asparagus and roasted vegetable mixture. For dressing, combine oil and vinegar; drizzle over mixture and toss to coat.

Oven-Roasted Spring Vegetable Medley

With potatoes, asparagus, squash and radishes, there's something for everyone in this dish. What a wonderful way to present a variety of spring veggies.

—**TRISHA KRUSE** EAGLE, ID

PREP: 15 MIN. • **BAKE:** 35 MIN.
MAKES: 10 SERVINGS

- 9 **small red potatoes, quartered**
- 2 **tablespoons olive oil**
- ½ **teaspoon salt**
- ¼ **teaspoon pepper**
- 1 **pound fresh asparagus, trimmed and cut into 1-inch pieces**
- 2 **small yellow summer squash, quartered and cut into ½-inch slices**
- 2 **small zucchini, quartered and cut into ½-inch slices**
- 6 **radishes, quartered**
- ⅓ **cup balsamic vinegar**
- 3 **tablespoons brown sugar**

1. Preheat oven to 425°. In a large bowl, toss potatoes with oil, salt and pepper. Transfer to a shallow roasting pan. Bake 15 minutes.
2. In same bowl, combine the remaining ingredients; add to pan. Bake 20-25 minutes longer or until vegetables are tender.

OVEN-ROASTED SPRING VEGETABLE MEDLEY

TOP TIP

Balsamic Basics

Balsamic vinegar is made from sweet white grapes and is aged in wooden barrels for at least 10 years. You can substitute cider vinegar or a mild red wine vinegar. White wine vinegar is much stronger and sharper, and it should be used sparingly if it's your only substitute.

Creamy Spinach Casserole

Creamed spinach is a beloved standby, but it's missing a salty crunch. Adding seasoned stuffing crumbs turns this dish into an ideal side dish for just about any event.

—ANNETTE MARIE YOUNG
WEST LAFAYETTE, IN

PREP: 10 MIN. • **BAKE:** 35 MIN.
MAKES: 10 SERVINGS

- 2 **cans (10¾ ounces each) reduced-fat reduced-sodium condensed cream of chicken soup, undiluted**
- 1 **package (8 ounces) reduced-fat cream cheese, cubed**
- ½ **cup fat-free milk**
- ½ **cup grated Parmesan cheese**
- 4 **cups herb seasoned stuffing cubes**
- 2 **packages (10 ounces each) frozen chopped spinach, thawed and squeezed dry**

1. Preheat oven to 350°. In a large bowl, beat soup, cream cheese, milk and Parmesan cheese until blended. Stir in stuffing cubes and spinach.
2. Spoon into a 2-qt. baking dish coated with cooking spray. Bake, uncovered, 35-40 minutes or until heated through.

Lemon Vinaigrette Potato Salad

I developed this recipe for a friend who wanted a potato salad without mayonnaise. I substituted fresh thyme for the basil, but any fresh herbs would work well.

—MELANIE CLOYD MULLICA HILL, NJ

PREP: 25 MIN. • **COOK:** 15 MIN.
MAKES: 12 SERVINGS

- 3 **pounds red potatoes, cut into 1-inch cubes**
- ½ **cup olive oil**
- 3 **tablespoons lemon juice**
- 2 **tablespoons minced fresh basil**
- 2 **tablespoons minced fresh parsley**
- 1 **tablespoon red wine vinegar**
- 1 **teaspoon grated lemon peel**
- ¾ **teaspoon salt**
- ½ **teaspoon pepper**
- 1 **small onion, finely chopped**

1. Place potatoes in a large saucepan and cover with water. Bring to a boil. Reduce heat; cover and simmer for 10-15 minutes or until tender. Meanwhile, in a small bowl, whisk the oil, lemon juice, herbs, vinegar, lemon peel, salt and pepper.
2. Drain potatoes. Place in a large bowl; add onion. Drizzle with vinaigrette; toss to coat. Serve warm or chill until serving.

CREAMY SPINACH CASSEROLE

SEAFOOD &
SHELLS SALAD

FAST FIX ▶
Seafood & Shells Salad

My family often asks for this salad during the summer months. The colors and flavor brighten up any potluck.
—**ROSALEE RAY** LANSING, MI

START TO FINISH: 30 MIN. • **MAKES:** 13 SERVINGS

- 2 **cups uncooked small pasta shells**
- 3 **packages (8 ounces each) imitation crabmeat**
- 1 **pound cooked small shrimp, peeled and deveined**
- ¼ **cup finely chopped sweet onion**
- ¼ **cup finely chopped celery**
- 3 **tablespoons each finely chopped green, sweet red and yellow pepper**
- 3 **tablespoons minced fresh parsley**
- 2 **tablespoons snipped fresh dill or 2 teaspoons dill weed**
- 1½ **cups fat-free mayonnaise**
- 2 **tablespoons lemon juice**
- ¼ **teaspoon salt**
- ¼ **teaspoon pepper**

1. Cook pasta according to package directions; drain and rinse in cold water.

2. In a large bowl, combine the crab, shrimp, onion, celery, peppers, parsley and dill. Stir in pasta. In a small bowl, combine the mayonnaise, lemon juice, salt and pepper. Pour over salad and toss to coat. Chill until serving.

FAST FIX ▶
Honey-Lime Berry Salad

I picked up this recipe a couple of years ago, and I really like the mint and fruit combo. Cilantro is one of my summer favorites, so sometimes I use it instead of mint.
—**KAYLA SPENCE** WILBER, NE

START TO FINISH: 15 MIN. • **MAKES:** 10 SERVINGS

- 4 **cups fresh strawberries, halved**
- 3 **cups fresh blueberries**
- 3 **medium Granny Smith apples, cubed**
- ⅓ **cup lime juice**
- ¼ **to ⅓ cup honey**
- 2 **tablespoons minced fresh mint**

In a large bowl, combine strawberries, blueberries and apples. In a small bowl, whisk lime juice, honey and mint. Pour over fruit; toss to coat.

Lemon Pecan Pilaf

Grated lemon peel brings delicate flavor to this rice dish, while pecans add a satisfying crunch. I'm so happy my sister shared the easy recipe.

—CINDIE EKSTRAND DUARTE, CA

START TO FINISH: 30 MIN. • **MAKES:** 10 SERVINGS

- 5 cups chicken broth
- 2½ cups uncooked long grain rice
- 2 tablespoons butter
- ½ cup pecan halves
- 3 tablespoons lemon juice
- 1 teaspoon grated lemon peel
- ¼ cup minced fresh parsley

In a saucepan, bring broth to a boil. Stir in rice; return to a boil. Reduce heat; cover and simmer for 20-25 minutes or until the rice is tender. Meanwhile, melt butter in a nonstick skillet. Add the pecans; saute until golden. Stir in the lemon juice and peel. Pour over rice and stir to coat. Sprinkle with parsley.

Texas Tabbouleh

I used to live in Texas, and ever since I moved away, I've missed those classic Tex-Mex flavors that were always a big part of my meals. I decided to create a fresh and healthy salad that reminds me of traditional pico de gallo. My friends love it because it's so different; it's always popular at our gatherings.

—TAMMY DAVIS ARLINGTON, VA

PREP: 40 MIN. + CHILLING • **MAKES:** 10 SERVINGS

- 1 cup bulgur
- 2 cups boiling water

TEXAS TABBOULEH

- 3 medium tomatoes
- 1 cup finely chopped red onion
- 2 green onions, thinly sliced
- ½ cup chopped sweet red pepper
- ½ cup chopped green pepper
- 2 jalapeno peppers, seeded and chopped
- ½ cup fresh cilantro leaves, chopped
- ¼ cup lime juice
- 3 tablespoons canola oil
- 2 garlic cloves, minced
- ¼ teaspoon salt
- ¼ teaspoon coarsely ground pepper
- 1 can (15 ounces) black beans, rinsed and drained
- 1 cup (4 ounces) crumbled queso fresco or feta cheese

1. Place bulgur in a large bowl; stir in boiling water. Let stand, covered, 30 minutes or until bulgur is tender and most of the liquid is absorbed. Drain well, pressing out excess water. Cool completely.

2. Stir in tomatoes, onions, peppers, cilantro, lime juice, oil and seasonings. Add beans; toss to combine. Refrigerate, covered, at least 30 minutes. Serve with the cheese.

NOTE *Wear disposable gloves when cutting hot peppers; the oils can burn skin. Avoid touching your face.*

Maple-Ginger Glazed Carrots

I first made this dish for my family and friends one Thanksgiving. Not only are the carrots lovely on any table, but they taste terrific, too.

—JEANNETTE SABO LEXINGTON PARK, MD

PREP: 15 MIN. • **COOK:** 25 MIN. • **MAKES:** 16 SERVINGS

- 4 pounds medium carrots, cut into ¼-inch slices
- ¼ cup water
- 3 tablespoons butter, divided
- 1 tablespoon minced fresh gingerroot
- ⅓ cup maple syrup
- 1 tablespoon cider vinegar
- ½ teaspoon salt
- ¼ teaspoon pepper
  Minced fresh parsley, optional

1. In a Dutch oven, combine the carrots, water, 2 tablespoons butter and ginger. Cover and cook for 10 minutes. Cook, uncovered, 6-8 minutes longer or until carrots are crisp-tender.

2. Stir in the syrup, vinegar, salt and pepper. Cook for 5-6 minutes, stirring frequently, or until sauce is thickened. Stir in remaining butter. Garnish with parsley if desired.

Company Rice

This colorful side dish is a proven favorite with family and friends. It's delicious served with grilled salmon, beef, turkey, lamb roast or ham.

—JAYNE SHILEY CAMPBELLSPORT, WI

PREP: 10 MIN. • **COOK:** 55 MIN.
MAKES: 10 SERVINGS

- 1 celery rib, thinly sliced
- 1 large carrot, finely chopped
- 1 small onion, finely chopped
- 2 tablespoons butter
- 5 cups chicken broth
- 1 cup uncooked wild rice
- 1 cup uncooked long grain rice
- ⅔ cup dried cherries or cranberries
- ½ cup chopped pecans, toasted

1. In a large saucepan, saute the celery, carrot and onion in butter until tender. Stir in broth and wild rice. Bring to a boil. Reduce heat; cover and simmer for 25 minutes.
2. Add long grain rice; cover and simmer 20 minutes longer. Stir in cherries; cook 5 minutes longer or until the liquid is absorbed.
3. Just before serving, stir in the toasted pecans.

TOP TIP

Quick Contribution

Rice side dishes and chilled rice salads make great contributions to church suppers. Not only is the variety of rice recipes endless, but they complement most entrees and travel well. In addition, many can be made in advance and can be served cold or at room temperature.

COMPANY RICE

Orange Gelatin Pretzel Salad

Salty pretzels pair nicely with the sweet fruit in this refreshing layered salad. It's a family tradition that's also a pretty potluck dish.
—**PEGGY BOYD** NORTHPORT, AL

PREP: 30 MIN. + CHILLING • **MAKES:** 15 SERVINGS

- 2 cups crushed pretzels
- 3 teaspoons plus ¾ cup sugar, divided
- ¾ cup butter, melted
- 2 packages (3 ounces each) orange gelatin
- 2 cups boiling water
- 2 cans (8 ounces each) crushed pineapple, drained
- 1 can (11 ounces) mandarin oranges, drained
- 1 package (8 ounces) cream cheese, softened
- 2 cups whipped topping
  Additional whipped topping, optional

1. Preheat oven to 350°. In a small bowl, combine pretzels and 3 teaspoons sugar; stir in butter. Press into an ungreased 13x9-in. baking dish. Bake 10 minutes. Cool on a wire rack.

2. In a large bowl, dissolve gelatin in boiling water. Add pineapple and oranges. Chill until partially set, about 30 minutes.

3. In a small bowl, beat cream cheese and remaining sugar until smooth. Fold in the whipped topping. Spread over crust. Gently spoon gelatin mixture over cream cheese layer. Cover and refrigerate 2-4 hours or until firm.

4. Cut into squares. Garnish with additional whipped topping if desired.

Strawberry Spinach Salad with Poppy Seed Dressing

Spinach salad looks best-dressed when it features luscious red strawberries and toasted pecans. Top it off with a sweet poppy seed dressing.
—**ERIN LOUGHMILLER** RIDGECREST, CA

PREP: 25 MIN. + CHILLING • **MAKES:** 10 SERVINGS

- ⅓ cup olive oil
- ¼ cup sugar
- 3 tablespoons white or balsamic vinegar
- 2 tablespoons sesame seeds
- 1 tablespoon poppy seeds
- 1 tablespoon chopped onion
- ¼ teaspoon paprika
- ¼ teaspoon Worcestershire sauce
- 1 package (9 ounces) fresh spinach, trimmed
- 4 cups fresh strawberries, sliced
- ¼ cup chopped pecans, toasted

1. Place the first eight ingredients in a jar with a tight-fitting lid; shake well. Refrigerate for 1 hour.

2. Just before serving, combine the remaining ingredients in a large bowl. Shake dressing and drizzle over salad; toss to coat.

FAST FIX

Peas a la Francaise

I love peas, and this recipe is a delightful way to fix them. It features tiny pearl onions touched with thyme and chervil, and its presentation is just lovely.
—**CHRISTINE FRAZIER** AUBURNDALE, FL

START TO FINISH: 30 MIN. • **MAKES:** 12 SERVINGS (½ CUP EACH)

- 1½ cups pearl onions, trimmed
- ¼ cup butter, cubed
- ¼ cup water
- 1 tablespoon sugar
- 1 teaspoon salt
- ¼ teaspoon dried thyme
- ¼ teaspoon dried chervil
- ¼ teaspoon pepper
- 2 packages (16 ounces each) frozen peas, thawed
- 2 cups shredded lettuce

1. In a Dutch oven, bring 6 cups water to a boil. Add pearl onions; boil for 3 minutes. Drain and rinse in cold water; peel and set aside.

2. In the same saucepan, melt butter over medium heat. Stir in the onions, water, sugar and seasonings. Add peas and lettuce; stir until blended. Cover and cook for 6-8 minutes or until vegetables are tender. Serve with a slotted spoon.

PEAS A LA FRANCAISE

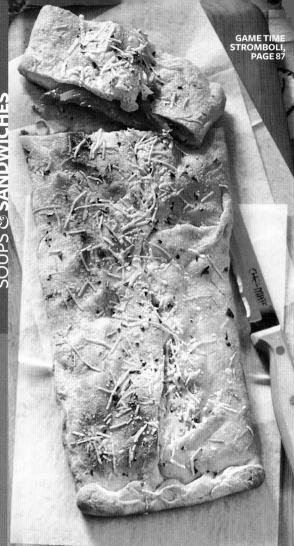

GAME TIME
STROMBOLI,
PAGE 87

HEARTY BUTTERNUT
SQUASH SOUP, PAGE 88

SPECIAL SANDWICH
LOAVES, PAGE 80

SOUPS & SANDWICHES

ITALIAN WEDDING
SOUP, PAGE 90

66 They devoted themselves
to the apostles' teaching
and fellowship, to the
breaking of bread and
the prayers. 99

ACTS 2:42

Cheese Tortellini and Kale Soup

My family and neighbors always welcome this soup. I often serve it when we get together to watch football games. I add crusty bread, sliced cheese and grapes to make it a meal.

—**MARLENA LIIMATAINEN** DENTON, MD

PREP: 30 MIN. • **COOK:** 45 MIN.
MAKES: 12 SERVINGS (3 QUARTS)

- 3 **Italian sausage links (4 ounces each), sliced**
- 1 **medium onion, finely chopped**
- 1 **cup chopped fennel bulb**
- 4 **garlic cloves, minced**
- 1½ **teaspoons minced fresh thyme**
- ½ **teaspoon crushed red pepper flakes**
- 2 **tablespoons olive oil**
- 2 **cartons (32 ounces each) reduced-sodium chicken broth**
- 1 **cup water**
- 4 **cups chopped fresh kale**
- 1 **can (15 ounces) white kidney or cannellini beans, rinsed and drained**
- 1 **package (9 ounces) refrigerated cheese tortellini**

1. In a large saucepan, cook the sausage, onion, fennel, garlic, thyme and pepper flakes in oil until sausage is no longer pink; drain. Add broth and water; bring to a boil.
2. Stir in kale and beans; return to a boil. Reduce the heat; simmer, uncovered, until kale is tender. Add the tortellini; simmer, uncovered, 7-9 minutes or until tender.

FAST FIX
Special Sandwich Loaves

These satisfying sub sandwiches are a study in simplicity. Serve the seasoned mayonnaise on the side so everyone can customize his or her own hoagie.
—*TASTE OF HOME* **TEST KITCHEN**

START TO FINISH: 30 MIN.
MAKES: 20 SANDWICHES

- 2 **loaves (1 pound each) French bread**
- 10 **slices deli smoked turkey, halved**
- 10 **slices deli roast beef, halved**
- 20 **small lettuce leaves**
- 10 **slices Colby-Monterey Jack cheese, halved**
- 10 **slices cheddar cheese, halved**
- 2 **cups roasted sweet red peppers, drained and patted dry**
- ¾ **cup mild pickled pepper rings**

GARLIC-LIME MAYONNAISE
- 1 **cup mayonnaise**
- ½ **cup sour cream**
- 1 **teaspoon lime juice**
- ½ **teaspoon minced garlic**
- ¼ **teaspoon chili powder**
- 1 **bottle (5 ounces) submarine sandwich dressing**

1. Cut each loaf into 22 slices, leaving slices attached at the bottom (cut off and discard end pieces). Between every other slice of bread, place a piece of turkey and beef, a lettuce leaf, a piece of each kind of cheese, red peppers and pepper rings.
2. In a small bowl, whisk the mayonnaise, sour cream, lime juice, garlic and chili powder. To serve, cut completely through the bread between the plain slices. Serve with mayonnaise mixture and submarine dressing.

SPECIAL SANDWICH LOAVES

VEGETABLE
BEEF SOUP

Ingredients (Broccoli Beer Cheese Soup, continued)

- 1 small onion, finely chopped
- 3 tablespoons butter
- 4 cans (14½ ounces each) chicken broth
- 4 cups fresh broccoli florets, chopped
- ¼ cup chopped sweet red pepper
- 1 teaspoon salt
- ½ teaspoon pepper
- ½ cup all-purpose flour
- ½ cup water
- 3 cups (12 ounces) shredded cheddar cheese
- 1 package (8 ounces) cream cheese, cubed
- 1 bottle (12 ounces) beer or nonalcoholic beer
  Optional toppings: cooked and crumbled bacon, chopped green onions, shredded cheddar cheese, sour cream and salad croutons

---

FAST FIX

Vegetable Beef Soup

Just brimming with veggies, my hearty soup will warm family and friends right to their toes! It's especially good served with corn bread and we think it's even better the second day.
—**MARIE CARLISLE** SUMRALL, MS

START TO FINISH: 30 MIN.
MAKES: 14 SERVINGS (3½ QUARTS)

- 4 cups cubed peeled potatoes
- 6 cups water
- 1 pound ground beef
- 5 teaspoons beef bouillon granules
- 1 can (10¾ ounces) condensed tomato soup, undiluted
- 2 cups frozen corn, thawed
- 2 cups frozen sliced carrots, thawed
- 2 cups frozen cut green beans, thawed
- 2 cups frozen sliced okra, thawed
- 3 tablespoons dried minced onion

1. In a Dutch oven, bring potatoes and water to a boil. Cover and cook 10-15 minutes or until tender.
2. Meanwhile, in a large skillet, cook beef over medium heat until no longer pink; drain.
3. Add bouillon, soup, vegetables, dried minced onion and beef to the undrained potatoes. Bring to a boil. Reduce heat; simmer, uncovered, for 8-10 minutes or until heated through, stirring occasionally.

FREEZE IT

Broccoli Beer Cheese Soup

Whether you use the beer or not, this soup tastes wonderful. I always make extra and pop individual servings in the freezer.
—**LORI LEE** BROOKSVILLE, FL

PREP: 15 MIN. • **COOK:** 40 MIN.
MAKES: 12 SERVINGS (3 QUARTS)

- 5 celery ribs, finely chopped
- 3 medium carrots, finely chopped

1. In a Dutch oven, saute celery, carrots and onion in butter until almost tender; add broth, broccoli, red pepper, salt and pepper. Combine flour and water until smooth; stir into pan. Bring to a boil. Reduce heat; simmer, uncovered, 30-40 minutes or until thickened and vegetables are tender.
2. Stir in cheeses and beer; cook until heated through and cheese is melted, stirring occasionally (do not boil). Serve with toppings of your choice.
FREEZE OPTION *Cool soup; transfer to freezer containers. Freeze for up to 3 months. To use, thaw in the refrigerator overnight. Transfer to a saucepan. Cover and cook over medium-low heat until heated through, stirring occasionally (do not boil).*

1. Preheat oven to 325°. Sprinkle roast with 1 teaspoon salt and ½ teaspoon pepper. In a Dutch oven, brown roast in oil on both sides; drain. Combine water, ketchup, onion, vinegar, Worcestershire sauce, chili powder, garlic and remaining salt and pepper; pour over meat.

2. Cover and bake 2½ to 3 hours or until meat is tender. Remove roast; let stand 5 minutes before slicing, Skim fat from cooking juices. Return meat to the pan; heat through. Serve on rolls.

Chunky Taco Soup

Here's one of my go-to soups for church suppers and potlucks. The crowd is always happy whenever I bring this easy-to-fix soup with a Southwestern zip. The flavor seems to improve in leftovers—if there are any!
—EVELYN BUFORD BELTON, MO

PREP: 20 MIN. • **COOK:** 20 MIN.
MAKES: 12 SERVINGS (ABOUT 3 QUARTS)

- 1½ **pounds beef top sirloin or round steak, cut into ¾-inch cubes**
- 1 **medium onion, chopped**
- 1 **tablespoon olive oil**
- 2 **cans (15 ounces each) pinto beans, rinsed and drained**
- 2 **cans (14½ ounces each) diced tomatoes and green chilies, undrained**
- 2 **cups water**
- 1 **can (15 ounces) black beans, rinsed and drained**
- 1 **can (14¾ ounces) cream-style corn**
- 1 **envelope ranch salad dressing mix**
- 1 **envelope taco seasoning**
- ¼ **cup minced fresh cilantro**

In a large stockpot or Dutch oven, brown beef and onion in oil. Add pinto beans, tomatoes, water, black beans, corn, salad dressing mix and taco seasoning. Bring to a boil. Reduce heat; cover and simmer 20-30 minutes or until the meat is tender. Sprinkle with cilantro.

Tangy Roast Beef Sandwiches

I've been making this recipe for years, and it never fails to win big grins from family and guests. The meat is tender, and the sauce is tangy with a little kick.
—LYNN HENDERSON POWELL, OH

PREP: 10 MIN. • **BAKE:** 2½ HOURS • **MAKES:** 12 SERVINGS

- 1 **boneless beef chuck roast (about 3 pounds)**
- 2 **teaspoons salt, divided**
- 1 **teaspoon pepper, divided**
- 2 **tablespoons canola oil**
- 2 **cups water**
- 1 **cup ketchup**
- 1 **large onion, chopped**
- ¼ **cup cider vinegar**
- ¼ **cup Worcestershire sauce**
- 1 **tablespoon chili powder**
- 1 **garlic clove, minced**
- 12 **kaiser rolls, split**

TOP TIP

Sandwiches for a Crowd

When you're hosting a large group, why not set up a sandwich bar? Let guests build their own sandwiches for a quick and simple fundraiser. Here are some guidelines for the amount you'll need. Allow 4 ounces of meat per person. For a professional look, roll up each slice of meat and stack them on a large serving platter. Order 2 ounces of cheese per person and 2 slices of bread or 1 roll for each guest. Besides mayonnaise, butter and mustard, allow each person to customize his or her sandwich with an assortment of toppers such as cheese spreads, pickles, peppers and strips of crispy bacon.

CHUNKY
TACO SOUP

Sally's West Coast Chili

We often have chili cook-offs at our church, so we trade lots of different recipes. I was always experimenting, trying to come up with an original recipe that would be a little different. That's how I developed this one, and I never fail to get compliments on it!

—**SALLY GRISHAM** MURRAY, KY

PREP: 30 MIN. • **COOK:** 3 HOURS
MAKES: 12 SERVINGS (4 QUARTS)

- 1 **pound sliced bacon, diced**
- 2 **pounds beef stew meat, cut into ¼-inch cubes**
- 2 **medium onions, chopped**
- 4 **garlic cloves, minced**
- 3 **cans (14½ ounces each) diced tomatoes, undrained**
- 1 **cup barbecue sauce**
- 1 **cup chili sauce**
- ½ **cup honey**
- 4 **teaspoons beef bouillon granules**
- 1 **bay leaf**
- 1 **tablespoon chili powder**
- 1 **tablespoon baking cocoa**
- 1 **tablespoon Worcestershire sauce**
- 1 **tablespoon Dijon mustard**
- 1½ **teaspoons ground cumin**
- ¼ **teaspoon cayenne powder, optional**
- 3 **cans (16 ounces each) kidney beans, rinsed and drained Shredded cheddar cheese**

1. In a Dutch oven, cook bacon over medium heat until crisp; remove to paper towels to drain. Reserve 3 tablespoons drippings.

2. Brown beef in drippings. Add onions; cook until tender. Add the garlic; cook 1 minute longer. Return bacon to pan. Stir in the next 12 ingredients.

3. Bring to a boil. Reduce heat; cover and simmer until meat is tender, about 3 hours.

4. Add beans and heat through. Discard bay leaf. Garnish with cheddar cheese.

SALLY'S
WEST COAST CHILI

Shredded Pork Barbecue

Pork shoulder roast is rubbed with seasonings and grilled, creating a crispy exterior that's lip-smacking good! The meat is delicious by itself but can also be topped with your favorite barbecue sauce.

—AMANDA MCLEMORE
MARYVILLE, TN

PREP: 15 MIN.
GRILL: 3½ HOURS + STANDING
MAKES: 16 SERVINGS

- 1½ teaspoons each white pepper, paprika and black pepper
- 1 teaspoon each onion powder, garlic powder and cayenne pepper
- 1 teaspoon dried thyme
- ½ teaspoon salt
- 1 boneless pork shoulder roast (4 to 5 pounds)
- 16 hard rolls, split
  Barbecue sauce, optional

1. Combine seasonings; rub over roast. Prepare grill for indirect heat, using a drip pan with 1 in. of water. Grill roast, covered, over medium-low heat for 3½ to 4 hours or until meat is tender.

2. When cool enough to handle, shred meat with two forks. Spoon ½ cup onto each bun; serve with barbecue sauce if desired.

Grandma's Chicken 'n' Dumpling Soup

I've enjoyed making this rich soup for over 40 years. Every time I serve it, I remember my grandma, who was very special to me and was known as a great cook.

—PAULETTE BALDA
PROPHETSTOWN, IL

PREP: 20 MIN. + COOLING
COOK: 2¾ HOURS
MAKES: 12 SERVINGS (3 QUARTS)

- 1 broiler/fryer chicken (3½ to 4 pounds), cut up
- 2¼ quarts cold water
- 5 chicken bouillon cubes
- 6 whole peppercorns
- 3 whole cloves
- 1 can (10¾ ounces) condensed cream of chicken soup, undiluted
- 1 can (10¾ ounces) condensed cream of mushroom soup, undiluted
- 1½ cups chopped carrots
- 1 cup fresh or frozen peas

- 1 cup chopped celery
- 1 cup chopped peeled potatoes
- ¼ cup chopped onion
- 1½ teaspoons seasoned salt
- ¼ teaspoon pepper
- 1 bay leaf

DUMPLINGS

- 2 cups all-purpose flour
- 4 teaspoons baking powder
- 1 teaspoon salt
- ¼ teaspoon pepper
- 1 egg, beaten
- 2 tablespoons butter, melted
- ¾ to 1 cup milk
  Snipped fresh parsley, optional

1. Place the chicken, water, bouillon, peppercorns and cloves in a stockpot. Cover and bring to a boil; skim foam. Reduce heat; cover and simmer 45-60 minutes or until chicken is tender. Strain broth; return to stockpot.

2. Remove chicken and set aside until cool enough to handle. Remove meat from bones; discard bones and skin and cut chicken into chunks. Cool broth and skim off fat.

3. Return chicken to stockpot with the soups, vegetables and seasonings; bring to a boil. Reduce heat; cover and simmer 1 hour. Uncover; increase heat to a gentle boil. Discard bay leaf.

4. For dumplings, combine dry ingredients in a medium bowl. Stir in egg, butter and enough milk to make a moist stiff batter. Drop by teaspoonfuls into soup. Cover and cook without lifting the lid for 18-20 minutes. Sprinkle with parsley if desired.

SHREDDED PORK BARBECUE

**KIELBASA
SPLIT PEA SOUP**

Kielbasa Split Pea Soup

Turkey kielbasa brings hearty flavor to this simple split pea soup. It's been a hit with my entire family—even our picky toddler enjoys it.
—**SANDRA BONDE** BRAINERD, MN

PREP: 15 MIN. • **COOK:** 55 MIN. • **MAKES:** 12 SERVINGS (3 QUARTS)

- 2 celery ribs, thinly sliced
- 1 medium onion, chopped
- 1 package (16 ounces) dried green split peas
- 9 cups water, divided
- 1 package (14 ounces) smoked turkey kielbasa, halved and sliced
- 4 medium carrots, halved and thinly sliced
- 2 medium potatoes, peeled and cubed
- 1 tablespoon minced fresh parsley
- 1 teaspoon dried basil
- 1½ teaspoons salt
- ½ teaspoon pepper

1. In a Dutch oven coated with cooking spray, cook celery and onion until tender. Stir in split peas and 6 cups water. Bring to a boil. Reduce heat; cover and simmer 25 minutes.
2. Stir in the kielbasa, carrots, potatoes, parsley, basil, salt, pepper and remaining water. Return to a boil. Reduce heat; cover and simmer for 20-25 minutes or until peas and vegetables are tender.

White Chili

This chili recipe has made the rounds. I got it from a friend who got it from a friend. And now I'm passing it out.
—**KAREN GARDINER** EUTAW, AL

PREP: 40 MIN. + SOAKING • **COOK:** 3½ HOURS
MAKES: 20 SERVINGS

- 2 pounds dried great northern beans
- 1½ cups diced onion
- 1 tablespoon canola oil
- 1 tablespoon ground oregano
- 2 teaspoons ground cumin
- 1½ teaspoons seasoned salt
- ½ teaspoon cayenne pepper
- 4½ quarts chicken broth
- 2 garlic cloves, minced
- 2 pounds boneless skinless chicken breast halves, cubed
- 2 cans (4 ounces each) chopped green chilies

1. Sort beans and rinse with cold water. Place beans in a Dutch oven; add water to cover by 2 in. Bring to a boil; boil 2 minutes. Remove from heat; cover and let stand 1 to 4 hours or until beans are softened. Drain and rinse beans, discarding liquid.
2. In a stockpot, saute onion in oil until tender. Combine seasonings; add half to onion mixture. Saute 1 minute. Add beans, broth and garlic; bring to a boil. Reduce heat; cover and simmer 2 hours.
3. Preheat oven to 350°. Coat chicken with remaining seasoning mixture; place in 15x10x1-in. baking pan. Bake 15 minutes or until chicken is no longer pink; add to beans. Stir in chilies. Cover and simmer 1½ to 2 hours or until flavors are blended.

**WHITE
CHILI**

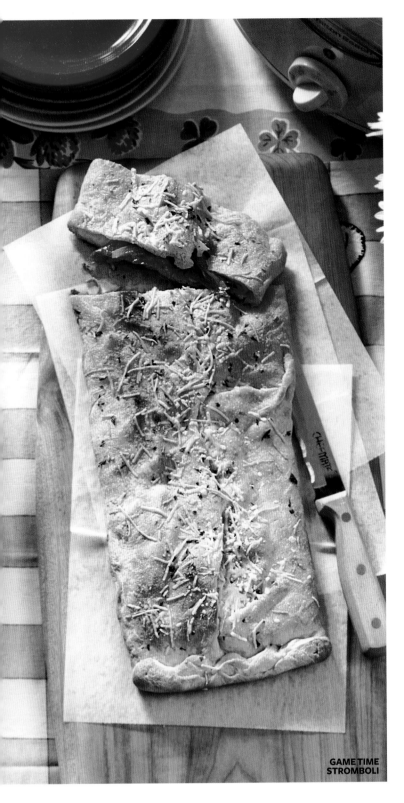

GAME TIME STROMBOLI

Game Time Stromboli

Make this hearty stromboli a game-time appetizer or serve as a light dinner with a green salad.
—**JANE WHITTAKER** PENSACOLA, FL

PREP: 30 MIN. • **BAKE:** 20 MIN.
MAKES: 2 STROMBOLI (6 SERVINGS EACH)

- 2 tubes (13.8 ounces each) refrigerated pizza crust
- 8 ounces thinly sliced part-skim mozzarella cheese
- 8 ounces thinly sliced mortadella
- 8 ounces thinly sliced capocollo or prosciutto
- 8 ounces thinly sliced hard salami
- 1 large green pepper, thinly sliced
- 2 tablespoons shredded Asiago cheese
- 1 teaspoon garlic powder
- 1 teaspoon dried parsley flakes
  Marinara sauce, warmed

1. Preheat oven to 425°. On a greased baking sheet, unroll one pizza crust and pat into a 16x13-in. rectangle. Layer half of the mozzarella cheese, deli meats and pepper lengthwise down center third of crust, leaving a ½-in. border at each end. Fold up long sides of crust over filling, pinching seam and ends to seal. Fold up ends. Cut slits in top. Repeat with remaining ingredients.
2. Sprinkle each with half of the Asiago cheese, garlic powder and parsley. Bake 16-20 minutes or until golden brown. Serve with marinara sauce.

1. In a stockpot, cook sausage, onion and red pepper over medium heat 9-11 minutes or until sausage is no longer pink and onion is tender, breaking up sausage into crumbles. Add garlic; cook 1 minute longer. Remove with a slotted spoon; discard drippings.
2. Add squash, 1½ cups corn, water and chicken base to same pan; bring to a boil. Reduce heat; simmer, covered, 15-20 minutes or until squash is tender.
3. Remove soup from heat; cool slightly. Process in batches in a blender until smooth. Return to pot. Add beans, tomatoes, salt, pepper, sausage mixture and remaining corn; heat through. If desired, drizzle servings with cream and sprinkle with parsley.
FREEZE OPTION *Freeze cooled soup in freezer containers. To use, partially thaw in refrigerator overnight. Heat through in a saucepan, stirring occasionally and adding a little water if necessary.*
NOTE *Look for chicken base near the broth and bouillon.*

FAST FIX
Chicken Salad Party Sandwiches
My famous chicken salad arrives at the party chilled in a plastic container. When it's time to set out the food, I stir in the pecans and assemble the sandwiches. They're great for buffet-style potlucks.
—**TRISHA KRUSE** EAGLE, ID

START TO FINISH: 20 MIN. • **MAKES:** 15 SERVINGS

- 4 **cups cubed cooked chicken breast**
- 1½ **cups dried cranberries**
- 2 **celery ribs, finely chopped**
- 2 **green onions, thinly sliced**
- ¼ **cup chopped sweet pickles**
- 1 **cup fat-free mayonnaise**
- ½ **teaspoon curry powder**
- ¼ **teaspoon coarsely ground pepper**
- ½ **cup chopped pecans, toasted**
- 15 **whole wheat dinner rolls**
  Torn leaf lettuce
  Frilled toothpicks, optional

1. In a large bowl, combine the first five ingredients. In a small bowl, combine the mayonnaise, curry and pepper. Add to chicken mixture; toss to coat. Chill until serving.
2. Stir pecans into chicken salad. Serve on rolls lined with lettuce. Secure with toothpicks if desired.

FREEZE IT
Hearty Butternut Squash Soup
The comforting combination of squash, meat, beans and veggies make this my standby soup in fall. It's full of good-for-you ingredients.
—**JAYE BEELER** GRAND RAPIDS, MI

PREP: 20 MIN. • **COOK:** 40 MIN.
MAKES: 12 SERVINGS (4½ QUARTS)

- 1 **pound bulk Italian sausage**
- 1 **medium onion, chopped**
- 1 **medium sweet red pepper, chopped**
- 4 **garlic cloves, minced**
- 1 **large butternut squash (about 5 pounds), peeled, seeded and cut into 1-inch pieces**
- 1 **package (16 ounces) frozen corn, divided**
- 4 **cups water**
- 1 **tablespoon chicken base**
- 2 **cans (15½ ounces each) great northern beans, rinsed and drained**
- 2 **cans (14½ ounces each) fire-roasted diced tomatoes, undrained**
- 1 **teaspoon salt**
- ¼ **teaspoon pepper**
  Heavy whipping cream and minced fresh parsley, optional

**CHICKEN SALAD
PARTY SANDWICHES**

Italian Wedding Soup

Even in our hot Florida weather, this soup always satisfies!
I add cooked pasta at the end of the cooking time to keep
it from getting mushy.

—NANCY DUCHARME DELTONA, FL

PREP: 20 MIN. • **COOK:** 15 MIN.
MAKES: 12 SERVINGS (3 QUARTS)

- 1 egg
- ¾ cup grated Parmesan cheese
- ½ cup dry bread crumbs
- 1 small onion, chopped
- ¾ teaspoon salt, divided
- 1¼ teaspoons pepper, divided
- 1¼ teaspoons garlic powder, divided
- 2 pounds ground beef
- 2 quarts chicken broth
- ⅓ cup chopped fresh spinach
- 1 teaspoon onion powder
- 1 teaspoon dried parsley flakes
- 1¼ cups cooked medium pasta shells

1. In a large bowl, combine the egg, cheese, bread
crumbs, onion, ¼ teaspoon salt, ¼ teaspoon pepper
and ¼ teaspoon garlic powder. Crumble beef over
mixture and mix well. Shape into 1-in. balls.
2. In a Dutch oven, brown meatballs in small batches;
drain. Add the broth, spinach, onion powder, parsley
and remaining salt, pepper and garlic powder; bring to
a boil. Reduce heat; simmer, uncovered, 5 minutes. Stir
in pasta; heat through.

PEAR-WALNUT TEA SANDWICHES

Halibut Chowder

Several times a year I invite both my retired and current teaching friends to a dinner party with their spouses. I've served this halibut chowder at those parties and it's always a big hit.
—**TERESA LUECK** ONAMIA, MN

PREP: 25 MIN. • **COOK:** 30 MIN.
MAKES: 12 SERVINGS (3 QUARTS)

- 4 celery ribs, chopped
- 3 medium carrots, chopped
- 1 large onion, chopped
- ½ cup butter, cubed
- ½ cup all-purpose flour
- ¼ teaspoon white pepper
- 2 cups 2% milk
- 1 can (14½ ounces) chicken broth
- ¼ cup water
- 1 tablespoon chicken base
- 3 medium potatoes, peeled and chopped
- 1 can (15¼ ounces) whole kernel corn, drained
- 3 bay leaves
- 2 cups half-and-half cream
- 2 tablespoons lemon juice
- 1 pound halibut or other whitefish fillets, cut into 1-inch pieces
- 1 cup salad croutons
- ¾ cup grated Parmesan cheese
- ½ cup minced chives

1. In a large saucepan, saute the celery, carrots and onion in butter until tender. Stir in flour and pepper until blended; gradually add the milk, broth, water and chicken base. Bring to a boil; cook and stir 2 minutes or until thickened.

2. Add the potatoes, corn and bay leaves. Return to a boil. Reduce heat; cover and simmer 15-20 minutes or until potatoes are tender.

3. Stir in cream and lemon juice; return to a boil. Add halibut. Reduce heat; simmer, uncovered, 7-11 minutes or until the fish flakes easily with a fork. Discard the bay leaves.

4. Garnish servings with croutons, cheese and chives.

NOTE *Look for chicken base near the broth and bouillon.*

FAST FIX ▶

Pear-Walnut Tea Sandwiches

These satisfying tea sandwiches boast crunchy walnuts, chopped pear and deli chicken. Use white, pumpernickel and rye bread for variety.
—**DAVID BOSTEDT** ZEPHYRHILLS, FL

START TO FINISH: 20 MIN. • **MAKES:** 8 TEA SANDWICHES

- ½ cup mayonnaise
- ⅓ cup chopped peeled ripe pears
- 2 tablespoons minced fresh tarragon
- 2 tablespoons chopped walnuts, toasted
- 1 teaspoon Dijon mustard
- ¼ teaspoon salt
- ⅛ teaspoon pepper
- 16 slices white bread
- 16 slices deli chicken
- 2 cups fresh arugula

In a small bowl, combine the first seven ingredients; spread on one side of each bread slice. Layer half of the slices with chicken and arugula. Top with the remaining bread. Cut each sandwich with a 3-in. round cookie cutter.

Meat & Cheese Stromboli

This is the perfect item to take to a potluck. It's so quick to assemble and bake. When it's done, wrap it in foil to transport. Everyone who tastes it will marvel at each rich and cheesy slice!

—SUE SHEA DEFIANCE, OH

PREP: 25 MIN. • **BAKE:** 15 MIN.
MAKES: 2 LOAVES (8 SERVINGS EACH)

- 1 medium onion, sliced and separated into rings
- 1 medium green pepper, sliced into rings
- 1 tablespoon butter
- 2 loaves (16 ounces each) frozen bread dough, thawed
- ½ pound thinly sliced hard salami
- ½ pound thinly sliced deli ham
- 8 ounces sliced part-skim mozzarella cheese
- 8 ounces sliced cheddar cheese
- ½ teaspoon Italian seasoning
- ¼ teaspoon garlic powder
- ⅛ teaspoon pepper
- 1 egg, lightly beaten
- 1 teaspoon poppy seeds

1. Preheat oven to 400°. In a large skillet, saute onion and green pepper in butter until crisp-tender; set aside.
2. On two greased baking sheets, roll each loaf of dough into a 15x12-in. rectangle. Arrange salami, ham and cheeses lengthwise over half of each rectangle to within ½ in. of edges. Top with onion mixture; sprinkle with Italian seasoning, garlic powder and pepper. Fold dough over filling; pinch edges to seal.
3. Brush with egg and sprinkle with poppy seeds. Bake 15-20 minutes or until golden brown. Cool 5 minutes before slicing.

Rich Clam Chowder

I came across a chowder recipe I liked several years ago and have made just enough changes to give it a unique flavor—and feed a pretty large crowd. People always go back for seconds, then ask for the recipe.

—TERESA DASTRUP MERIDIAN, ID

PREP: 45 MIN. • **COOK:** 25 MIN.
MAKES: 22 SERVINGS (1 CUP EACH)

- 6 cups diced peeled red potatoes
- 3 large onions, finely chopped
- 6 celery ribs, finely chopped
- 3 cups water
- 6 cans (6½ ounces each) minced clams
- 1½ cups butter, cubed
- 1½ cups all-purpose flour
- 8 cups half-and-half cream
- ¼ cup red wine vinegar
- 2 tablespoons minced fresh parsley
- 3 teaspoons salt
- ¼ teaspoon pepper

1. In a stockpot, combine the potatoes, onions, celery and water. Drain clams, reserving juice; set clams aside. Add juice to potato mixture. Bring to a boil. Reduce heat; cover and simmer 10 minutes or until potatoes are tender.
2. Meanwhile, in a large saucepan, melt butter over medium heat. Whisk in flour. Cook and stir 5 minutes or until lightly browned. Gradually stir in cream. Bring to a boil; cook and stir 2 minutes or until thickened. Gradually stir into the potato mixture.
3. Add the vinegar, parsley, salt, pepper and clams. Cook 5-10 minutes longer or until heated through.

MEAT & CHEESE STROMBOLI

CREAMY VEGETABLE SOUP

Creamy Vegetable Soup

I tasted this delicious soup in a restaurant, but I couldn't get the chef to share the recipe, so I experimented on my own. Finally, I came up with this blend, which is very close to what I'd tasted—maybe even better!

—AUDREY NEMETH MOUNT VERNON, ME

START TO FINISH: 30 MIN.
MAKES: 12-16 SERVINGS (4 QUARTS)

- 1 **large onion, chopped**
- ¼ **cup butter**
- 3 **medium sweet potatoes, peeled and chopped**
- 3 **medium zucchini, chopped**
- 1 **bunch broccoli, chopped**
- 2 **cartons (32 ounces each) chicken broth**
- 2 **medium potatoes, peeled and shredded**
- 1 **teaspoon celery seed**
- 1 **to 2 teaspoons ground cumin**
- 2 **teaspoons salt**
- 1 **teaspoon pepper**
- 2 **cups half-and-half cream**

In a stockpot, saute onion in butter until transparent but not browned. Add sweet potatoes, zucchini and broccoli; saute lightly 5 minutes or until crisp-tender. Stir in broth; simmer for a few minutes. Add potatoes and seasonings; cook 10 minutes or until vegetables are tender. Stir in cream; heat through.

TOP TIP

Finishing Touches

Adding a garnish to soup before serving gives color and boosts the flavor and texture. Easy ideas include finely chopped green onions or chives; minced fresh parsley; shredded, grated or shaved cheese; a dollop of sour cream; and plain or seasoned croutons.

PEPPERONI
PIZZA CHILI

FREEZE IT

Pepperoni Pizza Chili

Pizza and chili go together—what could be better? Fill folks up at halftime when you set out bowls of this treat.

—**JENNIFER GELORMINO** PITTSBURGH, PA

PREP: 20 MIN. • **COOK:** 30 MIN.
MAKES: 12 SERVINGS (3 QUARTS)

- 2 **pounds ground beef**
- 1 **pound bulk hot Italian sausage**
- 1 **large onion, chopped**
- 1 **large green pepper, chopped**
- 4 **garlic cloves, minced**
- 1 **jar (16 ounces) salsa**
- 1 **can (16 ounces) hot chili beans, undrained**
- 1 **can (16 ounces) kidney beans, rinsed and drained**
- 1 **can (12 ounces) pizza sauce**
- 1 **package (8 ounces) sliced pepperoni, halved**
- 1 **cup water**
- 2 **teaspoons chili powder**
- ½ **teaspoon salt**
- ½ **teaspoon pepper**
- 3 **cups (12 ounces) shredded part-skim mozzarella cheese**

1. In a Dutch oven, cook the beef, sausage, onion, green pepper and garlic over medium heat until meat is no longer pink; drain.

2. Stir in the salsa, beans, pizza sauce, pepperoni, water, chili powder, salt and pepper. Bring to a boil. Reduce heat; cover and simmer 20 minutes or until heated through. Sprinkle servings with cheese.

FREEZE OPTION *Before adding cheese, cool chili. Freeze chili in freezer containers. To use, partially thaw in refrigerator overnight. Heat through in a saucepan, stirring occasionally and adding a little water if necessary. Sprinkle each serving with cheese.*

THREE-BEAN SOUP

Three-Bean Soup

When I was growing up, my mother prepared many different soups, each one seasoned just right. She often made this colorful combination chock-full of harvest-fresh goodness. It features an appealing assortment of beans, potatoes, carrots and spinach.
—**VALERIE LEE** SNELLVILLE, GA

PREP: 20 MIN. • **COOK:** 15 MIN.
MAKES: 12 SERVINGS (ABOUT 3 QUARTS)

- 1 **medium onion, chopped**
- 1 **tablespoon canola oil**
- 3 **small potatoes, peeled and cubed**
- 2 **medium carrots, sliced**
- 3 **cans (14½ ounces each) chicken or vegetable broth**
- 3 **cups water**
- 2 **tablespoons dried parsley flakes**
- 2 **teaspoons dried basil**
- 1 **teaspoon dried oregano**
- 1 **garlic clove, minced**
- ½ **teaspoon pepper**
- 1 **can (15½ ounces) great northern beans, rinsed and drained**
- 1 **can (15 ounces) pinto beans, rinsed and drained**
- 1 **can (15 ounces) garbanzo beans or chickpeas, rinsed and drained**
- 3 **cups chopped fresh spinach**

In a Dutch oven, saute onion in oil. Add the next nine ingredients. Simmer, uncovered, until vegetables are tender. Add beans and spinach; heat through.

Chunky Turkey Soup

This hearty recipe combining the earthy flavors of curry and cumin is the perfect answer to your Turkey Day leftovers. No one will mistake it for canned soup!
—**JANE SCANLON** MARCO ISLAND, FL

PREP: 20 MIN. + SIMMERING • **COOK:** 40 MIN.
MAKES: 12 SERVINGS (1⅓ CUPS EACH)

- 1 **leftover turkey carcass (from a 12- to 14-pound turkey)**
- 4½ **quarts water**
- 1 **medium onion, quartered**
- 1 **medium carrot, cut into 2-inch pieces**
- 1 **celery rib, cut into 2-inch pieces**

SOUP

- 2 **cups shredded cooked turkey**
- 4 **celery ribs, chopped**
- 2 **cups frozen corn**
- 2 **medium carrots, sliced**
- 1 **large onion, chopped**
- 1 **cup uncooked orzo pasta**
- 2 **tablespoons minced fresh parsley**
- 4 **teaspoons chicken bouillon granules**
- 1 **teaspoon salt**
- 1 **teaspoon curry powder**
- ½ **teaspoon ground cumin**
- ½ **teaspoon pepper**

1. Place the turkey carcass in a stockpot; add the water, onion, carrot and celery. Slowly bring to a boil over low heat; cover and simmer 1½ hours.
2. Discard the carcass. Strain broth through a cheesecloth-lined colander. If using immediately, skim fat. Or cool, then refrigerate 8 hours or overnight; remove fat from surface before using. (Broth may be refrigerated up to 3 days or frozen for 4-6 months.)
3. Place the soup ingredients in a stockpot; add the broth. Bring to a boil. Reduce heat; cover and simmer 30 minutes or until pasta and vegetables are tender.

Ham and Bean Soup

I learned to make this soup when we lived in Pennsylvania near several Amish families. It's a favorite way to use up ham and mashed potatoes, and it freezes well, too.

—AMANDA REED MILFORD, DE

PREP: 30 MIN. + SOAKING • **COOK:** 1½ HOURS
MAKES: 15 SERVINGS (3¾ QUARTS)

1   **pound dried navy beans**
2   **medium onions, chopped**
2   **teaspoons canola oil**
2   **celery ribs, chopped**
10 **cups water**
4   **cups cubed fully cooked ham**
1   **cup mashed potatoes (without added milk and butter)**
½   **cup shredded carrot**
2   **tablespoons Worcestershire sauce**
1   **teaspoon salt**
½   **teaspoon dried thyme**
½   **teaspoon pepper**
2   **bay leaves**
1   **meaty ham bone or 2 smoked ham hocks**
¼   **cup minced fresh parsley**

1. Place beans in a Dutch oven; add water to cover by 2 in. Bring to a boil; boil 2 minutes. Remove from heat; cover and let stand 1 to 4 hours or until the beans are softened. Drain and rinse beans, discarding liquid.

2. In the same pan, saute onions in oil 2 minutes. Add celery; cook until tender. Stir in beans, water, ham, potatoes, carrot, Worcestershire sauce, salt, thyme, pepper and bay leaves. Add ham bone. Bring to a boil. Reduce heat; cover and simmer 1¼ to 1½ hours or until beans are tender.

3. Discard bay leaves. Remove ham bone and set aside until cool enough to handle. Remove ham from bone and cut into cubes. Discard bone. Return ham to soup; heat through. Garnish soup with parsley.

Turkey & Swiss Biscuit Sliders

Experimenting in the kitchen is fun! I love to come up with new recipe ideas. I created these sliders while my sister was pregnant to satisfy a craving, and they really did the trick!

—CINDY ESPOSITO BLOOMFIELD, NJ

PREP: 35 MIN. + RISING • **BAKE:** 10 MIN. • **MAKES:** 16 SERVINGS

1   **package (¼ ounce) active dry yeast**
⅔   **cup warm buttermilk (110° to 115°)**
2   **tablespoons warm water (110° to 115°)**
2   **cups bread flour**
3   **tablespoons sugar**
1½   **teaspoons baking powder**
½   **teaspoon salt**
½   **cup shortening**
¾   **pound thinly sliced deli smoked turkey**
½   **pound slices Swiss cheese**
Dijon mustard, optional

1. In a small bowl, dissolve yeast in warm buttermilk and water. Place the flour, sugar, baking powder and salt in a food processor; pulse until blended. Add the shortening; pulse until shortening is the size of peas. While processing, gradually add yeast mixture and process just until dough forms a ball.

2. Turn dough onto a lightly floured surface; knead 8-10 times. Pat or roll to ½-in. thickness; cut with a floured 2-in. biscuit cutter. Place 2 in. apart on greased baking sheets. Let rise until almost doubled, about 30 minutes.

3. Preheat oven to 425°. Bake 7-9 minutes or until golden brown. Remove to wire racks to cool slightly. Preheat broiler.

4. Split biscuits in half; place bottoms on greased baking sheets. Layer with turkey and cheese. Broil 3-4 in. from heat 2-3 minutes or until the cheese is melted. Replace tops. If desired, serve with mustard.

TURKEY & SWISS
BISCUIT SLIDERS

Spicy Pork Chili

There's plenty of heft to this chili, which is loaded with white beans and cubes of pork. If you want more heat, top servings with shredded jalapeno jack cheese and finely diced onions.

—LARRY LAATSCH SAGINAW, MI

PREP: 10 MIN. • **COOK:** 1½ HOURS
MAKES: 15 SERVINGS

- 1½ **pounds pork tenderloin, cubed**
- 2 **tablespoons butter**
- 2 **large onions, diced**
- 4 **celery ribs, diced**
- 6 **cans (15½ ounces each) great northern beans, rinsed and drained**
- 4 **cans (14½ ounces each) chicken broth**
- 2 **cups water**
- 2 **jalapeno peppers, seeded and chopped**
- 2 **teaspoons chili powder**
- ½ **teaspoon each white pepper, cayenne pepper, ground cumin and pepper**
- 2 **garlic cloves, minced**
- ½ **teaspoon salt**
- ¼ **teaspoon dried parsley flakes**
- ¼ **teaspoon hot pepper sauce, optional**
- 1 **cup (4 ounces) shredded Monterey Jack cheese**

1. In a Dutch oven, brown the pork in butter in batches. Remove pork and keep warm.

2. In the same pan, saute onions and celery until tender. Stir in the beans, broth, water, jalapenos, spices, garlic, salt, parsley, pork and, if desired, hot pepper sauce. Bring to a boil. Reduce heat; cover and simmer 45-60 minutes or until pork is tender.

3. Uncover; simmer 30-40 minutes longer or until chili reaches desired consistency. Sprinkle with cheese.

NOTE *Wear disposable gloves when cutting hot peppers; the oils can burn skin. Avoid touching your face.*

SPICY
PORK CHILI

AUTHENTIC
CAJUN GUMBO

Authentic Cajun Gumbo

I learned to cook in Louisiana, and this chicken oyster gumbo is one of my favorites. I make huge batches and freeze portions or bring it to family cookouts.
—**PAUL MORRIS** KELSO, WA

PREP: 1 HOUR + SIMMERING • **COOK:** 45 MIN.
MAKES: 20 SERVINGS (1¼ CUPS EACH)

  6 **quarts water**
  1 **chicken (5 pounds), cut up**
  2 **large onions, quartered**
  4 **celery ribs, cut into 3-inch pieces**
  6 **garlic cloves, coarsely chopped**
  2 **tablespoons salt**
  1 **teaspoon garlic powder**
  ½ **teaspoon poultry seasoning**
  ½ **teaspoon cayenne pepper**
  ½ **teaspoon pepper**
  ¼ **teaspoon white pepper**
  1 **cup canola oil**
1½ **cups all-purpose flour**
  1 **large onion, finely chopped**
  1 **pound fully cooked andouille sausage links, chopped**
  2 **pounds sliced okra**
  2 **pints shucked oysters**
  3 **tablespoons gumbo file powder**
    Hot cooked rice

1. Place the first 11 ingredients in a stockpot; bring to a boil. Reduce heat; cover and simmer 1½ hours.
2. Remove chicken and allow to cool. Strain broth, discarding vegetables; skim fat. Remove meat from bones; cut chicken into bite-size pieces and set aside. Discard bones.
3. In the same pan, cook and stir oil and flour over medium heat until caramel-colored, about 14 minutes (do not burn). Add finely chopped onion; cook and stir 2 minutes longer. Gradually stir in broth. Bring to a boil.
4. Carefully stir in sausage and reserved chicken. Reduce heat; simmer, uncovered, 10 minutes. Stir in okra and oysters. Simmer, uncovered, 10-15 minutes longer or just until okra is tender. Stir in file powder. Serve with rice.
NOTE *Gumbo file powder, used to thicken and flavor Creole recipes, is available in spice shops. If you don't want to use gumbo file powder, combine 2 tablespoons each cornstarch and cold water until smooth. Gradually stir into gumbo. Bring to a boil; cook and stir 2 minutes or until thickened.*

Mom's Dynamite Sandwiches

Whenever we had a family get-together and my mom had a lot of people to feed, she'd make her delicious dynamite sandwiches. I'm from Woonsocket, Rhode Island, and this is a staple in our area. Dynamites are to Woonsocket what cheesesteaks are to Philadelphia.
—**KATHY HEWITT** CRANSTON, RI

PREP: 15 MIN. • **COOK:** 1 HOUR 20 MIN. • **MAKES:** 16 SERVINGS

2½ **pounds ground beef**
  5 **medium green peppers, finely chopped**
  4 **large onions, chopped (6 cups)**
  1 **can (28 ounces) crushed tomatoes in puree**
  1 **can (16 ounces) tomato sauce**
  1 **can (12 ounces) tomato paste**
  1 **cup water**
  2 **tablespoons sugar**
  2 **tablespoons garlic powder**
  1 **tablespoon Italian seasoning**
  1 **tablespoon dried oregano**
2¼ **teaspoons salt**
  2 **teaspoons hot pepper sauce**
1½ **teaspoons pepper**
  ½ **teaspoon crushed red pepper flakes, optional**
 12 **hoagie buns or other sandwich rolls, split**

1. In a Dutch oven, cook beef over medium-high heat 8-10 minutes or until no longer pink, breaking into crumbles; drain.
2. Stir in all remaining ingredients except buns. Bring to a boil. Reduce heat; simmer, uncovered, 1 hour or until mixture reaches desired consistency and flavors are blended, stirring occasionally. Serve on buns.

WINTER
COUNTRY SOUP

Winter Country Soup

My soup will warm your family up on the chilliest nights. Featuring smoked sausage, beans and other vegetables, it's a hearty way to start a meal or a satisfying lunch all by itself.

—JEANNETTE SABO LEXINGTON PARK, MD

PREP: 15 MIN. • **COOK:** 40 MIN.
MAKES: 12 SERVINGS (3 QUARTS)

- 1 package (14 ounces) smoked sausage, cut into ¼-inch slices
- 1 large sweet red pepper, cut into ½-inch pieces
- 8 shallots, chopped
- 1 tablespoon butter
- 8 cups chopped fresh kale
- 8 cups vegetable broth
- 3 cups frozen corn
- 1 can (15½ ounces) great northern beans, rinsed and drained
- ½ teaspoon cayenne pepper
- ¼ teaspoon pepper
- ¾ cup uncooked orzo pasta

1. In a Dutch oven, saute the sausage, red pepper and shallots in butter until vegetables are tender.
2. Add kale; cover and cook 2-3 minutes or until kale is wilted. Stir in the broth, corn, beans, cayenne and pepper. Bring to a boil. Reduce heat; simmer, uncovered, 20 minutes. Return to a boil. Stir in orzo. Cook 8-10 minutes longer or until pasta is tender.

Turkey Sloppy Joes for a Crowd

I found this recipe in my mother's recipe box. Sometimes I serve it over vegetables such as corn or green beans, but it's equally delicious on a bun.

—**JULIE CLEMES** ADRIAN, MI

PREP: 25 MIN. • **COOK:** 40 MIN.
MAKES: 16 SERVINGS

- 3 **pounds lean ground turkey**
- 3 **medium green peppers, chopped**
- 3 **medium onions, finely chopped**
- 2¼ **cups ketchup**
- ¾ **cup water**
- 3 **tablespoons white vinegar**
- 3 **tablespoons spicy brown mustard**
- 1 **jalapeno pepper, seeded and chopped**
- ½ **teaspoon pepper**
- 16 **whole wheat hamburger buns, split**

1. In a Dutch oven coated with cooking spray, cook the turkey, green peppers and onions over medium heat until meat is no longer pink and vegetables are tender; drain.
2. Stir in ketchup, water, vinegar, mustard, jalapeno and pepper. Bring to a boil. Reduce heat; cover and simmer 20-30 minutes; stir occasionally. Serve on buns.
NOTE *Wear disposable gloves when cutting hot peppers; the oils can burn skin. Avoid touching your face.*

Crowd-Pleasin' Muffuletta

A garlic-olive paste is the delicious difference in this unusual make-ahead sandwich.

—**JEANNIE YEE** FREMONT, CA

PREP: 1 HOUR + CHILLING
MAKES: 12-14 SERVINGS

- 1 **cup pimiento-stuffed olives, finely chopped**
- 1 **cup pitted ripe olives, finely chopped**

- ⅔ **cup olive oil**
- ½ **cup chopped roasted sweet red peppers**
- 3 **tablespoons minced fresh parsley**
- 2 **tablespoons red wine vinegar**
- 3 **garlic cloves, minced**
- 1 **round loaf (2 pounds) unsliced Italian bread**
- 1 **pound thinly sliced deli turkey**
- 12 **ounces thinly sliced part-skim mozzarella cheese (about 16 slices)**
- 1 **pound thinly sliced hard salami**
- 1 **pound thinly sliced deli ham**

1. In a large bowl, combine the first seven ingredients; set aside. Cut bread in half horizontally. Carefully hollow out top and bottom, leaving a 1-in. shell (save removed bread for another use).
2. Spread 1½ cups olive mixture over bottom bread shell. Spread remaining olive mixture over cut side of top bread shell. In bottom bread shell, layer the turkey, half of the cheese, salami, remaining cheese and ham. Replace bread top. Wrap tightly in plastic wrap. Refrigerate 4 hours or overnight. Cut into wedges to serve.

TURKEY SLOPPY JOES FOR A CROWD

ITALIAN MEATBALL
TORTES, PAGE 119

MIXED GRILL
FAJITAS, PAGE 113

BRATWURST
SUPPER, PAGE 127

HEARTY MAIN DISHES

HEARTY
MAIN DISHES

CREAMED TURKEY WITH PUFF PASTRY, PAGE 126

66 So I commend enjoyment, for there is nothing better for people under the sun than to eat, and drink, and enjoy themselves, for this will go with them in their toil through the days of life that God gives them under the sun. 99

ECCLESIASTES 8:15

FAST FIX

Ham It Up Primavera

I adapted my primavera from a cookbook my husband and I received when we got married. We love all the veggies, especially fresh asparagus.
—**ANGELIA HOLLAND** PLANO, TX

START TO FINISH: 30 MIN.
MAKES: 12 SERVINGS

- 1 package (16 ounces) spaghetti
- 1 pound fresh asparagus, trimmed and cut into 1-inch pieces
- 2 medium carrots, cut into ¼-inch slices
- ½ cup butter, cubed
- ½ pound sliced fresh mushrooms
- 2 medium zucchini, halved and cut into ¼-inch slices
- 2 cups cubed fully cooked ham
- 1 package (10 ounces) frozen peas, thawed
- 8 green onions, chopped
- 3 teaspoons dried basil
- 1½ teaspoons salt
- ¼ teaspoon white pepper
- ¼ teaspoon ground nutmeg
- 1½ cups heavy whipping cream
- 1 cup grated Parmesan cheese, divided

1. Cook spaghetti according to package directions.
2. Meanwhile, in a large skillet, saute asparagus and carrots in butter 3 minutes. Add mushrooms and zucchini; saute until vegetables are crisp-tender.
3. Stir in the ham, peas, onions, basil, salt, pepper and nutmeg. Add cream. Bring to a boil; cook and stir 2 minutes.
4. Drain spaghetti; place in a large bowl. Add vegetable mixture and ½ cup cheese; toss to combine. Serve with remaining cheese.

HAM IT UP PRIMAVERA

NO-FUSS CHICKEN

PEPPERED BEEF TENDERLOIN

No-Fuss Chicken

This quick and easy recipe is perfect when you need to feed a crowd. The chicken boasts a tangy flavor, and no one will know you used convenient ingredients like a bottle of salad dressing and onion soup mix.

—**MARILYN DICK** CENTRALIA, MO

PREP: 5 MIN. • **BAKE:** 40 MIN. • **MAKES:** 16 SERVINGS

- 1 bottle (16 ounces) Russian or Catalina salad dressing
- ⅔ cup apricot preserves
- 2 envelopes onion soup mix
- 16 boneless skinless chicken breast halves
  Hot cooked rice

Preheat oven to 350°. In a bowl, combine dressing, preserves and soup mix. Place chicken in two ungreased 11x7-in. baking pans; top with dressing mixture. Cover and bake 20 minutes; baste. Bake, uncovered, 20 minutes longer or until chicken juices run clear. Serve over rice.

Peppered Beef Tenderloin

A pepper rub gives this moist, tender beef a bit of a zippy taste. It takes just minutes to prepare, and the meat slices well. Lining the baking pan with foil makes it a breeze to clean up, too.

—**DENISE BITNER** REEDSVILLE, PA

PREP: 10 MIN. • **BAKE:** 45 MIN. + STANDING
MAKES: 10-12 SERVINGS

- 3 tablespoons coarsely ground pepper
- 2 tablespoons olive oil
- 1 tablespoon grated lemon peel
- 1 teaspoon salt
- 2 garlic cloves, minced
- 1 beef tenderloin roast (3 to 4 pounds)

1. Preheat oven to 400°. Combine pepper, oil, lemon peel, salt and garlic; rub over tenderloin. Place on a greased rack in a foil-lined roasting pan.
2. Bake, uncovered, 45-65 minutes or until beef reaches desired doneness (for medium-rare, a thermometer should read 145°; medium, 160°; well-done, 170°). Cover and let stand 10 minutes before slicing.

Chicken Time-Saver

Buying skinned and boned chicken breasts can cut up to 15 minutes off your cooking time. Save money by buying larger packages when they're on sale, then rewrap each breast individually or in family-size portions and freeze. Pull out and thaw whenever you need a quick chicken dinner.

Irish Beef Stew

Rich and hearty, this stew is my husband's favorite. The beef is incredibly tender. Served with crusty bread, it's an ideal cool-weather meal and perfect for any Irish holiday.
—**CARRIE KARLEEN** ST. NICOLAS, QC

PREP: 40 MIN. • **COOK:** 3¼ HOURS
MAKES: 15 SERVINGS (3¾ QUARTS)

- 8 **bacon strips, diced**
- ⅓ **cup all-purpose flour**
- 1 **teaspoon salt**
- ½ **teaspoon pepper**
- 3 **pounds beef stew meat, cut into 1-inch cubes**
- 1 **pound whole fresh mushrooms, quartered**
- 3 **medium leeks (white portion only), chopped**
- 2 **medium carrots, chopped**
- ¼ **cup chopped celery**
- 1 **tablespoon canola oil**
- 4 **garlic cloves, minced**
- 1 **tablespoon tomato paste**
- 4 **cups reduced-sodium beef broth**
- 1 **cup dark stout beer or additional reduced-sodium beef broth**
- 2 **bay leaves**
- 1 **teaspoon dried thyme**
- 1 **teaspoon dried parsley flakes**
- 1 **teaspoon dried rosemary, crushed**
- 2 **pounds Yukon Gold potatoes, cut into 1-inch cubes**
- 2 **tablespoons cornstarch**
- 2 **tablespoons cold water**
- 1 **cup frozen peas**

1. In a stockpot, cook bacon over medium heat until crisp. Using a slotted spoon, remove to paper towels. In a large resealable plastic bag, combine flour, salt and pepper. Add beef, a few pieces at a time, and shake to coat. Brown beef in the bacon drippings. Remove and set aside.

2. In the same pan, saute the mushrooms, leeks, carrots and celery in oil until tender. Add garlic; cook 1 minute longer. Stir in tomato paste until blended. Add the broth, beer, bay leaves, thyme, parsley and rosemary. Return beef and bacon to pan. Bring to a boil. Reduce heat; cover and simmer 2 hours or until beef is tender.

3. Add potatoes. Return to a boil. Reduce heat; cover and simmer 1 hour longer or until potatoes are tender. Combine cornstarch and water until smooth; stir into stew. Bring to a boil; cook and stir 2 minutes or until thickened. Add peas; heat through. Discard bay leaves.

Fish Tacos

A cool sauce with just a bit of zing tops these crispy, spicy fish tacos. It's a dinnertime solution that's delicious, guilt-free and doesn't break the bank.
—**LENA LIM** SEATTLE, WA

PREP: 30 MIN. • **COOK:** 20 MIN. • **MAKES:** 8 SERVINGS

- ¾ **cup fat-free sour cream**
- 1 **can (4 ounces) chopped green chilies**
- 1 **tablespoon fresh cilantro leaves**
- 1 **tablespoon lime juice**
- 4 **tilapia fillets (4 ounces each)**
- ½ **cup all-purpose flour**
- 1 **egg white, beaten**
- ½ **cup panko (Japanese) bread crumbs**
- 1 **tablespoon canola oil**
- ½ **teaspoon salt**
- ½ **teaspoon each white pepper, cayenne pepper and paprika**
- 8 **corn tortillas (6 inches), warmed**
- 1 **large tomato, finely chopped**

1. Place the sour cream, chilies, cilantro and lime juice in a food processor; cover and process until blended. Set aside.

2. Cut each tilapia fillet lengthwise into two portions. Place the flour, egg white and bread crumbs in separate shallow bowls. Dip tilapia in flour, then egg white, then crumbs.

3. In a large skillet over medium heat, cook tilapia in oil in batches for 4-5 minutes on each side or until fish flakes easily with a fork. Combine the seasonings; sprinkle over fish.

4. Place a portion of fish on each tortilla; top with about 2 tablespoons of sour cream mixture. Sprinkle with tomato.

CHICKEN RIGGIES

Chicken Riggies

Rigatoni cooked with cream and cream cheese spells comfort when combined with chicken marinated in sherry and garlic.

—JACKIE SCANLAN DAYTON, OH

PREP: 30 MIN. + MARINATING • **COOK:** 15 MIN.
MAKES: 12 SERVINGS (1¾ CUPS EACH)

- ½ cup dry sherry
- 2 tablespoons olive oil
- 3 garlic cloves, minced
- 1 teaspoon dried oregano
- 2 pounds boneless skinless chicken breasts, cubed

SAUCE

- 2 tablespoons butter
- 1 each medium sweet red and green pepper, chopped
- 4 pickled hot cherry peppers, chopped
- 1 medium onion, chopped
- 2 garlic cloves, minced
- 1 cup dry sherry
- 2 cans (one 29 ounces, one 15 ounces) tomato puree
- ¼ teaspoon salt
- ⅛ teaspoon pepper
- 2 packages (16 ounces each) uncooked rigatoni
- 1½ cups heavy whipping cream
- 6 ounces cream cheese, cut up
- 1½ cups grated Romano cheese

1. In a large resealable plastic bag, combine sherry, oil, garlic and oregano. Add chicken; seal bag and turn to coat. Refrigerate 1 hour.

2. Drain chicken, discarding marinade. Heat a Dutch oven over medium-high heat. Add chicken in batches; cook and stir until no longer pink. Remove from pan.

3. In same pan, heat butter over medium-high heat. Add peppers, onion and garlic; cook and stir until tender. Add sherry; bring to a boil. Stir in tomato puree, salt and pepper; return to a boil. Reduce heat; simmer 8-10 minutes or until slightly thickened, stirring occasionally. Add chicken; heat through.

4. Meanwhile, in a stockpot, cook rigatoni according to package directions. In a small saucepan, combine cream and cream cheese over medium heat; cook and stir until blended. Add to chicken mixture; stir in Romano cheese.

5. Drain rigatoni; return to stockpot. Add sauce to pasta; toss to combine.

Hollywood Pizza

My father and I used to order a pizza like this from a place in Tinseltown. Here's my homemade version of that delicious pie.

—**MICHAEL WILLIAMS** MORENO VALLEY, CA

PREP: 20 MIN. • **BAKE:** 20 MIN. • **MAKES:** 12 SERVINGS

- 1 loaf (1 pound) frozen bread dough, thawed
- 2 tablespoons olive oil
- ½ pound lean ground beef (90% lean)
- 1 can (7 ounces) pizza sauce
- ½ cup sliced fresh mushrooms
- ½ cup chopped green pepper
- 1 can (2¼ ounces) sliced ripe olives, drained
- 1 can (14½ ounces) stewed tomatoes, drained
- ¼ cup sliced seeded jalapeno peppers, optional
- 2 cups (8 ounces) shredded part-skim mozzarella cheese

1. Preheat oven to 400°. On a greased baking sheet, roll bread dough into a 14x10-in. rectangle, building edges up slightly. Prick thoroughly with a fork. Brush dough with olive oil. Bake 10-12 minutes or until lightly browned.
2. Meanwhile, in a large skillet, cook beef over medium heat until no longer pink; drain. Spread pizza sauce over crust. Top with beef, mushrooms, green pepper, olives, tomatoes and, if desired, jalapeno peppers; sprinkle with cheese. Bake 20-25 minutes or until cheese is melted.
NOTE *Wear disposable gloves when cutting hot peppers; the oils can burn skin. Avoid touching your face.*

Garlic Rosemary Turkey

The aroma in our house is incredible while the bird is roasting, and my family can hardly wait to eat. The garlic, herbs and lemon are such simple additions, but they're all you really need to make this holiday turkey shine.
—**CATHY DOBBINS** RIO RANCHO, NM

PREP: 10 MIN. • **BAKE:** 3 HOURS + STANDING • **MAKES:** 10 SERVINGS

- 1 whole turkey (10 to 12 pounds)
- 6 to 8 garlic cloves, peeled
- 2 large lemons, halved
- 2 tablespoons olive oil
- 2 teaspoons dried rosemary, crushed
- 1 teaspoon rubbed sage

1. Preheat oven to 325°. Cut six to eight small slits in turkey skin; insert garlic under the skin. Squeeze two lemon halves inside the turkey; squeeze remaining halves over outside of turkey. Place lemons in the cavity.
2. Tuck wings under turkey; tie drumsticks together. Place on a rack in a shallow roasting pan, breast side up. Brush with oil; sprinkle with rosemary and sage. Roast 1 hour.
3. Cover turkey with foil; roast 2 to 2½ hours longer or until a thermometer inserted in thickest part of thigh reads 170°-175°. Baste occasionally with pan drippings.
4. Remove turkey from oven. Let stand 20 minutes before carving. If desired, skim fat and thicken pan drippings for gravy. Serve with turkey.

Spice-Rubbed Ribs

I recommend this rub for grilling. It's made with a wonderful blend of spices. If you have some left after making ribs, put it in a shaker and use it another day on pork or beef roasts, tenderloins, steaks and more.
—**CHERYL EWING** ELLWOOD CITY, PA

PREP: 10 MIN. • **GRILL:** 1 HOUR **MAKES:** 10 SERVINGS

- 3 tablespoons paprika
- 2 tablespoons plus 1 teaspoon salt
- 2 tablespoons plus 1 teaspoon garlic powder
- 2 tablespoons cayenne pepper
- 4 teaspoons onion powder
- 4 teaspoons dried oregano
- 4 teaspoons dried thyme
- 4 teaspoons pepper
- 10 pounds pork baby back ribs

1. In a small bowl, combine seasonings; rub over ribs.
2. Prepare grill for indirect heat, using a drip pan. Grill ribs, covered, over indirect medium heat for 1 hour or until meat is tender, turning occasionally.

GARLIC ROSEMARY TURKEY

Yankee Pot Roast

Here's a traditional main dish that's tried and true. It's been a favorite with my family for years.
—**VERA BURKE** WEST PITTSTON, PA

PREP: 20 MIN. • **COOK:** 2½ HOURS
MAKES: 12-14 SERVINGS

- 1 **boneless beef chuck roast (4 to 5 pounds)**
- 1 **tablespoon canola oil**
- 2 **large onions, coarsely chopped**
- 2 **cups sliced carrots**
- 2 **celery ribs, sliced**
- 2 **cans (14½ ounces each) Italian stewed tomatoes**
- 1¾ **cups water**
- 1 **teaspoon salt**
- ½ **teaspoon dried thyme**
- ¼ **teaspoon pepper**
- 4 **medium potatoes, peeled and cut into eighths**

1. In a Dutch oven, brown roast on all sides over medium-high heat in oil. Remove roast and set aside.

2. Add the onions, carrots, celery, tomatoes, water, salt, thyme and pepper to the pan. Bring to a boil. Return roast to pan. Reduce heat; cover and simmer 2 hours.

3. Add potatoes. Cover; cook 30-40 minutes longer or until meat and vegetables are tender.

TOP TIP

Add Zip to Pot Roast

Using a sharp knife, cut small slits in a pot roast and insert slivers of garlic cloves into each one. The garlic not only seasons the beef but gives the vegetables and broth for gravy a wonderful flavor.
—**JOYCE CHAMBERS**
PLEASANTON, CA

YANKEE POT ROAST

Turkey Potpies

With their golden brown crust and scrumptious filling, these comforting potpies will warm you down to your toes. Because the recipe makes two, you can eat one now and freeze the other for later. They bake and cut beautifully.

—**LAURIE JENSEN** CADILLAC, MI

PREP: 40 MIN.
BAKE: 40 MIN. + STANDING
MAKES: 2 PIES (6 SERVINGS EACH)

- 2 **medium potatoes, peeled and cut into 1-inch pieces**
- 3 **medium carrots, cut into 1-inch slices**
- 1 **medium onion, chopped**
- 1 **celery rib, diced**
- 2 **tablespoons butter**
- 1 **tablespoon olive oil**
- 6 **tablespoons all-purpose flour**
- 3 **cups chicken broth**
- 4 **cups cubed cooked turkey**
- ⅔ **cup frozen peas**
- ½ **cup plus 1 tablespoon heavy whipping cream, divided**
- 1 **tablespoon minced fresh parsley**
- 1 **teaspoon garlic salt**
- ¼ **teaspoon pepper**
- 1 **package (15 ounces) refrigerated pie pastry**
- 1 **egg**

1. Preheat oven to 375°. In a Dutch oven, saute potatoes, carrots, onion and celery in butter and oil until tender. Stir in flour until blended; gradually add broth. Bring to a boil; cook and stir 2 minutes or until thickened. Stir in turkey, peas, ½ cup cream, parsley, garlic salt and pepper.

2. Spoon into two ungreased 9-in. pie plates. Roll out pastry to fit top of each pie; place over filling. Trim, seal and flute edges. Cut out a decorative center or cut slits in pastry. In a small bowl, whisk egg and remaining cream; brush over pastry.

3. Bake 40-45 minutes or until golden brown. Let stand 10 minutes before cutting.

FREEZE OPTION *Cover and freeze unbaked potpies up to 3 months. To use, remove from freezer 30 minutes before baking (do not thaw). Preheat oven to 425°. Place pie on a baking sheet; cover edge loosely with foil. Bake 30 minutes. Reduce oven setting to 350°; remove foil. Bake 55-60 minutes longer or until golden brown and a thermometer inserted in center reads 165°.*

Picnic Chicken with Yogurt Dip

I made this well-seasoned chicken one evening for dinner and served it hot from the oven. While raiding the fridge the next day, I discovered how delicious it was cold and created the yogurt dip to go with it.

—**AMI OKASINSKI** MEMPHIS, TN

PREP: 20 MIN. • **COOK:** 1 HOUR
MAKES: 24 SERVINGS

- 3 **eggs**
- 3 **tablespoons water**
- 1½ **cups dry bread crumbs**
- 2 **teaspoons paprika**
- 1 **teaspoon salt**
- ½ **teaspoon each dried marjoram, thyme and rosemary, crushed**
- ½ **teaspoon pepper**
- 1 **cup butter, melted**
- 12 **chicken drumsticks**
- 12 **bone-in chicken thighs**

CREAMY LEEK DIP:
- 1 **cup heavy whipping cream**
- 1½ **cups plain yogurt**
- 1 **envelope leek soup mix**
- 1 **cup (4 ounces) shredded Colby cheese**

1. Preheat oven to 375°. In a bowl, whisk eggs and water. In another shallow bowl, combine bread crumbs and seasonings. Divide butter between two 13x9-in. baking dishes.

2. Dip chicken pieces in egg mixture, then coat with crumb mixture. Place in prepared pans. Bake, uncovered, 1 hour or until a thermometer reads 170°-175°, turning once. Cool for 30 minutes; refrigerate until chilled.

3. For dip, in a small bowl, beat cream until stiff peaks form. In another bowl, combine yogurt, soup mix and cheese; fold in whipped cream. Cover and refrigerate until serving. Serve with cold chicken.

TURKEY POTPIES

Beef Bolognese with Linguine

After much research, tasting and tweaking, I finally came up with this sauce, which is based on a dish from an Italian restaurant where I worked. It's perfect for feeding a house full of guests.

—**CHRISTINE WENDLAND** BROWNS MILLS, NJ

PREP: 30 MIN. • **COOK:** 3½ HOURS
MAKES: 18 SERVINGS (1 CUP EACH)

- 3 **pounds lean ground beef (90% lean)**
- ⅓ **cup olive oil**
- 3 **medium onions, chopped**
- 3 **large carrots, chopped**
- 6 **celery ribs, chopped**
- 1 **can (12 ounces) tomato paste, divided**
- 9 **garlic cloves, sliced**
- 3 **tablespoons dried parsley flakes**
- 5 **teaspoons kosher salt**
- 3 **teaspoons dried basil**
- 3 **teaspoons dried marjoram**
- 1½ **teaspoons coarsely ground pepper**
- ¼ **teaspoon crushed red pepper flakes**
- 1½ **cups dry red wine**

**BEEF BOLOGNESE
WITH LINGUINE**

- 3 **cans (28 ounces each) diced tomatoes, undrained**
- 1½ **cups beef stock**
- 6 **bay leaves**
- 3 **cups 2% milk**
- ¾ **cup grated Parmesan cheese**
  Hot cooked linguine
  Additional grated Parmesan cheese, optional

1. In a stockpot, cook half of the beef over medium heat 8-10 minutes or until no longer pink, breaking into crumbles. Remove beef with a slotted spoon; set aside. Pour off drippings. Repeat with remaining beef.
2. In the same stockpot, heat oil over medium heat. Add the onions, carrots and celery; cook and stir until tender. Stir in 1 cup tomato paste; cook and stir 3 minutes longer. Add the garlic, seasonings and beef.
3. Stir in wine. Bring to a boil; cook until almost evaporated. Add tomatoes, stock and bay leaves; return to a boil. Reduce heat; simmer, uncovered, for 3 hours or until desired consistency, stirring in milk halfway through cooking.
4. Remove bay leaves. Stir in cheese and remaining tomato paste; heat through. Serve with linguine and, if desired, additional cheese.

Ham with Spiced-Cherry Sauce

This showstopping entree will have everyone coming back for more. It's a simple treatment that lends an appealing sweet-tart flavor to tender ham.

—**SHERRY THOMPSON** SENECA, SC

PREP: 15 MIN. • **BAKE:** 2 HOURS 20 MIN. + STANDING
MAKES: 18 SERVINGS

- 1 **boneless fully cooked ham (6 pounds)**
- 2 **jars (12 ounces each) cherry preserves**
- ½ **cup cider vinegar**
- ¼ **cup packed brown sugar**
- ¼ **cup water**
- ½ **teaspoon each ground cinnamon, nutmeg and allspice**

1. Preheat oven to 325°. Place ham on a rack in a shallow roasting pan. Score the surface of ham, making diamond shapes ½ in. deep. Bake, uncovered, 2 hours.
2. Meanwhile, in a small saucepan, combine preserves, vinegar, brown sugar, water and spices. Bring to a boil. Reduce heat; cover and simmer 3-4 minutes or until sugar is dissolved.
3. Pour ¾ cup sauce mixture over the ham. Bake 20-30 minutes longer or until a thermometer reads 140°. Serve with remaining sauce.

MIXED GRILL FAJITAS

FAST FIX
Mixed Grill Fajitas

Everyone loves to make their own fajitas with this assortment of tasty meats and veggies. The recipe is my original creation, but I have found that there's really no wrong way to make these!
—**KAREN HAEN** STURGEON BAY, WI

START TO FINISH: 30 MIN. • **MAKES:** 12 SERVINGS

- 1 **each medium green, sweet red and yellow peppers, julienned**
- 2 **medium red onions, sliced**
- 3 **tablespoons olive oil**
- 1 **cup (8 ounces) sour cream**
- 2 **teaspoons ground cumin**
- 2 **garlic cloves, minced**
- ½ **teaspoon salt**
- ½ **teaspoon pepper**
- ½ **teaspoon chili powder**
- 6 **boneless skinless chicken breast halves (4 ounces each)**
- 3 **Italian sausage links**
- 2 **beef cubed steaks (4 ounces each)**
- 24 **flour tortillas (8 inches), warmed**
- 6 **cups (24 ounces) shredded cheddar cheese**

1. In a large skillet, saute peppers and onions in oil until tender; keep warm. In a small bowl, combine the sour cream, cumin and garlic; chill until serving.

2. Combine the salt, pepper and chili powder; sprinkle over chicken, sausages and steaks. Grill chicken and sausages, covered, over medium heat 5-8 minutes on each side or until a thermometer inserted in chicken reads 165° and the sausage is no longer pink. Slice and keep warm.

3. Grill steaks, covered, over medium heat for 2-3 minutes on each side or until meat reaches desired doneness (for medium-rare, a thermometer should read 145°; medium, 160°; well-done, 170°). Slice and keep warm.

4. Divide meats and vegetables among tortillas; sprinkle with cheese. Roll up; serve fajitas with sour cream mixture.

Brisket in a Bag

This tender brisket is served with a savory cranberry gravy that's made right in the bag. I like to serve the slices with mashed potatoes and drizzle the gravy over them.

—**PEGGY STIGERS** FORT WORTH, TX

PREP: 15 MIN. • **BAKE:** 2½ HOURS
MAKES: 12 SERVINGS

- 3 **tablespoons all-purpose flour, divided**
- 1 **large oven roasting bag**
- 1 **fresh beef brisket (5 pounds), trimmed**
- 1 **can (14 ounces) whole-berry cranberry sauce**
- 1 **can (10¾ ounces) condensed cream of mushroom soup, undiluted**
- 1 **can (8 ounces) tomato sauce**
- 1 **envelope onion soup mix**

1. Preheat oven to 325°. Place 1 tablespoon flour in oven bag; shake to coat. Place bag in an ungreased 13x9-in. baking pan; place brisket in bag.
2. Combine cranberry sauce, soup, tomato sauce, soup mix and remaining flour; pour over beef. Seal bag. Cut slits in top of bag according to package directions.
3. Bake 2½ to 3 hours or until meat is tender. Carefully remove brisket from bag. Let stand 5 minutes before slicing. Thinly slice meat across the grain; serve with gravy.
NOTE *This is a fresh beef brisket, not corned beef.*

TOP TIP

Slicing Beef Roasts

To slice boneless roasts, slice the meat vertically across the grain into ¼-in. to ½-in. slices. If the roast is tied, remove the string as you carve to help hold the roast together.

TURKEY LATTICE PIE

Turkey Lattice Pie

With its pretty lattice crust, this cheesy baked dish is as eye-catching as it is delicious. It's easy to make, too, since it uses convenient crescent roll dough. It's a fun and different way to dress up leftover turkey.

—**LORRAINE NAIG** EMMETSBURG, IA

PREP: 20 MIN. • **BAKE:** 20 MIN.
MAKES: 12 SERVINGS

- 3 **tubes (8 ounces each) refrigerated crescent rolls**
- 4 **cups cubed cooked turkey**
- 1½ **cups (6 ounces) shredded cheddar or Swiss cheese**
- 3 **cups frozen chopped broccoli, thawed and drained**
- 1 **can (10¾ ounces) condensed cream of chicken soup, undiluted**
- 1⅓ **cups milk**
- 2 **tablespoons Dijon mustard**
- 1 **tablespoon dried minced onion**
- ½ **teaspoon salt**
- Dash pepper
- 1 **egg, lightly beaten**

1. Preheat oven to 375°. Unroll two tubes of crescent roll dough; separate into rectangles. Place rectangles in an ungreased 15x10x1-in. baking pan. Press onto the bottom and ¼ in. up the sides of pan to form a crust, sealing seams and perforations. Bake 5-7 minutes or until light golden brown.
2. Meanwhile, in a large bowl, combine turkey, cheese, broccoli, soup, milk, mustard, onion, salt and pepper. Spoon over crust.
3. Unroll remaining dough; divide into rectangles. Seal perforations. Cut each rectangle into four 1-in. strips. Using strips, make a lattice design on top of turkey mixture. Brush with egg. Bake 17-22 minutes longer or until top crust is golden brown and filling is bubbly.

Creamy Beef Enchiladas

These American-style enchiladas are rich, creamy and loaded with cheese. Kids will like the texture and the fact that they have just a touch of south-of-the-border heat.

—BELINDA MORAN WOODBURY, TN

PREP: 25 MIN. • **BAKE:** 20 MIN.
MAKES: 12 SERVINGS

- 2 **pounds lean ground beef (90% lean)**
- 1 **cup chopped onion**
- 1 **can (10¾ ounces) condensed cream of mushroom soup, undiluted**
- 1 **cup (8 ounces) sour cream**
- 1 **can (4 ounces) chopped green chilies**
- 3 **cups (12 ounces) shredded cheddar cheese, divided**
- 3 **cans (10 ounces each) enchilada sauce, divided**
- 12 **flour tortillas (8 inches), warmed**

1. Preheat oven to 350°. In a Dutch oven, cook beef and onion over medium heat until meat is no longer pink; drain. Add soup, sour cream, chilies, 1 cup cheese and ½ cup enchilada sauce; heat through.
2. Spread ¼ cup enchilada sauce into each of two ungreased 13x9-in. baking dishes. Place ½ cup beef mixture down the center of each tortilla. Roll up and place seam side down in prepared dishes.
3. Pour remaining enchilada sauce over top; sprinkle with the remaining cheese. Bake, uncovered, 20-25 minutes or until heated through.

Stuffed-Crust Chicken Pizza

Talk about a clever idea that just couldn't be quicker or easier! String cheese is the secret behind my yummy stuffed-crust chicken pizza.

—PAM BROOKS
SOUTH BERWICK, ME

PREP: 35 MIN. • **BAKE:** 10 MIN.
MAKES: 12 PIECES

- 2 **tubes (13.8 ounces each) refrigerated pizza crust**
- 10 **pieces string cheese**
- ½ **pound boneless skinless chicken breasts, cut into ½-inch cubes**

- 1 **small onion, chopped**
- 2 **tablespoons olive oil**
- 3 **garlic cloves, minced**
- ½ **cup oil-packed sun-dried tomatoes, julienned**
- 1 **teaspoon dried rosemary, crushed**
- ½ **teaspoon salt**
- ½ **teaspoon pepper**
- ¾ **cup pizza sauce**
- 2 **cups (8 ounces) shredded part-skim mozzarella cheese**
- ½ **cup pitted ripe olives, chopped**

1. Preheat oven to 425°. Unroll both pizza crusts and place in a greased 15x10x1-in. baking pan, letting dough drape 1 in. over the edges. Pinch center seam to seal.
2. Place string cheese around edges of pan. Fold dough over cheese; pinch to seal. Bake for 5 minutes.
3. In a large skillet, saute chicken and onion in oil until the chicken is no longer pink. Add garlic; cook 1 minute. Stir in the tomatoes, rosemary, salt and pepper.
4. Spread sauce over crust. Top with chicken mixture. Sprinkle with mozzarella and olives.
5. Bake 10-15 minutes or until cheese is melted and crust is golden brown.

CREAMY BEEF ENCHILADAS

Crab Cakes with Red Pepper Sauce

Don't forget to have lemons on hand so you and your guests can squeeze some fresh lemon juice over these succulent crab cakes.

—**JOYLYN TRICKEL** HELENDALE, CA

PREP: 30 MIN. + CHILLING • **COOK:** 20 MIN.
MAKES: 10 SERVINGS

- ¼ **cup mayonnaise**
- ¼ **cup minced chives**
- 2 **tablespoons minced fresh parsley**
- 1 **tablespoon lemon juice**
- ½ **teaspoon seafood seasoning**
- ⅛ **teaspoon cayenne pepper**
  Dash pepper
- 1 **pound lump crabmeat, cartilage removed**
- 4 **to 5 slices French bread (1 inch thick), crust removed**

RED PEPPER SAUCE

- ¼ **cup mayonnaise**
- ¼ **cup Dijon mustard**
- 2 **tablespoons honey**
- 1 **tablespoon lemon juice**
- ½ **cup chopped sweet red pepper**
- ¼ **cup chopped green onions**
- 2 **tablespoons minced shallots**
- 2 **tablespoons minced fresh parsley**
  Salt and pepper to taste
- 2 **tablespoons butter**
- 1 **tablespoon olive oil**
  Lemon wedges

1. In a large bowl, combine first seven ingredients; stir in crab. In a food processor, process bread slices, a few at a time, until fine crumbs form (total volume should be 2½ cups). Add 1 cup to the crab mixture.
2. Shape ¼ cupfuls of crab mixture into patties. Coat both sides of patties with remaining bread crumbs, pressing to adhere. Place on a baking sheet; cover and refrigerate for up to 6 hours.
3. Meanwhile, for sauce, in a blender, combine the mayonnaise, mustard, honey, lemon juice, red pepper, onions, shallots, parsley, salt and pepper; cover and process until finely chopped. Refrigerate until serving.
4. In a large skillet, melt half of the butter and half of the oil. Place half of the crab cakes in skillet. Cook over medium heat for 5 minutes on each side or until lightly browned (carefully turn the delicate cakes over). Repeat with remaining butter, oil and crab cakes. Serve with sauce and lemon wedges.
NOTE *Chilling these delicate crab cakes makes them less fragile during frying.*

FREEZE IT

Honey-Dijon Chicken

Smothered in a sauce that gets its sweetness from honey and pineapple juice, these chicken breasts are a favorite, even for picky eaters. I like to serve them over egg noodles.

—**BARBARA LEVENTHAL** HAUPPAUGE, NY

PREP: 15 MIN. • **BAKE:** 20 MIN
MAKES: 2 CASSEROLES (12 SERVINGS, 6 PER CASSEROLE)

- 12 **boneless skinless chicken breast halves (4 ounces each)**
- 4 **garlic cloves, minced**
- 2 **teaspoons dried thyme**
  Salt and pepper to taste
- 1 **tablespoon canola oil**
- 2 **tablespoons cornstarch**
- 1½ **cups pineapple juice**
- ½ **cup water**
- ½ **cup Dijon mustard**
- ⅓ **cup honey**
  Hot cooked rice or noodles

Rub chicken with garlic and thyme. Sprinkle with salt and pepper. In a large skillet, cook chicken in oil until a thermometer reads 165°. In a small bowl, combine cornstarch, pineapple juice and water until smooth. Stir in mustard and honey. Add to skillet. Bring to a boil; cook and stir 2 minutes or until thickened. Serve with rice or noodles.
FREEZE OPTION *Divide chicken between two 11x7-in. baking dishes. Cool. Cover and freeze up to 3 months. To use, completely thaw in refrigerator. Remove from refrigerator 30 minutes before baking. Preheat oven to 350°. Cover and bake 35 minutes or until heated through.*

Stuffed Pork Loin with Currant Sauce

When you're looking for a special entree, try this pork loin. It looks so pretty with the red currant sauce and the fresh parsley garnish.

—GLORIA BRADLEY NAPERVILLE, IL

PREP: 30 MIN. • **BAKE:** 1 HOUR + STANDING
MAKES: 12 SERVINGS (1¼ CUPS SAUCE)

- ¾ cup chopped walnuts, toasted
- ¾ pound bulk pork sausage
- 1 medium apple, peeled and finely chopped
- 1 garlic clove, minced
- 1 egg, beaten
- 1 tablespoon minced fresh parsley
- ¼ teaspoon salt
- ¼ teaspoon pepper
- 1 boneless whole pork loin roast (3 to 4 pounds)
- ⅓ cup apple butter

SAUCE
- 1 cup red currant jelly
- 2 tablespoons honey
- 1 tablespoon dried currants
- 2 teaspoons cider vinegar
- ¼ teaspoon hot pepper sauce

1. Preheat oven to 350°. Place walnuts in a food processor; cover and process until ground. Set aside.

2. Cook sausage, apple and garlic over medium heat in a large skillet until meat is no longer pink. Drain; cool slightly. Stir in ground walnuts, egg, parsley, salt and pepper.

3. Cut a lengthwise slit down the center of the roast to within ½ in. of bottom. Open roast so it lies flat. Starting at the center, split each half of roast horizontally to within ½ in. of edge. Open halves so roast lies flat. Cover with plastic wrap. Flatten to ½-in. thickness. Remove plastic.

4. Brush roast with apple butter; spoon sausage mixture over the top. Roll up jelly-roll style, starting with a long side. Tie with kitchen string at 2-in. intervals. Place on a rack in a shallow baking pan.

5. Bake, uncovered, 1 to 1½ hours or until a meat thermometer reads 145°. Let stand 10-15 minutes before slicing. In a small saucepan, heat the sauce ingredients until smooth. Serve with roast.

NOTE *This recipe was tested with commercially prepared apple butter.*

Lamb Stew

My grandmother used to make this stew as a special Sunday meal. It's also a memorable treat from Ireland. If you like your stew thick and rich, you've got to try this.
—**VICKIE DESOURDY** WASHINGTON, NC

PREP: 40 MIN. • **BAKE:** 1½ HOURS
MAKES: 8 SERVINGS (2½ QUARTS)

- 2 pounds lamb stew meat, cut into 1-inch cubes
- 1 tablespoon butter
- 1 tablespoon olive oil
- 1 pound carrots, sliced
- 2 medium onions, thinly sliced
- 2 garlic cloves, minced
- 1½ cups reduced-sodium chicken broth
- 1 bottle (12 ounces) Guinness stout or additional reduced-sodium chicken broth
- 6 medium red potatoes, peeled and cut into 1-inch cubes
- 4 bay leaves
- 2 fresh thyme sprigs
- 2 fresh rosemary sprigs
- 2 teaspoons salt
- 1½ teaspoons pepper
- ¼ cup heavy whipping cream

1. Preheat oven to 325°. In an ovenproof Dutch oven, brown lamb in butter and oil in batches. Remove and keep warm. In the same pan, saute carrots and onions in drippings until crisp-tender. Add garlic; cook 1 minute. Gradually add broth and beer. Stir in lamb, potatoes, bay leaves, thyme, rosemary, salt and pepper.
2. Cover and bake 1½ to 2 hours or until meat and vegetables are tender, stirring every 30 minutes. Discard bay leaves, thyme and rosemary. Stir in cream; heat through.
FREEZE OPTION *Place individual portions of stew in freezer containers and freeze up to 3 months. To use, partially thaw in refrigerator overnight. Heat through in a saucepan, stirring occasionally and adding a little water if necessary.*

ITALIAN
MEATBALL TORTES

Italian Meatball Tortes

With classic Italian flavor, these hearty dinner pies filled with tomatoes, mozzarella and savory homemade meatballs will be a hit with your family. Preparation takes some time, but the results are well worth it.

—**SANDY BLESSING** OCEAN SHORES, WA

PREP: 1¼ HOURS + RISING • **BAKE:** 30 MIN.
MAKES: 2 TORTES (6 SERVINGS EACH)

- 1 package (¼ ounce) active dry yeast
- ¼ cup warm water (110° to 115°)
- ¾ cup warm milk (110° to 115°)
- ¼ cup sugar
- ¼ cup shortening
- 1 egg
- 1 teaspoon salt
- 3½ to 3¾ cups all-purpose flour

MEATBALLS
- 1 can (5 ounces) evaporated milk
- 2 eggs, lightly beaten
- 1 cup quick-cooking oats
- 1 cup crushed saltines
- ½ cup chopped onion
- ½ cup chopped celery
- 2 teaspoons salt
- 2 teaspoons chili powder
- ½ teaspoon garlic powder
- ½ teaspoon pepper
- 3 pounds ground beef

FILLING
- 1 can (15 ounces) crushed tomatoes
- ½ cup chopped onion
- ⅓ cup grated Parmesan cheese
- 1½ teaspoons dried basil
- 1½ teaspoons dried oregano
- 1 teaspoon minced fresh parsley
- 1 teaspoon salt
- 1½ cups (6 ounces) shredded part-skim mozzarella cheese

1. In a large bowl, dissolve yeast in warm water. Add the milk, sugar, shortening, egg, salt and 2 cups flour. Beat until smooth. Stir in enough remaining flour to form a soft dough.

2. Turn onto a floured surface; knead until smooth and elastic, about 6-8 minutes. Place in a greased bowl, turning once to grease the top. Cover and let rise in a warm place until doubled, 1 to 1½ hours.

3. In a large bowl, combine the milk, eggs, oats, saltines, onion, celery and seasonings. Crumble beef over mixture and mix well. Shape into 1½-in. balls. In a large skillet over medium heat, cook meatballs in batches until no longer pink.

4. Meanwhile, place tomatoes and onion in a small saucepan. Bring to a boil. Reduce heat; simmer, uncovered, for 10 minutes or until slightly thickened. Stir in the Parmesan cheese, herbs and salt.

5. Punch dough down. Divide into three portions. Roll two portions into 11-in. circles; line the bottoms and press partially up the sides of two greased 9-in. springform pans. Roll third portion into a 12x10-in. rectangle; cut into twelve 10x1-in. strips.

6. Place meatballs in prepared crusts; top with tomato mixture and mozzarella cheese. Make lattice crusts with strips of dough; trim and seal edges. Cover and let rise for 30 minutes.

7. Preheat oven to 350°. Bake 30-35 minutes or until golden brown. Cut into wedges.

TOP TIP

Making Meatballs of Equal Size

For meatballs to cook evenly, it's important for them to be the same size. One way to do this is to lightly pat meat mixture into a 1-in.-thick rectangle. Cut the rectangle into the same number of squares as meatballs in the recipe. Gently roll each square into a ball. Or, using a 1½- or 1¾-in.-diameter scoop, scoop the mixture into portions of equal size. Gently roll each into a ball.

FREEZE IT

All-American Meat Loaf

My family loves this classic stick-to-your-ribs version of meat loaf. It's down-home good!

—**MARGIE WILLIAMS** MOUNT JULIET, TN

PREP: 30 MIN. • **BAKE:** 50 MIN.+STANDING
MAKES: 2 LOAVES (8 SERVINGS EACH)

- 1 large green pepper, chopped
- 1 large onion, chopped
- 2 teaspoons olive oil
- 4 garlic cloves, minced
- 2 eggs, lightly beaten
- 1 cup 2% milk
- 6 slices bread, cubed
- 1½ cups (6 ounces) shredded cheddar cheese
- 2¼ teaspoons dried rosemary, crushed
- 2 teaspoons salt
- 1 teaspoon pepper
- 2 pounds lean ground beef (90% lean)
- 1 pound ground pork
- 1½ cups ketchup
- ¼ cup packed brown sugar
- 2 teaspoons cider vinegar

1. Saute green pepper and onion in oil in a large skillet until tender. Add garlic; cook 1 minute longer. Transfer to a large bowl; cool to room temperature.
2. Preheat oven to 350°. Add eggs, milk, bread, cheese, rosemary, salt and pepper to sauteed vegetables. Crumble beef and pork over mixture and mix well.
3. Pat into two greased 9x5-in. loaf pans. Combine ketchup, brown sugar and vinegar in a small bowl. Spread over tops.
4. Bake, uncovered, 50-55 minutes or until no pink remains and a thermometer reads 160°. Let stand 10 minutes before slicing.
FREEZE OPTION *Shape meat loaves in plastic wrap-lined loaf pan; cover and freeze until firm. Remove from pan and wrap securely in foil; return to freezer. Freeze up to 3 months. To use, preheat oven to 350°. Unwrap meat loaf and place in pan. Bake, uncovered, 1¼ to 1½ hours or until a thermometer inserted in center reads 160°.*

Herbed Standing Rib Roast

We're a meat-and-potatoes family, so this roast is right up our alley. It really is the highlight of an elegant dinner for special guests. Leftovers are great for sandwiches, too.

—**CAROL STEVENS** BASYE, VA

PREP: 10 MIN.
BAKE: 2¼ HOURS + STANDING
MAKES: 12 SERVINGS

- 3 tablespoons grated onion
- 2 tablespoons olive oil
- 4 garlic cloves, minced
- 2 teaspoons celery seed
- 1 teaspoon coarsely ground pepper
- 1 teaspoon paprika
- ¼ teaspoon dried thyme
- 1 bone-in beef rib roast (6 to 7 pounds)
- 2 large onions, cut into wedges
- 2 large carrots, cut into 2-inch pieces
- 2 celery ribs, cut into 2-inch pieces
- ¼ cup red wine or beef broth Assorted herbs and fruit, optional

1. Preheat oven to 350°. In a small bowl, combine the first seven ingredients; rub over roast. Place onions, carrots and celery in a large roasting pan; place roast over vegetables.
2. Bake, uncovered, 2¼ to 3 hours or until meat reaches desired doneness (for medium-rare, a thermometer should read 145°; medium, 160°; well-done, 170°).
3. Remove roast to a serving platter and keep warm; let stand 15 minutes before slicing.
4. Meanwhile, for au jus, strain and discard vegetables. Pour drippings into a measuring cup; skim fat. Add wine to roasting pan, stirring to remove any browned bits. Stir in drippings; heat through. Serve with roast. Garnish platter with herbs and fruit.

HERBED STANDING RIB ROAST

BLACK BEAN TURKEY ENCHILADAS

2. Place ½ cup turkey mixture off center on each tortilla. Roll up and place in two 13x9-in. baking dishes coated with cooking spray, seam side down. Top with enchilada sauce; sprinkle with remaining cheese.

3. Bake casseroles, uncovered, 15-20 minutes or until heated through. Sprinkle with cilantro; serve with yogurt.

FREEZE OPTION *Cool unbaked casseroles; cover and freeze up to 3 months. To use, partially thaw in refrigerator overnight. Remove from refrigerator 30 minutes before baking. Preheat oven to 375°. Bake casseroles, as directed, increasing time to 20-25 minutes or until heated through and a thermometer inserted in center reads 165°.*

FREEZE IT

Black Bean Turkey Enchiladas

My best friend and I created this recipe because we wanted a meal that was easy to prepare, affordable and nutritious. We both have hectic schedules, so when we're feeling crunched for time, it's a relief to have these wholesome enchiladas waiting for us in the freezer.
—**HOLLY BABER** SEATTLE, WA

PREP: 35 MIN. • **BAKE:** 15 MIN. • **MAKES:** 14 SERVINGS

- 1¼ pounds lean ground turkey
- 1 small onion, chopped
- 1 teaspoon reduced-sodium taco seasoning
- ½ teaspoon ground cumin
- ¼ teaspoon pepper
- 1 package (8 ounces) reduced-fat cream cheese, cubed
- 1 cup (4 ounces) shredded Mexican cheese blend, divided
- 1 can (15 ounces) black beans, rinsed and drained
- 1½ cups frozen corn, thawed
- 1 can (14½ ounces) fire-roasted diced tomatoes, drained
- 2 cans (4 ounces each) chopped green chilies
- ¼ cup salsa
- 14 whole wheat tortillas (8 inches), warmed
- 2 cans (10 ounces each) enchilada sauce
  Minced fresh cilantro
- ¾ cup reduced-fat plain Greek yogurt

1. Preheat oven to 375°. In a large nonstick skillet, cook turkey, onion and seasonings over medium heat 6-8 minutes or until turkey is no longer pink and onion is tender. Stir in cream cheese and ½ cup Mexican cheese blend until melted. Stir in beans, corn, tomatoes, chilies and salsa.

Zippy Coconut Baked Fish

Fish fillets are a good choice for a quick, healthy meal. I like this recipe because the fish is baked and I can avoid hot oil splatters on the stovetop. The chutney dipping sauce adds some heat to this tropical dish.
—**PAT SCHMELING** GERMANTOWN, WI

PREP: 20 MIN. • **BAKE:** 15 MIN. • **MAKES:** 8 SERVINGS

- ⅓ cup butter, melted
- 3 tablespoons orange juice
- 2 tablespoons lemon juice
- 2 teaspoons garlic powder
- 2 teaspoons ground ginger
- 1 to 2 teaspoons crushed red pepper flakes
- ½ teaspoon salt
- ½ teaspoon pepper
- 1½ cups flaked coconut
- 1 cup dry bread crumbs
- 8 red snapper, bass or turbot fillets (6 ounces each)

CHUTNEY SAUCE
- ½ cup mayonnaise
- ¼ cup mango chutney
- 1 tablespoon lemon juice
- 1 teaspoon curry powder

1. Preheat oven to 425°. In a shallow bowl, combine the first eight ingredients. In another shallow bowl, combine coconut and bread crumbs. Dip fillets in butter mixture, then coat with coconut mixture. Transfer to a 15x10x1-in. baking pan coated with cooking spray.

2. Bake 15-20 minutes or until fish flakes easily with a fork. Meanwhile, in a small bowl, combine the chutney sauce ingredients. Serve with fish.

NOTES *Because fish fillets vary in thickness, the baking time may vary depending on what type of fish you use.*

Potato-Bar Chili

Everyone will love this mild chili, especially when scooped over a baked potato. This thick, hearty sauce really does eat like a meal!

—ALCY THORNE LOS MOLINOS, CA

PREP: 10 MIN. • **COOK:** 30 MIN. • **MAKES:** 7 CUPS

- 1½ **pounds ground beef**
- 2 **medium onions, chopped**
- 1 **medium green pepper, chopped**
- 1 **can (28 ounces) diced tomatoes, undrained**
- 1 **can (16 ounces) chili beans, undrained**
- 2 **tablespoons sugar**
- 2 **teaspoons chili powder**
- ¼ **teaspoon salt**
- ¼ **teaspoon pepper**
  Baked potatoes

1. In a Dutch oven, cook the beef, onions and green pepper over medium heat until meat is no longer pink; drain. Add the tomatoes, beans, sugar and seasonings.
2. Bring to a boil. Reduce heat; simmer, uncovered, for 20 minutes. Serve with potatoes.

Italian Pot Roast

This tender roast with its rich, savory gravy fills the entire house with a wonderful aroma as it cooks and will have the family waiting at the table for dinner. Serve it with a crusty loaf of bread and tossed salad.

—KAREN SCHULTZ BREDA NEEDHAM, MA

PREP: 15 MIN. • **COOK:** 2¾ HOURS **MAKES:** 12 SERVINGS

- 1 **beef rump roast or bottom round roast (3 pounds)**
- 1½ **cups water**

- 6 **garlic cloves, minced**
- 2 **bay leaves**
- 2 **tablespoons dried basil**
- 4½ **teaspoons dried oregano**
- 1½ **teaspoons salt**
- ½ **teaspoon crushed red pepper flakes**
- ½ **teaspoon garlic powder**
- 1 **tablespoon cornstarch**
- 3 **tablespoons cold water**

1. In a Dutch oven coated with cooking spray, brown roast on all sides; drain. Combine the water, garlic and seasonings; pour over roast. Bring to a boil. Reduce heat; cover and simmer for 2¾ to 3¼ hours or until meat is tender.
2. Discard bay leaves. Remove roast to a serving platter; let stand for 10 minutes. Meanwhile, for gravy, pour pan drippings and loosened browned bits into a measuring cup; skim and discard fat. Transfer to a small saucepan. Combine cornstarch and cold water until smooth; gradually stir into drippings. Bring to a boil; cook and stir for 2 minutes or until thickened. Slice beef; serve with gravy.

Homemade Meatless Spaghetti Sauce

I get so excited when my homegrown tomatoes ripen because it's time to make my homemade spaghetti sauce.

—SONDRA BERGY LOWELL, MI

PREP: 20 MIN. • **COOK:** 3¼ HOURS • **MAKES:** 2 QUARTS

- 4 **medium onions, chopped**
- ½ **cup canola oil**
- 12 **cups chopped peeled fresh tomatoes**
- 4 **garlic cloves, minced**
- 3 **bay leaves**
- 4 **teaspoons salt**
- 2 **teaspoons dried oregano**
- 1¼ **teaspoons pepper**
- ½ **teaspoon dried basil**
- 2 **cans (6 ounces each) tomato paste**
- ⅓ **cup packed brown sugar**
  Hot cooked spaghetti

1. In a Dutch oven, saute onions in oil until tender. Add the tomatoes, garlic, bay leaves, salt, oregano, pepper and basil. Bring to a boil. Reduce heat; cover and simmer for 2 hours, stirring occasionally.
2. Add tomato paste and brown sugar; simmer, uncovered, for 1 hour. Discard bay leaves. Serve with spaghetti.
NOTE *Browned ground beef or Italian sausage can be added to cooked sauce if desired. The sauce also freezes well.*

MUFFIN-CUP CHEDDAR BEEF PIES

Muffin-Cup Cheddar Beef Pies

My clan can't get enough of these beef rolls, so I make extra to have on hand whenever they get a craving. The pies heat up quickly and taste especially good with dipping sauce—my kids ask for spaghetti sauce or ranch dressing.
—**KIMBERLY FARMER** WICHITA, KS

PREP: 25 MIN. + STANDING • **BAKE:** 20 MIN.
MAKES: 20 MEAT PIES

- 2 **loaves (1 pound each) frozen bread dough**
- 2 **pounds ground beef**
- 1 **can (8 ounces) mushroom stems and pieces, drained**
- 1¼ **cups (5 ounces) shredded cheddar cheese**
- 1½ **teaspoons Italian seasoning**
- 1 **teaspoon garlic powder**
- ½ **teaspoon salt**
- ¼ **teaspoon pepper**
  Spaghetti sauce, warmed

1. Let dough stand at room temperature 30 minutes or until softened. Preheat oven to 350°. Meanwhile, in a Dutch oven, cook beef over medium heat 12-15 minutes or until no longer pink, breaking into crumbles; drain. Stir in mushrooms, cheese and seasonings.

2. Divide each loaf into 10 portions; roll each into a 4-in. circle. Top with ¼ cup filling; bring edges of dough up over filling and pinch to seal.

3. Place meat pies in greased muffin cups, seam side down. Bake 20-25 minutes or until golden brown. Serve with spaghetti sauce.

FREEZE OPTION *Freeze cooled beef pies in a resealable plastic freezer bag. To use, reheat beef pies on greased baking sheets in a preheated 350° oven until heated through.*

Hometown Pasty Pies

I prepare these in advance and freeze them for a quick dinner later—or to share with a friend. The meaty baked pies make a hot, substantial meal.
—**JEN HATLEN** EDGERTON, WI

PREP: 70 MIN. + CHILLING
BAKE: 45 MIN. + STANDING
MAKES: 2 PIES (8 SERVINGS EACH)

- 5 **cups all-purpose flour**
- 1 **tablespoon sugar**
- 1½ **teaspoons salt**
- 2 **cups butter-flavored shortening**
- 7 **tablespoons cold water**
- 1 **egg**
- 1 **tablespoon white vinegar**

FILLING

- 2 **cups cubed peeled potatoes**
- 2 **cups finely chopped fresh carrots**
- 1 **pound ground beef**
- 1 **pound bulk pork sausage**
- 1 **cup sliced fresh mushrooms**
- 1 **medium onion, chopped**
- 1 **can (10¾ ounces) condensed cream of mushroom soup, undiluted**
- 1 **can (10¾ ounces) condensed cream of chicken soup, undiluted**
- 1 **cup frozen peas**
- 1 **tablespoon sherry or chicken broth**
- ½ **teaspoon salt**
- ½ **teaspoon seasoned salt**
- ¼ **teaspoon pepper**
- ½ **cup shredded Colby cheese**
- ½ **cup sour cream**

1. In a large bowl, combine flour, sugar and salt; cut in shortening until crumbly. Whisk water, egg and vinegar; gradually add to flour mixture, tossing with a fork until dough forms a ball. Divide dough in quarters so that two of the portions are slightly larger than the other two; wrap each in plastic wrap. Refrigerate for 1 hour or until easy to handle.

HOMETOWN
PASTY PIES

2. Meanwhile, place potatoes in a large saucepan and cover with water. Bring to a boil. Reduce heat; cover and cook 5 minutes. Add carrots; cook 6-9 minutes longer or until vegetables are tender. Drain and set aside.
3. In a Dutch oven, cook beef and sausage over medium heat until meat is no longer pink. Remove from pan with a slotted spoon; drain, reserving 1 tablespoon drippings. Saute mushrooms and onion in drippings until tender. Add soups, peas, sherry, salt, seasoned salt, pepper, beef mixture and potato mixture; heat through.
4. Preheat oven to 375°. Roll out one of the larger portions of dough to fit a 9-in. pie plate. Transfer pastry to pie plate. Trim pastry even with edge. Fill with half of the meat mixture. Repeat with remaining larger portion of dough and filling.
5. Roll out smaller portions of dough to fit tops of pies. Place over filling. Trim, seal and flute edges. Cut slits in pastry.
6. Bake 45-50 minutes or until crust is golden brown. Cover edges with foil during the last 15 minutes to prevent overbrowning if necessary. Sprinkle tops with cheese; let stand 10 minutes. Serve with sour cream.

Pepper Sausage Pizza

Fresh spinach gives this recipe a tasty twist. That leafy green plus yellow peppers, snow-white mushrooms and tomato sauce make this a colorful addition to you pizza buffet table.

—*TASTE OF HOME* TEST KITCHEN

PREP: 30 MIN. • **BAKE:** 20 MIN.
MAKES: 15 SLICES

- 3 to 4 cups all-purpose flour, divided
- 1 package (¼ ounce) quick-rise yeast
- 1 teaspoon sugar
- 1 cup warm water (120° to 130°)
- ¼ cup olive oil
- 2 teaspoons salt
- 1 teaspoon dried basil
- ½ teaspoon pepper
- ½ cup shredded Parmesan cheese, divided
- 3 cups torn fresh spinach
- 1 can (15 ounces) pizza sauce
- 4 cups (16 ounces) shredded mozzarella cheese, divided
- ½ pound bulk pork sausage, cooked and drained
- 1 medium onion, chopped
- ½ pound fresh mushrooms, sliced
- ½ medium sweet yellow pepper, chopped
- 1½ teaspoons pizza seasoning or Italian seasoning
- 3 tablespoons minced fresh basil, optional

1. Preheat oven to 450°. In a bowl, combine 1 cup flour, yeast and sugar. Add water; beat until smooth. Add the oil, salt, dried basil, pepper, ¼ cup Parmesan cheese and 2 cups flour; beat until blended. Stir in enough remaining flour to form a soft dough. Turn onto a floured surface; knead until smooth and elastic, about 6-8 minutes. Cover and let rest 5 minutes.

2. Meanwhile, place spinach in a microwave-safe bowl; cover and microwave on high 30 seconds or just until wilted. Uncover and set aside.

3. Press dough into a greased 15x10x1-in. baking pan. Spread with pizza sauce; sprinkle with 2½ cups mozzarella cheese, sausage, onion, spinach, mushrooms and yellow pepper. Top with remaining Parmesan and mozzarella cheeses. Sprinkle with pizza seasoning. Bake 20 minutes or until crust is golden brown. Sprinkle with fresh basil if desired. Cut into squares.

PEPPER SAUSAGE PIZZA

TOP TIP

Perk Up Pizza

To make mouthwatering homemade pizza, saute the vegetables (peppers, onions, mushrooms, etc.) in butter with garlic and herbs before putting them on the pizza. It makes the flavor come alive.

—**PATRICIA F.** SYRACUSE, NY

CREAMED TURKEY WITH PUFF PASTRY

FREEZE IT **FAST FIX**

Creamed Turkey with Puff Pastry

Warm and hearty with lots of veggies in every creamy bite, this dish is comfort food at its best. It tastes a lot like potpie but is much quicker to prepare.
—**NILA GRAHL** GURNEE, IL

START TO FINISH: 25 MIN. • **MAKES:** 12 SERVINGS

- 1 **package (17.3 ounces) frozen puff pastry**
- 4 **cans (18.8 ounces each) chunky chicken corn chowder soup**
- 4 **cups cubed cooked turkey**
- 2 **packages (16 ounces each) frozen peas and carrots, thawed**
- 1 **package (8 ounces) cream cheese, cubed**
- ¼ **teaspoon pepper**

1. Thaw one sheet of puff pastry.

2. Preheat oven to 400°. Cut pastry into six squares. Cut each square in half diagonally; transfer to two greased baking sheets. Bake 10-15 minutes or until golden brown.

3. Meanwhile, in a Dutch oven, combine soup, turkey, peas and carrots, cream cheese and pepper. Bring to a boil, stirring frequently. Reduce heat; simmer, uncovered, 5 minutes or until cream cheese is melted. Serve half of the turkey mixture with puff pastry triangles. Cool the remaining turkey mixture; transfer to freezer containers. May be frozen for up to 3 months.

TO USE FROZEN TURKEY MIXTURE *Thaw mixture in the refrigerator overnight. Thaw remaining puff pastry; prepare and bake pastry triangles as directed. Place turkey mixture in a large saucepan and heat through. Serve with puff pastry triangles.*

Crispy Cajun Panfish

My mother was happiest with a fishing rod in her hands, and her method of frying her catch was always a hit. I turn to her recipe whenever I buy fish from the market or am lucky enough to receive it fresh from someone who loves fishing as much as she did.

—**GAYLE COOK** MINOT, ND

PREP: 10 MIN. • **COOK:** 30 MIN. • **MAKES:** 8 SERVINGS

- 2 cups all-purpose flour
- 2 teaspoons salt
- 2 teaspoons Cajun seasoning
- 1½ teaspoons pepper
- ⅛ teaspoon ground cinnamon
- 2 pounds bass or perch fillets
- 2 eggs
- ¼ cup water
- 2 cups mashed potato flakes
- 6 tablespoons canola oil

1. In a large resealable plastic bag, combine the first five ingredients. Add fish, one piece at a time; shake to coat. Whisk eggs and water in a shallow dish. Place potato flakes in another shallow dish. Dip each fillet in eggs, then coat with potato flakes. Dip fish again in eggs and potato flakes.

2. In a large skillet, heat 3 tablespoons oil over medium-high heat. Cook fish in batches for 3-4 minutes on each side or until fish flakes easily with a fork, adding oil as needed.

Bratwurst Supper

This meal-in-one grills to perfection in heavy-duty foil packets and is ideal for camping. Loaded with chunks of bratwurst, red potatoes, mushrooms and carrots, it's easy to season with onion soup mix and a little soy sauce.

—**JANICE MEYER** MEDFORD, WI

PREP: 10 MIN. • **GRILL:** 45 MIN. • **MAKES:** 12 SERVINGS

- 3 pounds uncooked bratwurst links
- 3 pounds small red potatoes, cut into wedges
- 1 pound baby carrots
- 1 large red onion, sliced and separated into rings
- 2 jars (4½ ounces each) whole mushrooms, drained
- ¼ cup butter, cubed
- 1 envelope onion soup mix
- 2 tablespoons soy sauce
- ½ teaspoon pepper

1. For each of two foil packets, arrange a double thickness of heavy-duty foil (about 17x15 in.) on a flat surface.

2. Cut brats into thirds. Divide the brats, potatoes, carrots, onion and mushrooms evenly between the two double-layer foil pieces. Dot with butter. Sprinkle with soup mix, soy sauce and pepper. Bring edges of foil together; crimp to seal, forming two large packets. Seal tightly; turn to coat.

3. Grill, covered, over medium heat for 23-28 minutes on each side or until vegetables are tender and sausage is no longer pink.

CRISPY CAJUN PANFISH

BRATWURST SUPPER

SUNDAY POT ROAST, PAGE 134

TURKEY CHILI, PAGE 144

SWEET & TANGY CHICKEN WINGS, PAGE 147

SLOW-COOKER
FAVORITES

**CHICAGO-STYLE
BEEF ROLLS, PAGE 132**

66 Your words were found,
and I ate them, and your
words became to me a joy and
the delight of my heart; for
I am called by your name, O
Lord, God of hosts.99

JEREMIAH 15:16

Tropical Pulled Pork Sliders

I used what I had in my cupboard to make this pork, and the results were fantastic! I enjoy transforming an inexpensive cut of meat into something extraordinary.
—**SHELLY MITCHELL** GRESHAM, OR

PREP: 15 MIN. • **COOK:** 8 HOURS
MAKES: 12 SERVINGS

- 1 **boneless pork shoulder butt roast (3 pounds)**
- 2 **garlic cloves, minced**
- ½ **teaspoon lemon-pepper seasoning**
- 1 **can (20 ounces) unsweetened crushed pineapple, undrained**
- ½ **cup orange juice**
- 1 **jar (16 ounces) mango salsa**
- 24 **whole wheat dinner rolls, split**

1. Rub roast with garlic and lemon pepper. Transfer to a 4-qt. slow cooker; top with pineapple and orange juice. Cook, covered, on low 8-10 hours or until meat is tender.

2. Remove roast; cool slightly. Skim fat from cooking juices. Shred pork with two forks. Return pork and cooking juices to slow cooker. Stir in salsa; heat through. Serve with rolls.

TOP TIP

Quick Pork Roast

Whole bay leaves make my pork roast special. I simply cut small slits in the roast and insert three or four bay leaves. They add great flavor and wonderful aroma as the pork is cooking. It couldn't be easier!
—**JOANN SWOPE**
WESTERVILLE, OH

TROPICAL PULLED PORK SLIDERS

Chicken Thighs with Ginger-Peach Sauce

This slightly sweet Asian chicken has become one of my favorite recipes to prepare on Sunday. It's easy to make, requires very little cleanup and leaves me plenty of time to do other things.
—**LISA RENSHAW** KANSAS CITY, MO

PREP: 15 MIN. • **COOK:** 4 HOURS
MAKES: 10 SERVINGS

- 10 boneless skinless chicken thighs (about 2½ pounds)
- 1 cup sliced peeled fresh or frozen peaches
- 1 cup golden raisins
- 1 cup peach preserves
- ⅓ cup chili sauce
- 2 tablespoons minced crystallized ginger
- 1 tablespoon reduced-sodium soy sauce
- 1 tablespoon minced garlic
  Hot cooked rice, optional

1. Place chicken in a 4-qt. slow cooker coated with cooking spray. Top with peaches and raisins. In a small bowl, combine the preserves, chili sauce, ginger, soy sauce and garlic. Spoon over top.
2. Cover and cook on low for 4-5 hours or until chicken is tender. Serve with rice if desired.

Black-Eyed Peas & Ham

We have these black-eyed peas regularly at our house. They're supposed to bring good luck!
—**DAWN FRIHAUF** FORT MORGAN, CO

PREP: 20 MIN. • **COOK:** 6 HOURS
MAKES: 12 SERVINGS (¾ CUP EACH)

- 1 package (16 ounces) dried black-eyed peas, rinsed and sorted
- ½ pound fully cooked boneless ham, finely chopped
- 1 medium onion, finely chopped
- 1 medium sweet red pepper, finely chopped
- 5 bacon strips, cooked and crumbled
- 1 large jalapeno pepper, seeded and finely chopped
- 2 garlic cloves, minced
- 1½ teaspoons ground cumin
- 1 teaspoon reduced-sodium chicken bouillon granules
- ½ teaspoon salt
- ½ teaspoon cayenne pepper
- ¼ teaspoon pepper
- 6 cups water
  Minced fresh cilantro, optional
  Hot cooked rice

In a 6-qt. slow cooker, combine the first 13 ingredients. Cover and cook on low for 6-8 hours or until peas are tender. Sprinkle with cilantro if desired. Serve with rice.
NOTE *Wear disposable gloves when cutting hot peppers; the oils can burn skin. Avoid touching your face.*

CHICKEN THIGHS WITH GINGER-PEACH SAUCE

Slow-Cooker Beef Bourguignonne

I've wanted to make beef Burgundy ever since I got one of Julia Child's cookbooks, but I wanted to find a way to fix it in a slow cooker. My version of the popular beef stew is still rich, hearty and delicious, but without the need to watch on the stovetop or in the oven.

—**CRYSTAL BRUNS** ILIFF, CO

PREP: 30 MIN. + MARINATING • **COOK:** 8 HOURS
MAKES: 12 SERVINGS (⅔ CUP EACH)

- 3 **pounds beef stew meat**
- 1¾ **cups dry red wine**
- 3 **tablespoons olive oil**
- 3 **tablespoons dried minced onion**
- 2 **tablespoons dried parsley flakes**
- 1 **bay leaf**
- 1 **teaspoon dried thyme**
- ¼ **teaspoon pepper**
- 8 **bacon strips, chopped**
- 1 **pound whole fresh mushrooms, quartered**
- 24 **pearl onions, peeled (about 2 cups)**
- 2 **garlic cloves, minced**
- ⅓ **cup all-purpose flour**
- 1 **teaspoon salt**
  Hot cooked whole wheat egg noodles, optional

1. Place beef in a large resealable plastic bag; add wine, oil and seasonings. Seal bag and turn to coat. Refrigerate overnight.
2. In a large skillet, cook bacon over medium heat until crisp, stirring occasionally. Remove with a slotted spoon; drain on paper towels. Discard drippings, reserving 1 tablespoon in pan.
3. Add mushrooms and onions to drippings; cook and stir over medium-high heat until tender. Add garlic; cook 1 minute longer.
4. Drain beef, reserving marinade; transfer beef to a 4- or 5-qt. slow cooker. Sprinkle beef with flour and salt; toss to coat. Top with bacon and mushroom mixture. Add reserved marinade.
5. Cook, covered, on low 8-10 hours or until beef is tender. Remove bay leaf. If desired, serve stew with noodles.

Chicago-Style Beef Rolls

I have fond memories of eating these big, messy sandwiches at a neighbor's house when I was growing up. The recipe makes a lot, so the beef is great to share!

—**TRISHA KRUSE** EAGLE, ID

PREP: 20 MIN. • **COOK:** 8 HOURS • **MAKES:** 16 SERVINGS

- 1 **boneless beef chuck roast (4 to 5 pounds)**
- 1 **tablespoon olive oil**
- 3 **cups beef broth**
- 1 **medium onion, chopped**
- 1 **package Italian salad dressing mix**
- 3 **garlic cloves, minced**
- 1 **tablespoon Italian seasoning**
- ½ **teaspoon crushed red pepper flakes**
- 16 **sourdough rolls, split**
  Sliced pepperoncini and pickled red pepper rings, optional

1. Brown roast in oil on all sides in a large skillet; drain. Transfer beef to a 5-qt. slow cooker. Combine the broth, onion, dressing mix, garlic, Italian seasoning and pepper flakes in a large bowl; pour over roast.
2. Cover and cook on low for 8-10 hours or until tender. Remove meat; cool slightly. Skim fat from cooking juices. Shred beef with two forks and return to slow cooker; heat through. Place ½ cup on each roll, using a slotted spoon. Serve with pepperoncini and pepper rings if desired.

SLOW-COOKER
BEEF BOURGUIGNONNE

SUNDAY
POT ROAST

Sunday Pot Roast

With the help of a slow cooker, you can prepare a down-home dinner for a large group anytime—not just Sundays. The roast always turns out tender and savory .
—**BRANDY SCHAEFER** GLEN CARBON, IL

PREP: 10 MIN. + CHILLING • **COOK:** 8 HOURS
MAKES: 14 SERVINGS

- 1 teaspoon dried oregano
- ½ teaspoon onion salt
- ½ teaspoon caraway seeds
- ½ teaspoon pepper
- ¼ teaspoon garlic salt
- 1 boneless pork loin roast (3½ to 4 pounds), trimmed
- 6 medium carrots, peeled and cut into 1½-inch pieces
- 3 large potatoes, peeled and quartered
- 3 small onions, quartered

- 1½ cups beef broth
- ⅓ cup all-purpose flour
- ⅓ cup cold water
- ¼ teaspoon browning sauce, optional

1. In a small bowl, combine the first five ingredients; rub over roast. Wrap in plastic wrap and refrigerate overnight.

2. Place carrots, potatoes and onions in a 6-qt. slow cooker; add broth. Unwrap roast; place in slow cooker. Cook, covered, on low 8-10 hours or until meat and vegetables are tender.

3. Transfer roast and vegetables to a serving platter; tent with foil. Pour cooking juices into a small saucepan. In a small bowl, mix flour and water until smooth; stir into pan. Bring to a boil; cook and stir 2 minutes or until thickened. If desired, add browning sauce. Serve roast with gravy.

MEXICAN POT ROAST FILLING

Mexican Pot Roast Filling

My son's friends always requested this recipe when they came over and are still talking about it more than a decade later! The meat absorbs the juices, which gives it a fantastic taste. It's perfect as a filling for tacos, burritos or enchiladas and freezes well.
—**CONNIE DICAVOLI** SHAWNEE, KS

PREP: 25 MIN. • **COOK:** 8 HOURS • **MAKES:** 9 SERVINGS

- 1½ teaspoons chili powder
- 1 teaspoon ground cumin
- ½ teaspoon smoked paprika
- ½ teaspoon crushed red pepper flakes
- ¼ teaspoon salt
- 1 boneless beef chuck roast (3 pounds)
- 1 can (4 ounces) chopped green chilies
- ½ cup chopped sweet onion
- 2 garlic cloves, minced
- ¾ cup beef broth
  Taco shells or flour tortillas (8 inches)
  Chopped tomatoes, shredded lettuce and shredded Mexican cheese blend

1. In a small bowl, combine the first five ingredients. Cut roast in half; rub spice mixture over meat. Transfer to a 3-qt. slow cooker. Top with chilies, onion and garlic. Pour broth over meat. Cover and cook on low for 8-10 hours or until meat is tender.

2. Remove meat from slow cooker; shred with two forks. Skim fat from cooking juices. Return meat to slow cooker; heat through. Using a slotted spoon, place ½ cup meat mixture on each taco shell. Top with tomatoes, lettuce and cheese.

Spicy Cowboy Chili

Toasting the peppers for this chili releases their earthy flavors. Keep it in the slow cooker and take it to your next potluck, charity function or party.
—**RACHEL SPRINKEL** HILO, HI

PREP: 45 MIN. • **COOK:** 7 HOURS
MAKES: 14 SERVINGS (3½ QUARTS)

- 1 whole garlic bulb
- 2 to 3 tablespoons olive oil, divided
- 2 dried ancho chilies
- 2 dried chipotle chilies
- 1 bottle (12 ounces) dark beer
- 3 pounds beef stew meat, cut into ¾-inch pieces
- 2 large onions, chopped
- 3 cans (16 ounces each) kidney beans, rinsed and drained
- 3 cans (14½ ounces each) diced tomatoes, undrained
- 2 cans (8 ounces each) tomato sauce
- 2 tablespoons Worcestershire sauce
- 1 tablespoon chili powder
- 1 teaspoon pepper
- ½ teaspoon salt
  Shredded cheddar cheese, optional

1. Preheat oven to 425°. Remove papery outer skin from garlic bulb, but do not peel or separate the cloves. Cut off top of garlic bulb, exposing individual cloves. Brush cut cloves with 1 teaspoon oil. Wrap in foil. Bake 30-35 minutes or until cloves are soft. Unwrap and cool garlic slightly. Squeeze garlic from skins; mash with a fork.

2. Meanwhile, in a large dry skillet over medium-high heat, toast chilies on both sides until puffy, about 3-6 minutes. (Do not blacken.) Cool. Remove stems and seeds; coarsely chop chilies. Place in a small bowl; cover with beer. Let stand to soften, about 30 minutes.

3. In the same skillet, heat 1 tablespoon oil over medium-high heat. Brown beef in batches, adding additional oil if needed; transfer to a 6-qt. slow cooker. In the skillet, heat 2 teaspoons oil over medium heat. Add onions; cook and stir until tender. Add to beef.

4. Stir in the remaining ingredients, mashed garlic and dried chilies mixture. Cover and cook on low 7-9 hours or until meat is tender. If desired, serve with cheese.

NOTE *One-half teaspoon ground chipotle pepper may be substituted for the dried chipotle chilies; add ground chipotle with mashed garlic and beer mixture to slow cooker.*

Meat-Lover's Pizza Hot Dish

I make this hearty casserole for the men who help us out during harvest time. Every year they say it's the best, hands down. Throw in any pizza toppings your family likes. Canadian bacon, black olives and green peppers are some of our picks.

—**BROOK BOTHUN** CANBY, MN

PREP: 25 MIN. • **COOK:** 3¼ HOURS • **MAKES:** 10 SERVINGS

- 1 **pound ground beef**
- 1 **pound bulk Italian sausage**
- 1 **medium onion, chopped**
- 1 **cup sliced fresh mushrooms**
- 4 **cans (8 ounces each) no-salt-added tomato sauce**
- 2 **cans (15 ounces each) pizza sauce**
- 1 **package (16 ounces) penne pasta**
- 1 **cup water**
- 1 **can (6 ounces) tomato paste**
- 1 **package (3½ ounces) sliced pepperoni**
- 1 **teaspoon Italian seasoning**
- 2 **cups (8 ounces) shredded part-skim mozzarella cheese, divided**
- 2 **cups (8 ounces) shredded cheddar cheese, divided**

1. In a large skillet, cook beef, sausage, onion and mushrooms over medium heat 10-12 minutes or until meat is no longer pink and vegetables are tender, breaking up meat into crumbles; drain.

2. Transfer meat mixture to a greased 6-qt. slow cooker. Stir in tomato sauce, pizza sauce, pasta, water, tomato paste, pepperoni and Italian seasoning. Cook, covered, on low 3-4 hours or until pasta is tender.

MEAT-LOVER'S PIZZA HOT DISH

3. Stir thoroughly; mix in 1 cup mozzarella cheese and 1 cup cheddar cheese. Sprinkle remaining cheese over top. Cook, covered, 15-20 minutes longer or until cheese is melted.

Navy Bean Vegetable Soup

My family really likes bean soup, so I came up with this enticing version. The leftovers are, dare I say, even better the next day!

—**ELEANOR MIELKE** MITCHELL, SD

PREP: 15 MIN. • **COOK:** 9 HOURS
MAKES: 12 SERVINGS (3 QUARTS)

- 4 **medium carrots, thinly sliced**
- 2 **celery ribs, chopped**
- 1 **medium onion, chopped**
- 2 **cups cubed fully cooked ham**
- 1½ **cups dried navy beans**
- 1 **envelope vegetable recipe mix (Knorr)**
- 1 **envelope onion soup mix**
- 1 **bay leaf**
- ½ **teaspoon pepper**
- 8 **cups water**

In a 5-qt. slow cooker, combine the first nine ingredients. Stir in water. Cover and cook on low for 9-10 hours or until beans are tender. Discard bay leaf.

Hot Cocoa for a Crowd

What a great contribution to a cool-weather event! This simply delicious cocoa has a hint of cinnamon that offers just the right amount of sweetness.

—**DEBORAH CANADAY** MANHATTAN, KS

PREP: 10 MIN. • **COOK:** 3 HOURS
MAKES: 12 SERVINGS (1 CUP EACH)

- 5 **cups nonfat dry milk powder**
- ¾ **cup sugar**
- ¾ **cup baking cocoa**
- 1 **teaspoon vanilla extract**
- ¼ **teaspoon ground cinnamon**
- 11 **cups water**
  Miniature marshmallows and peppermint candy sticks, optional

1. In a 5- or 6-qt. slow cooker, combine the milk powder, sugar, cocoa, vanilla and cinnamon; gradually whisk in water until smooth. Cover and cook on low for 3-4 hours or until heated through.

2. Garnish with marshmallows and use peppermint sticks for stirrers if desired.

Elvis' Pudding Cake

I love the flavors of peanut butter and banana together, and this slow cooker pudding cake is just like eating an Elvis sandwich—only sweeter! Banana chips add a surprisingly crunchy texture—find them near the dried fruit in the grocery store.
—**LISA RENSHAW** KANSAS CITY, MO

PREP: 10 MIN. • **COOK:** 3 HOURS + STANDING
MAKES: 12 SERVINGS

- 3 **cups cold 2% milk**
- 1 **package (3.4 ounces) instant banana cream pudding mix**
- 1 **package banana cake mix (regular size)**
- ½ **cup creamy peanut butter**
- 2 **cups peanut butter chips**
- 1 **cup chopped dried banana chips**

1. In a small bowl, whisk milk and pudding mix for 2 minutes. Let stand for 2 minutes or until soft-set. Transfer to a greased 5-qt. slow cooker.

2. Prepare cake mix batter according to package directions, adding peanut butter before mixing. Pour over pudding. Cover and cook on low for 3 to 3½ hours or until a toothpick inserted near the center comes out with moist crumbs.

3. Sprinkle with peanut butter chips; cover and let stand for 15-20 minutes or until partially melted. Top with banana chips.

TOP TIP

Slow-Cooker Secrets

Try your best to keep the lid on the slow cooker while your specialty is simmering. Locking in heat and steam is key for slow cooking, particularly with desserts such as pudding cakes. Lifting the lid can greatly increase cooking time.

ELVIS' PUDDING CAKE

BACON & SAUSAGE STUFFING

Bacon & Sausage Stuffing

This dish was inspired by my mother's stuffing recipe. It smells like heaven while you're making it, and people can never seem to get enough.

—**SCOTT RUGH** PORTLAND, OR

PREP: 25 MIN. • **COOK:** 4 HOURS + STANDING
MAKES: 20 SERVINGS (¾ CUP EACH)

- 1 **pound bulk pork sausage**
- 1 **pound thick-sliced bacon strips, chopped**
- ½ **cup butter, cubed**
- 1 **large onion, chopped**
- 3 **celery ribs, sliced**
- 10½ **cups unseasoned stuffing cubes**
- 1 **cup sliced fresh mushrooms**
- 1 **cup chopped fresh parsley**
- 4 **teaspoons dried sage leaves**
- 4 **teaspoons dried thyme**
- 6 **eggs**
- 2 **cans (10¾ ounces each) condensed cream of chicken soup, undiluted**
- 1¼ **cups chicken stock**

1. In a large skillet, cook sausage over medium heat for 6-8 minutes or until no longer pink, breaking into crumbles. Remove with a slotted spoon; drain on paper towels. Discard drippings.

2. Add bacon to pan; cook over medium heat until crisp. Remove to paper towels to drain. Discard drippings. Wipe out pan. In same pan, heat butter over medium-high heat. Add onion and celery; cook and stir 6-8 minutes or until tender. Remove from heat.

3. In a large bowl, combine stuffing cubes, sausage, bacon, onion mixture, mushrooms, parsley, sage and thyme. In a small bowl, whisk eggs, soup and stock; pour over stuffing mixture and toss to coat.

4. Transfer to a greased 6-qt. slow cooker. Cook, covered, on low 4-5 hours or until a thermometer reads 160°. Remove lid; let stand 15 minutes before serving.

MAPLE-WALNUT SWEET POTATOES

EASY BEANS & POTATOES WITH BACON

Maple-Walnut Sweet Potatoes

Sweet potatoes with dried cherries and walnuts make this just so delectable! It's a wonderful side dish when you need to contribute something to a buffet or a dinner with lots of guests.

—**SARAH HERSE** BROOKLYN, NY

PREP: 15 MIN. • **COOK:** 5 HOURS
MAKES: 12 SERVINGS (¾ CUP EACH)

- 4 **pounds sweet potatoes (about 8 medium)**
- ¾ **cup coarsely chopped walnuts, divided**
- ½ **cup packed light brown sugar**
- ½ **cup dried cherries, coarsely chopped**
- ½ **cup maple syrup**
- ¼ **cup apple cider or juice**
- ¼ **teaspoon salt**

1. Peel and cut sweet potatoes lengthwise in half; cut crosswise into ½-in. slices. Place in a 5-qt. slow cooker. Add ½ cup walnuts, brown sugar, cherries, syrup, cider and salt; toss to combine.
2. Cook, covered, on low 5-6 hours or until potatoes are tender. Sprinkle with remaining walnuts.

Easy Beans & Potatoes with Bacon

I love the combination of green beans and bacon, so I came up with this recipe. It's great for when you have company, because you can start the side dish in the slow cooker and continue preparing the rest of your dinner.

—**BARBARA BRITTAIN** SANTEE, CA

PREP: 15 MIN. • **COOK:** 6 HOURS • **MAKES:** 10 SERVINGS

- 8 **bacon strips, chopped**
- 1½ **pounds fresh green beans, trimmed and cut into 2-inch pieces (about 4 cups)**
- 4 **medium potatoes, peeled and cubed (½-inch)**
- 1 **small onion, halved and sliced**
- ¼ **cup reduced-sodium chicken broth**
- ½ **teaspoon salt**
- ¼ **teaspoon pepper**

1. In a large skillet, cook bacon over medium heat until crisp, stirring occasionally. Remove to paper towels with a slotted spoon; drain, reserving 1 tablespoon drippings. Cover and refrigerate bacon until serving.
2. In a 5-qt. slow cooker, combine the remaining ingredients; stir in reserved drippings. Cover and cook on low for 6-8 hours or until potatoes are tender. Stir in bacon; heat through.

FREEZE IT

Slow-Simmered Meat Ragu

After a day of cooking in the slow cooker, this ragu is not your typical spaghetti sauce. It's so hearty, that it's almost like a stew.

—LAURIE LACLAIR NORTH RICHLAND HILLS, TX

PREP: 30 MIN. • **COOK:** 6 HOURS • **MAKES:** 10 SERVINGS

- 1 jar (24 ounces) tomato basil pasta sauce
- 1 can (14½ ounces) Italian diced tomatoes, undrained
- 2 jars (6 ounces each) sliced mushrooms, drained
- 1 can (8 ounces) tomato sauce
- 1 jar (3½ ounces) prepared pesto
- 1½ pounds chicken tenderloins
- 1 medium sweet red pepper, chopped
- ½ cup chopped pepperoni
- ½ cup pitted ripe olives, halved
- 1 teaspoon dried oregano
- ½ teaspoon hot pepper sauce
- 1 pound Italian sausage links, cut into 1-inch pieces
- 1 medium onion, chopped
  Hot cooked angel hair pasta

1. In a 5- or 6-qt. slow cooker, combine the first 11 ingredients. Heat a large skillet over medium heat. Add sausage and onion; cook and stir until sausage is no longer pink and onion is tender. Drain. Add to slow cooker.

2. Cook, covered, on low 6-8 hours or until chicken is tender. Serve with pasta.

FREEZE OPTION *Do not cook or add pasta. Freeze cooled sauce in freezer containers. To use, partially thaw in refrigerator overnight. Cook pasta according to package directions. Place meat mixture in a large saucepan; heat through, stirring occasionally and adding a little water if necessary. Proceed as directed.*

Easy Chili Verde

I love chili verde, and I order it whenever I can at restaurants. As such, I created an easy, tasty version to enjoy at home. You can eat it with a fork or wrap it up in tortillas with a variety of toppings such as cheese, cilantro, minced onions or even slices of lime. There are never leftovers when I prepare it.

—JULIE ROWLAND SALT LAKE CITY, UT

PREP: 10 MIN. • **COOK:** 5 HOURS • **MAKES:** 12 SERVINGS (3 QUARTS)

- 1 boneless pork shoulder roast (4 to 5 pounds), cut into 1-inch pieces
- 3 cans (10 ounces each) green enchilada sauce
- 1 cup salsa verde
- 1 can (4 ounces) chopped green chilies
- ½ teaspoon salt
  Hot cooked rice
  Sour cream, optional

In a 5-qt. slow cooker, combine pork, enchilada sauce, salsa verde, green chilies and salt. Cook, covered, on low 5-6 hours or until pork is tender. Serve with rice. If desired, top with sour cream.

TOP TIP

Mix Things Up With Chili Verde

Chili verde is a stew that's native to Mexico. Most often, it features a cut of pork that slowly simmers in liquid, such as a broth, until the meat is exceptionally tender. The cooked meat and its flavorful sauce can be served alone, over rice or wrapped in tortillas. Sometimes the meat is served with tortillas chips. Chili verde usually involves green sauces, chilies or tomatillos, and some versions feature poultry instead of pork.

SLOW-SIMMERED MEAT RAGU

SLOW-COOKER
TURKEY BREAST

Slow-Cooker Turkey Breast

Here's an easy recipe to try when you're craving turkey.
It uses pantry ingredients, which is handy.
—MARIA JUCO MILWAUKEE, WI

PREP: 10 MIN. • **COOK:** 5 HOURS • **MAKES:** 14 SERVINGS

- 1 **bone-in turkey breast (6 to 7 pounds), skin removed**
- 1 **tablespoon olive oil**
- 1 **teaspoon dried minced garlic**
- 1 **teaspoon seasoned salt**
- 1 **teaspoon paprika**
- 1 **teaspoon Italian seasoning**
- 1 **teaspoon pepper**
- ½ **cup water**

Brush turkey with oil. Combine the garlic, seasoned salt, paprika, Italian seasoning and pepper; rub over turkey. Transfer to a 6-qt. slow cooker; add water. Cover and cook on low for 5-6 hours or until tender.

Honey-Butter Peas and Carrots

This classic combination of peas and carrots is made special with a handful of flavor enhancers. Slow cooking allows the ingredients to meld for maximum taste.
—THERESA KREYCHE TUSTIN, CA

PREP: 15 MIN. • **COOK:** 5¼ HOURS
MAKES: 12 SERVINGS (½ CUP EACH)

- 1 **pound carrots, sliced**
- 1 **large onion, chopped**
- ¼ **cup water**
- ¼ **cup butter, cubed**
- ¼ **cup honey**
- 4 **garlic cloves, minced**
- 1 **teaspoon salt**
- 1 **teaspoon dried marjoram**
- ⅛ **teaspoon white pepper**
- 1 **package (16 ounces) frozen peas**

In a 3-qt. slow cooker, combine the first nine ingredients. Cook, covered, on low 5 hours. Stir in peas. Cook, covered, on high 15-25 minutes or until vegetables are tender.

Pork Roast with Plum Sauce

The flavors in this slow cooker dish blend perfectly to create a subtle hint of Asian flair. This juicy roast lends itself to variation so an alternative to the plum jam might be apricot preserves.

—**JEANNIE KLUGH** LANCASTER, PA

PREP: 20 MIN. • **COOK:** 5 HOURS + STANDING • **MAKES:** 10 SERVINGS

- 1 boneless whole pork loin roast (4 pounds)
- 2 tablespoons canola oil
- 1 cup sherry
- 2 tablespoons dried thyme
- 2 tablespoons soy sauce
- 4 garlic cloves, minced
- 1 tablespoon ground mustard
- 1½ teaspoons ground ginger
- 1 teaspoon garlic salt
- ½ teaspoon salt
- ½ teaspoon pepper
- ½ cup plum jam
- 2 tablespoons cornstarch
- ¼ cup cold water

1. Cut roast in half. In a large skillet, brown roast in oil on all sides; drain. Transfer to a 4-qt. slow cooker.
2. In a small bowl, combine sherry, thyme, soy sauce, garlic, mustard, ginger, garlic salt, salt and pepper; pour over pork. Cover and cook on low for 5 to 6 hours or until a meat is tender. Remove meat to a serving platter; keep warm. Let stand for 10-15 minutes before slicing.
3. Skim fat from cooking juices; transfer to a small saucepan. Add jam. Bring to a boil. Combine cornstarch and water until smooth. Gradually stir into the pan. Bring to a boil; cook and stir for 2 minutes or until thickened. Serve with gravy.

Chuck Wagon Beans

I followed the lead of cooks from the Old Western cattle ranges to come up with these savory beans. Sweet and smoky, they're made extra hearty with sausage.

—**NANCY MOORE** BUCKLIN, KS

PREP: 15 MIN. • **COOK:** 8 HOURS
MAKES: 24 SERVINGS (⅔ CUP EACH)

- 2 cans (28 ounces each) baked beans
- 3 cans (16 ounces each) kidney beans, rinsed and drained
- 2 cans (15 ounces each) pinto beans, rinsed and drained
- 1 pound smoked kielbasa or Polish sausage, sliced
- 1 jar (12 ounces) pickled jalapeno slices, drained
- 1 medium onion, chopped

- 1 cup barbecue sauce
- ½ cup spicy brown mustard
- ¼ cup steak seasoning

In a greased 6-qt. slow cooker, combine all ingredients. Cover and cook on low for 8-10 hours or until heated through.
NOTE *This recipe was tested with McCormick's Montreal Steak Seasoning. Look for it in the spice aisle.*

Warm Apple-Cranberry Dessert

Served with ice cream, this heartwarming dessert promises to become a favorite with all that try it! The dessert practically makes itself which is terrific.

—**MARY JONES** WILLIAMSTOWN, WV

PREP: 20 MIN. • **COOK:** 2 HOURS • **MAKES:** 10 SERVINGS

- 5 large apples, peeled and sliced
- 1 cup fresh or frozen cranberries, thawed
- ¾ cup packed brown sugar, divided
- 2 tablespoons lemon juice
- ½ cup all-purpose flour
  Dash salt
- ⅓ cup cold butter
  Vanilla ice cream
  Toasted chopped pecans

1. In a greased 5-qt. slow cooker, combine apples, cranberries, ¼ cup brown sugar and lemon juice. In a small bowl, mix flour, salt and remaining brown sugar; cut in butter until crumbly. Sprinkle over fruit mixture.
2. Cook, covered, on high 2 to 2½ hours or until apples are tender. Serve with ice cream and pecans.

WARM APPLE-CRANBERRY DESSERT

Turkey Chili

I've taken my mother's milder recipe for chili and made it thicker and more robust. It's a favorite, especially for fall and winter parties.

—CELESTA ZANGER
BLOOMFIELD HILLS, MI

PREP: 20 MIN. • **COOK:** 6½ HOURS
MAKES: 13 SERVINGS

- 1 **pound lean ground turkey**
- ¾ **cup each chopped onion, celery and green pepper**
- 1 **can (28 ounces) diced tomatoes, undrained**
- 1 **jar (26 ounces) meatless spaghetti sauce**
- 1 **can (16 ounces) hot chili beans, undrained**
- 1½ **cups water**
- ½ **cup frozen corn**
- 2 **tablespoons chili powder**
- 1 **teaspoon ground cumin**
- ¼ **teaspoon pepper**
- ⅛ **to ¼ teaspoon cayenne pepper**
- 1 **can (16 ounces) kidney beans, rinsed and drained**
- 1 **can (15 ounces) pinto beans, rinsed and drained**
  Sour cream, optional

1. In a large nonstick skillet, cook the turkey, onion, celery and green pepper over medium heat until meat is no longer pink and vegetables are tender; drain.

2. Transfer to a 5-qt. slow cooker. Add the tomatoes, spaghetti sauce, chili beans, water, corn and seasonings. Cover and cook on high for 1 hour.

3. Reduce heat to low; cook for 5-6 hours. Add kidney and pinto beans; cook 30 minutes longer. Garnish with sour cream if desired.

TURKEY CHILI

HONEY-GLAZED HAM

CHERRY & SPICE RICE PUDDING

Honey-Glazed Ham

Here's an easy solution for feeding a large group. The simple ham is perfect for large family dinners where time in the kitchen is as valuable as space in the oven.
—**JACQUIE STOLZ** LITTLE SIOUX, IA

PREP: 10 MIN. • **COOK:** 4½ HOURS • **MAKES:** 14 SERVINGS

- 1 **boneless fully cooked ham (4 pounds)**
- 1½ **cups ginger ale**
- ¼ **cup honey**
- ½ **teaspoon ground mustard**
- ½ **teaspoon ground cloves**
- ¼ **teaspoon ground cinnamon**

1. Cut ham in half; place in a 5-qt. slow cooker. Pour ginger ale over ham. Cover and cook on low for 4-5 hours or until heated through.
2. Combine the honey, mustard, cloves and cinnamon; stir until smooth. Spread over ham; cook 30 minutes longer.

Cherry & Spice Rice Pudding

Cinnamon and cherries sweeten the deal in this homey dessert. If you've never made rice pudding, this an excellent place to start.
—**DEB PERRY** TRAVERSE CITY, MI

PREP: 10 MIN. • **COOK:** 2 HOURS • **MAKES:** 12 SERVINGS

- 4 **cups cooked long grain rice**
- 1 **can (12 ounces) evaporated milk**
- 1 **cup 2% milk**
- ⅓ **cup sugar**
- ¼ **cup water**
- ¾ **cup dried cherries**
- 3 **tablespoons butter, softened**
- 2 **teaspoons vanilla extract**
- ½ **teaspoon ground cinnamon**
- ¼ **teaspoon ground nutmeg**

1. In a large bowl, combine the rice, evaporated milk, milk, sugar and water. Stir in the remaining ingredients. Transfer to a 3-qt. slow cooker coated with cooking spray.
2. Cover and cook on low for 2-3 hours or until mixture is thickened. Stir lightly before serving. Serve warm or cold. Refrigerate leftovers.

Warm Fruit Salad

I use canned goods and my slow cooker to whip up an old-fashioned side dish that's loaded with sweet fruits. It makes a heartwarming accompaniment to holiday menus.
—**MARY ANN JONNS** MIDLOTHIAN, IL

PREP: 10 MIN. • **COOK:** 2 HOURS
MAKES: 14-18 SERVINGS

- 2 **cans (29 ounces each) sliced peaches, drained**
- 2 **cans (29 ounces each) pear halves, drained and sliced**
- 1 **can (20 ounces) pineapple chunks, drained**
- 1 **can (15¼ ounces) apricot halves, drained and sliced**
- 1 **can (21 ounces) cherry pie filling**

In a 5-qt. slow cooker, combine the peaches, pears, pineapple and apricots. Top with pie filling. Cover and cook on high for 2 hours or until heated through. Serve with a slotted spoon.

Garlic Lover's Beef Stew

Red wine lends a mellow flavor to this stew that has tender pieces of beef and carrots. We like to serve it over mashed potatoes, but you could also use noodles.
—**ALISSA BROWN**
FT. WASHINGTON, PA

PREP: 30 MIN. • **COOK:** 8 HOURS
MAKES: 10 SERVINGS

- 1 **boneless beef chuck roast (3 pounds), cut into 2-inch pieces**
- 1¼ **teaspoons salt**
- ¾ **teaspoon coarsely ground pepper**
- ½ **cup all-purpose flour**
- 2 **tablespoons olive oil**
- 12 **garlic cloves, minced**
- 1 **cup dry red wine or reduced-sodium beef broth**
- 2 **cans (14½ ounces each) diced tomatoes, undrained**
- 1 **can (14½ ounces) reduced-sodium beef broth**
- 6 **medium carrots, thinly sliced**
- 2 **medium onions, chopped**
- 2 **tablespoons tomato paste**
- 2 **teaspoons minced fresh rosemary or ½ teaspoon dried rosemary, crushed**
- 2 **teaspoons minced fresh thyme or ½ teaspoon dried thyme**
- 2 **bay leaves**
  Dash ground cloves
  Hot mashed potatoes

1. Sprinkle beef with salt, pepper and flour; toss to coat.
2. In a large skillet, heat oil over medium-high heat. Brown beef in batches. Remove with a slotted spoon. Reduce heat to medium. Add garlic; cook and stir 1 minute.
3. Add wine to skillet; stirring to loosen browned bits from pan. Transfer to a 5- or 6-qt. slow cooker. Stir in tomatoes, broth, carrots, onions, tomato paste, rosemary, thyme, bay leaves, cloves and beef.
4. Cook, covered, on low 8-10 hours or until beef is tender. Remove bay leaves. Serve with mashed potatoes.

GARLIC LOVER'S BEEF STEW

SWEET & TANGY CHICKEN WINGS

Guinness Corned Beef and Cabbage

A dear friend of my mother's gave her this recipe years ago. My husband and kids request it for special occasions like birthdays and, of course, St. Patrick's Day.

—**KARIN BRODBECK** RED HOOK, NY

PREP: 20 MIN. • **COOK:** 8 HOURS
MAKES: 9 SERVINGS

- 2 **pounds red potatoes, quartered**
- 1 **pound carrots, cut into 3-inch pieces**
- 2 **celery ribs, cut into 3-inch pieces**
- 1 **small onion, quartered**
- 1 **corned beef brisket with spice packet (3 to 3½ pounds)**
- 8 **whole cloves**
- 6 **whole peppercorns**
- 1 **bay leaf**
- 1 **bottle (12 ounces) Guinness stout or reduced-sodium beef broth**
- ½ **small head cabbage, thinly sliced**
  Prepared horseradish

1. In a 6-qt. slow cooker, combine potatoes, carrots, celery and onion. Add corned beef (discard spice packet or save for another use).
2. Place cloves, peppercorns and bay leaf on a double thickness of cheesecloth. Gather corners of cloth to enclose seasonings; tie securely with string. Place in slow cooker. Pour stout over top.
3. Cook, covered, on low 8-10 hours or until meat and vegetables are tender, adding cabbage during the last hour of cooking. Discard spice bag.
4. Cut beef diagonally across the grain into thin slices. Serve beef with vegetables and horseradish.

FREEZE IT

Sweet & Tangy Chicken Wings

Here's a festive recipe that's perfect for parties. Put the wings in before you prepare for the party, and in a few hours, you'll have wonderful appetizers to share.

—**IDA TUEY** SOUTH LYON, MI

PREP: 20 MIN. • **COOK:** 3¼ HOURS
MAKES: ABOUT 2½ DOZEN

- 3 **pounds chicken wingettes (about 30)**
- ½ **teaspoon salt, divided**
  Dash pepper
- 1½ **cups ketchup**
- ¼ **cup packed brown sugar**
- ¼ **cup red wine vinegar**
- 2 **tablespoons Worcestershire sauce**
- 1 **tablespoon Dijon mustard**
- 1 **teaspoon minced garlic**
- 1 **teaspoon liquid smoke, optional**
  Sesame seeds, optional

1. Sprinkle chicken wings with a dash of salt and pepper. Broil 4-6 in. from the heat for 5-10 minutes on each side or until golden brown. Transfer to a greased 5-qt. slow cooker.
2. Combine the ketchup, brown sugar, vinegar, Worcestershire sauce, mustard, garlic, liquid smoke if desired and remaining salt; pour over wings. Toss with chicken to coat.
3. Cover and cook on low for 3¼ to 3¾ hours or until chicken juices run clear. Sprinkle with sesame seeds if desired.
FREEZE OPTION *Freeze cooled fully-cooked wings in freezer containers. To use, partially thaw in refrigerator overnight. Preheat oven to 325°. Reheat wings in a foil-lined 15x10x1-in. baking pan until heated through, covering if necessary to prevent browning. Serve as directed.*

Italian Shredded Pork Stew

Need a warm meal for a blustery night? Throw together this slow-cooked stew loaded with nutritious sweet potatoes and kale. The shredded pork is so tender, you'll want to make the recipe time and again.

—ROBIN JUNGERS CAMPBELLSPORT, WI

PREP: 20 MIN. • **COOK:** 8 HOURS
MAKES: 9 SERVINGS (3½ QUARTS)

- 2 medium sweet potatoes, peeled and cubed
- 2 cups chopped fresh kale
- 1 large onion, chopped
- 3 garlic cloves, minced
- 1 boneless pork shoulder butt roast (2½ to 3½ pounds)
- 1 can (14 ounces) white kidney or cannellini beans, rinsed and drained
- 1½ teaspoons Italian seasoning
- ½ teaspoon salt
- ½ teaspoon pepper
- 3 cans (14½ ounces each) chicken broth
  Sour cream, optional

1. Place the sweet potatoes, kale, onion and garlic in a 5-qt. slow cooker. Place roast on vegetables. Add the beans and seasonings. Pour broth over top. Cover and cook on low for 8-10 hours or until meat is tender.

2. Remove meat; cool slightly. Skim fat from cooking juices. Shred pork with two forks and return to slow cooker; heat through. Garnish servings with sour cream if desired.

SLOW-COOKER
CHICKEN CACCIATORE

Slow-Cooker Chicken Cacciatore

Treat company to this perfect Italian meal. You'll have time to visit with guests while it simmers, and it often earns me rave reviews. I like to serve it with couscous and green beans. Mangia!

—MARTHA SCHIRMACHER
STERLING HEIGHTS, MI

PREP: 15 MIN. • **COOK:** 8½ HOURS
MAKES: 12 SERVINGS

- 12 boneless skinless chicken thighs (about 3 pounds)
- 2 medium green peppers, chopped
- 1 can (14½ ounces) diced tomatoes with basil, oregano and garlic, undrained
- 1 can (6 ounces) tomato paste
- 1 medium onion, sliced
- ½ cup reduced-sodium chicken broth
- ¼ cup dry red wine or additional reduced-sodium chicken broth
- 3 garlic cloves, minced
- ¾ teaspoon salt
- ⅛ teaspoon pepper
- 2 tablespoons cornstarch
- 2 tablespoons cold water

1. Place chicken in a 4- or 5-qt. slow cooker. In a small bowl, combine green peppers, tomatoes, tomato paste, onion, broth, wine, garlic, salt and pepper; pour over chicken. Cook, covered, on low 8-10 hours or until chicken is tender.

2. In a small bowl, mix cornstarch and water until smooth; gradually stir into slow cooker. Cook, covered, on high 30 minutes or until sauce is thickened.

Spiced Cran-Apple Brisket

Kids seem to love this recipe the most, although every adult who tastes it becomes an instant fan as well. The apple and cranberry flavors are perfect for winter.

—AYSHA SCHURMAN AMMON, ID

PREP: 20 MIN. • **COOK:** 8 HOURS
MAKES: 9 SERVINGS

- 1 fresh beef brisket (4 pounds)
- ½ cup apple butter
- ¼ cup ruby port wine
- 2 tablespoons cider vinegar
- 1 teaspoon coarsely ground pepper
- ½ teaspoon salt
- 1 medium tart apple, peeled and cubed
- 1 celery rib, chopped
- 1 small red onion, chopped
- ⅓ cup dried apples, diced
- ⅓ cup dried cranberries
- 2 garlic cloves, minced
- 1 tablespoon cornstarch
- 3 tablespoons cold water

1. Cut brisket in half; place in a 5-quart slow cooker.
2. In a large bowl, combine the apple butter, wine, vinegar, pepper and salt. Stir in the tart apple, celery, onion, dried apples, cranberries and garlic. Pour over brisket. Cover and cook on low for 8-10 hours or until meat is tender.
3. Remove meat to a serving platter; keep warm. Skim fat from cooking juices; transfer to a small saucepan. Bring liquid to a boil.
4. Combine cornstarch and water until smooth. Gradually stir into the pan. Bring to a boil; cook and stir for 2 minutes or until thickened. Serve with meat.
NOTE *This is a fresh beef brisket, not corned beef. This recipe was tested with commercially prepared apple butter.*

Meaty Slow-Cooked Jambalaya

It sure makes life easy having this wonderful, full-of-flavor dish stashed away in the freezer! Another plus, you throw it all in the slow cooker. There's no need for a skillet.

—DIANE SMITH PINE MOUNTAIN, GA

PREP: 25 MIN. • **COOK:** 7¼ HOURS
MAKES: 12 SERVINGS (3½ QUARTS)

- 1 can (28 ounces) diced tomatoes, undrained
- 1 cup reduced-sodium chicken broth
- 1 large green pepper, chopped
- 1 medium onion, chopped
- 2 celery ribs, sliced
- ½ cup white wine or additional reduced-sodium chicken broth
- 4 garlic cloves, minced
- 2 teaspoons Cajun seasoning
- 2 teaspoons dried parsley flakes
- 1 teaspoon dried basil
- 1 teaspoon dried oregano
- ¾ teaspoon salt
- ½ to 1 teaspoon cayenne pepper
- 2 pounds boneless skinless chicken thighs, cut into 1-inch pieces
- 1 package (12 ounces) fully cooked andouille or other spicy chicken sausage links
- 2 pounds uncooked medium shrimp, peeled and deveined
- 8 cups hot cooked brown rice

1. In a large bowl, combine the first 13 ingredients. Place chicken and sausage in a 6-qt. slow cooker. Pour tomato mixture over top. Cook, covered, on low 7-9 hours or until chicken is tender.
2. Stir in shrimp. Cook, covered, 15-20 minutes longer or until shrimp turn pink. Serve with rice.

SPICED CRAN-APPLE BRISKET

Hot Spiced Cherry Cider

This three-ingredient cider is great to have in the slow cooker after being out in the cold all day.

—**MARLENE WICZEK** LITTLE FALLS, MN

PREP: 5 MIN. • **COOK:** 4 HOURS
MAKES: 4 QUARTS

- 1 gallon apple cider or juice
- 2 cinnamon sticks (3 inches)
- 2 packages (3 ounces each) cherry gelatin

Place cider in a 6-qt. slow cooker; add cinnamon sticks. Cover and cook on high for 3 hours. Stir in gelatin; cook 1 hour longer. Discard cinnamon sticks before serving.

Slow-Cooked Pulled Pork with Mojito Sauce

This Cuban twist on slow-cook pulled pork will knock the socks off any man! Serve it with rice and beans.

—**KRISTINA WILEY** JUPITER, FL

PREP: 15 MIN. + MARINATING
COOK: 9 HOURS
MAKES: 12 SERVINGS (1½ CUPS SAUCE)

- 2 large onions, quartered
- 12 garlic cloves
- 1 bottle (18 ounces) Cuban-style mojo sauce and marinade
- ½ cup lime juice
- ½ teaspoon salt
- ¼ teaspoon pepper

- 1 bone-in pork shoulder butt roast (5 to 5¼ pounds)
  MOJITO SAUCE
- ¾ cup canola oil
- 1 medium onion, finely chopped
- 6 garlic cloves, finely chopped
- ⅓ cup lime juice
- ½ teaspoon salt
- ¼ teaspoon pepper
  Additional chopped onion and lime wedges, optional

1. Place onions and garlic in a food processor; process until finely chopped. Add mojo marinade, lime juice, salt and pepper; process until blended. Pour half of the marinade into a large resealable plastic bag. Cut roast into quarters; add to bag. Seal bag and turn to coat. Refrigerate 8 hours or overnight. Transfer remaining marinade to a small bowl; refrigerate, covered, while marinating meat.

2. Drain pork, discarding marinade in bag. Place pork in a 5-qt. slow cooker coated with cooking spray. Top with reserved marinade. Cook, covered, on low 8-10 hours or until meat is tender.

3. For sauce, in a small saucepan, heat oil over medium heat 2½ to 3 minutes or until a thermometer reads 200°. Carefully add onion; cook 2 minutes, stirring occasionally. Stir in garlic; remove from heat. Stir in lime juice, salt and pepper.

4. Remove pork from slow cooker; cool slightly. Skim fat from cooking juices. Remove meat from bone; discard bone. Shred pork with two forks. Return cooking juices and pork to slow cooker; heat through.

5. Using tongs, remove pork to a platter. Serve with chopped onion, lime wedges and mojito sauce, stirring just before serving.

SLOW-COOKED PULLED PORK WITH MOJITO SAUCE

LEMON CHICKEN & RICE SOUP

Lemon Chicken & Rice Soup

When buying chicken for this soup, take it to the butcher counter and ask the butcher to cube it for you. It'll save you time in chopping!
—**KRISTIN CHERRY** BOTHELL, WA

PREP: 35 MIN. • **COOK:** 4¼ HOURS
MAKES: 12 SERVINGS (4 QUARTS)

- 2 **tablespoons olive oil**
- 2 **pounds boneless skinless chicken breasts, cut into ½-inch pieces**
- 5 **cans (14½ ounces each) reduced-sodium chicken broth**
- 8 **cups coarsely chopped Swiss chard, kale or spinach**
- 2 **large carrots, finely chopped**
- 1 **small onion, chopped**
- 1 **medium lemon, halved and thinly sliced**
- ¼ **cup lemon juice**
- 4 **teaspoons grated lemon peel**
- ½ **teaspoon pepper**
- 4 **cups cooked brown rice**

1. In a large skillet, heat 1 tablespoon oil over medium-high heat. Add half of the chicken; cook and stir until browned. Transfer to a 6-qt. slow cooker. Repeat with remaining oil and chicken.
2. Stir broth, vegetables, lemon slices, lemon juice, peel and pepper into chicken. Cook, covered, on low 4-5 hours or until chicken is tender. Stir in rice; heat through.

TOP TIP

Church Supper Slow Cookers

Taking your church-supper contribution to the event in a slow cooker? Bring along an extension cord or two. You'll save the day as this is something the organizers may have forgotten.

THE BEST EGGPLANT
PARMESAN, PAGE 157

OVERNIGHT BRUNCH
CASSEROLE, PAGE 160

BASIL CORN & TOMATO
BAKE, PAGE 167

COMFORTING
CASSEROLES

CORDON BLEU
CASSEROLE, PAGE 159

66 Day by day, as they spent much time together in the temple, they broke bread at home and ate their food with glad and generous hearts, praising God and having the goodwill of all the people. 99

ACTS 2:46-47

Deluxe Baked Macaroni and Cheese

By adding diced ham, tomatoes, several cheeses and a hint of Dijon mustard, I turned this super creamy mac and cheese into the ultimate comfort food.

—KATHY YAROSH APOPKA, FL

PREP: 30 MIN. • **BAKE:** 25 MIN.
MAKES: 12 SERVINGS

- 1 package (16 ounces) elbow macaroni
- ¼ cup all-purpose flour
- 2 cups 2% milk
- ½ cup heavy whipping cream
- 1 package (8 ounces) process cheese (Velveeta), cubed
- 1 cup (4 ounces) shredded cheddar cheese
- ⅔ cup whipped cream cheese
- ¼ cup grated Parmesan cheese
- 1 can (14½ ounces) diced tomatoes, drained
- 1½ cups cubed fully cooked ham
- 1 cup (8 ounces) sour cream
- 1 teaspoon Dijon mustard

TOPPING

- 1½ cups soft bread crumbs
- ¼ cup grated Parmesan cheese
- 2 tablespoons butter, melted

1. Preheat oven to 350°. Cook macaroni according to package directions. In a Dutch oven, whisk flour, milk and cream until smooth. Bring to a boil; cook and stir for 2 minutes or until thickened.
2. Stir in cheeses until melted. Add tomatoes, ham, sour cream and mustard. Drain macaroni; add to cheese mixture and toss to coat.
3. Transfer to a greased 13x9-in. baking dish. In a small bowl, mix topping ingredients; sprinkle over the top. Bake, uncovered, for 25-30 minutes or until bubbly and bread crumbs are lightly browned.
NOTE *To make soft bread crumbs, tear bread into pieces and place in a food processor or blender. Cover and pulse until crumbs form. One slice of bread yields ½ to ¾ cup crumbs.*

TWICE-BAKED CHEDDAR POTATO CASSEROLE

Twice-Baked Cheddar Potato Casserole

Here's a side dish that will have people talking! I simply jazzed up mashed potatoes with bacon, cheddar and sour cream. It's one of our standards for the holidays.

—KYLE COX SCOTTSDALE, AZ

PREP: 70 MIN. • **BAKE:** 15 MIN.
MAKES: 12 SERVINGS (⅔ CUP EACH)

- 8 medium baking potatoes (about 8 ounces each)
- ½ cup butter, cubed
- ⅔ cup sour cream
- ⅔ cup 2% milk
- 1 teaspoon salt
- ¾ teaspoon pepper
- 10 bacon strips, cooked and crumbled, divided
- 2 cups (8 ounces) shredded cheddar cheese, divided
- 4 green onions, chopped, divided

1. Preheat oven to 425°. Scrub potatoes; pierce several times with a fork. Bake 45-60 minutes or until tender. Remove from oven; reduce oven setting to 350°.
2. When potatoes are cool enough to handle, cut each potato lengthwise in half. Scoop out pulp and place in a large bowl; discard shells. Mash pulp with butter; stir in sour cream, milk, salt and pepper.
3. Reserve ¼ cup crumbled bacon for topping. Gently fold remaining bacon, 1 cup cheese and half of the green onions into potato mixture (do not overmix).
4. Transfer mixture to a greased 11x7-in. baking dish. Top with the remaining cheese and green onions; sprinkle with reserved bacon. Bake 15-20 minutes or until heated through and cheese is melted.

Aunt May's Lasagna

Lasagna is always a hit at large gatherings. You can make it ahead of time, it travels well and it feeds a lot. What more could you ask for?
—**ANGIE ESTES** ELKO, NV

PREP: 1 HOUR • **BAKE:** 35 MIN. + STANDING
MAKES: 12 SERVINGS

- 1 **pound ground beef**
- 1 **large onion, chopped**
- 2 **garlic cloves, minced**
- 1 **can (28 ounces) stewed tomatoes**
- 2 **cans (6 ounces each) tomato paste**
- 1 **teaspoon dried basil**
- ½ **teaspoon dried oregano**
- ¼ **teaspoon pepper**
- 1 **bay leaf**
- 9 **lasagna noodles**
- 1 **can (6 ounces) pitted ripe olives, drained and coarsely chopped**
- 2 **cups (8 ounces) shredded part-skim mozzarella cheese**
- ½ **cup grated Parmesan cheese**

1. In a large saucepan, cook beef and onion over medium heat until meat is no longer pink. Add garlic; cook 1 minute longer; drain. Stir in tomatoes, tomato paste, basil, oregano, pepper and bay leaf. Bring to a boil. Reduce heat; cover and simmer 40-50 minutes or until thickened.

2. Meanwhile, preheat oven to 350°. Cook noodles according to package directions; drain. Discard bay leaf from meat sauce. Stir in olives.

3. Spread a fourth of the sauce in a greased 13x9-in. baking dish. Top with three noodles and a third of the mozzarella and Parmesan cheese. Repeat layers. Top with remaining noodles, sauce and cheese.

4. Bake, uncovered, 35-40 minutes or until bubbly. Let stand 15 minutes before cutting.

Mallow Sweet Potato Bake

I put a light spin on a Thanksgiving classic with this recipe. This festive side captures the flavors of sweet potatoes and marshmallows and is perfect for bring-a-dish dinners.
—**DELORES NICKERSON** MUSKOGEE, OK

PREP: 70 MIN. • **BAKE:** 40 MIN.
MAKES: 12 SERVINGS

- 6 **large sweet potatoes**
- 3 **tablespoons butter**
- 1 **can (8 ounces) unsweetened crushed pineapple, undrained**
- ½ **cup dried cranberries, divided**
- ⅓ **cup orange juice**
- ¾ **teaspoon salt**
- ⅔ **cup miniature marshmallows**
- ⅓ **cup chopped pecans**

1. Preheat oven to 400°. Scrub and pierce sweet potatoes. Bake 45-55 minutes or until tender. Reduce oven setting to 350°.

2. Cut potatoes in half; scoop out pulp and place in a large bowl. Stir in butter until melted. Stir in the pineapple, ¼ cup cranberries, orange juice and salt.

3. Transfer to an 11x7-in. baking dish coated with cooking spray. Cover and bake 30 minutes.

4. Uncover; sprinkle with marshmallows, pecans and remaining cranberries. Bake 8-10 minutes longer or just until marshmallows are puffed and lightly browned.

AUNT MAY'S LASAGNA

Sausage Spinach Pasta Bake

Here's a yummy pasta crowd-pleaser. I've sometimes swapped in other meats, such as chicken sausage, veal or ground pork, and I've added summer squash, zucchini, green beans and mushrooms. A variety of fresh herbs also add a lot to the dish.

—**KIM FORNI** LACONIA, NH

PREP: 35 MIN. • **BAKE:** 25 MIN. • **MAKES:** 10 SERVINGS

- 1 package (16 ounces) whole wheat spiral pasta
- 1 pound Italian turkey sausage links, casings removed
- 1 medium onion, chopped
- 5 garlic cloves, minced
- 1 can (28 ounces) crushed tomatoes
- 1 can (14½ ounces) diced tomatoes, undrained
- 1 teaspoon dried oregano
- 1 teaspoon dried basil
- ¼ teaspoon pepper
- 1 package (10 ounces) frozen chopped spinach, thawed and squeezed dry
- ½ cup half-and-half cream
- 2 cups (8 ounces) shredded part-skim mozzarella cheese
- ½ cup grated Parmesan cheese

SAUSAGE SPINACH PASTA BAKE

1. Preheat oven to 350°. Cook pasta according to package directions.

2. Meanwhile, in a large skillet, cook turkey and onion over medium heat until meat is no longer pink. Add garlic. Cook 1 minute longer; drain. Stir in tomatoes, oregano, basil and pepper. Bring to a boil. Reduce heat; simmer, uncovered, 10 minutes.

3. Drain pasta; stir into turkey mixture. Add spinach and cream; heat through. Transfer to a 13x9-in. baking dish coated with cooking spray. Sprinkle with cheeses. Bake, uncovered, for 25-30 minutes or until golden brown.

Lightened-Up Green Bean Casserole

Try this take on green bean casserole at your next get-together, and you'll never go back to the old version again. Best of all, it's lighter than the original.

—**LAURA FALL-SUTTON** BUHL, ID

PREP: 40 MIN. • **BAKE:** 15 MIN. **MAKES:** 12 SERVINGS

- 8 cups cut fresh green beans (about 2 pounds)
- ½ pound sliced fresh mushrooms
- 2 tablespoons butter
- 2 tablespoons all-purpose flour
- 1 teaspoon dried minced onion
- ½ teaspoon pepper
- ½ cup fat-free milk
- 1 cup reduced-fat sour cream
- 1 teaspoon Worcestershire sauce
- 1½ cups (6 ounces) shredded reduced-fat Swiss cheese

TOPPING
- ⅓ cup slivered almonds
- ⅓ cup crushed cornflakes
- 1 tablespoon butter, melted

1. Place beans in a Dutch oven and cover with water; bring to a boil. Cover and cook for 3-5 minutes or until crisp-tender; drain and set aside.

2. Preheat oven to 400°. In a large skillet, saute mushrooms in butter until tender. Stir in flour, onion and pepper until blended. Gradually stir in milk. Bring to a boil; cook and stir 1-2 minutes or until thickened. Remove from heat; stir in sour cream and Worcestershire sauce. Stir in beans and cheese until blended.

3. Transfer to an 11x7-in. baking dish coated with cooking spray (dish will be full). Combine topping ingredients; sprinkle over the top.

4. Bake, uncovered, 12-16 minutes or until bubbly and heated through.

The Best Eggplant Parmesan

I love eggplant and have many recipes, but this truly delicious dish is one of my favorites. The cheeses and seasonings make it simply unforgettable.

—DOTTIE KILPATRICK WILMINGTON, NC

PREP: 1¼ HOURS • **BAKE:** 35 MIN. + STANDING
MAKES: 2 CASSEROLES (8 SERVINGS EACH)

- 3 garlic cloves, minced
- ⅓ cup olive oil
- 2 cans (28 ounces each) crushed tomatoes
- 1 cup pitted ripe olives, chopped
- ¼ cup thinly sliced fresh basil leaves or 1 tablespoon dried basil
- 3 tablespoons capers, drained
- 1 teaspoon crushed red pepper flakes
- ¼ teaspoon pepper

EGGPLANT

- 1 cup all-purpose flour
- 4 eggs, beaten
- 3 cups dry bread crumbs
- 1 tablespoon garlic powder
- 1 tablespoon minced fresh oregano or 1 teaspoon dried oregano
- 4 small eggplants (about 1 pound each), peeled and cut lengthwise into ½-inch slices
- 1 cup olive oil

CHEESE

- 2 eggs, beaten
- 2 cartons (15 ounces each) ricotta cheese
- 1¼ cups shredded Parmesan cheese, divided
- ½ cup thinly sliced fresh basil leaves or 2 tablespoons dried basil
- ½ teaspoon pepper
- 8 cups (32 ounces) shredded part-skim mozzarella cheese

1. In a Dutch oven over medium heat, cook garlic in oil 1 minute. Stir in tomatoes, olives, basil, capers, pepper flakes and pepper. Bring to a boil. Reduce heat; simmer, uncovered, 45-60 minutes or until thickened.

2. Meanwhile, for eggplant, place flour and eggs in separate shallow bowls. In another bowl, combine bread crumbs, garlic powder and oregano. Dip eggplant in flour, eggs, then bread crumb mixture.

3. In a large skillet, cook eggplant in batches in oil for 5 minutes on each side or until tender. Drain on paper towels. In a large bowl, combine the eggs, ricotta, ½ cup Parmesan cheese, basil and pepper.

4. Preheat oven to 350°. In each of two greased 13x9-in. baking dishes, layer 1½ cups tomato sauce, four eggplant slices, 1 cup ricotta mixture and 2 cups mozzarella cheese. Repeat layers. Sprinkle each with remaining Parmesan cheese. Bake, uncovered, 35-40 minutes or until bubbly. Let stand 10 minutes before cutting.

FREEZE IT

Ham & Noodle Casseroles

I got this recipe from my mother, and I love it because it's easy and I've usually got the ingredients on hand. Also, it freezes well so I can have an extra pan handy whenever I need a quick potluck contribution. Everyone seems to like it, because there are never leftovers to deal with.

—**JAN SCHOSHKE** BROOKVILLE, KS

PREP: 20 MIN. • **BAKE:** 25 MIN.
MAKES: 2 CASSEROLES (8 SERVINGS EACH)

- 1½ **pounds uncooked egg noodles**
- 3 **pounds cubed fully cooked ham**
- 4 **cans (10¾ ounces each) condensed cream of chicken soup, undiluted**
- 4 **cups frozen cut green beans, thawed**
- 1 **cup 2% milk**
- ¼ **cup butter, melted**
- 2 **cups (8 ounces) shredded Colby-Monterey Jack cheese**

1. Preheat oven to 350°. Cook pasta according to package directions.
2. Meanwhile, in a large bowl, combine ham, soup, beans and milk. Drain pasta; pour over ham mixture and toss to coat. Transfer to two greased 13x9-in. baking dishes.
3. Drizzle each with butter; sprinkle with cheese. Bake, uncovered, 25-30 minutes or until heated through.
FREEZE OPTION *Cool unbaked casseroles; cover and freeze up to 3 months. To use, partially thaw in refrigerator overnight. Remove from refrigerator 30 minutes before baking. Preheat oven to 350°. Bake, uncovered, 40-45 minutes or until heated through and a thermometer inserted in center reads 165°.*

Saucy Calico Beans

A picnic favorite, this saucy bean medley isn't overly sweet like some versions. The dish will be empty before you know it!

—**PAT PRICE COOK**
MISSION VIEJO, CA

PREP: 30 MIN. • **BAKE:** 1 HOUR
MAKES: 12 SERVINGS (¾ CUP EACH)

- 4 **medium onions, halved and sliced**
- 5 **bacon strips, diced**
- 2 **garlic cloves, minced**
- 1 **cup packed dark brown sugar**
- ½ **cup cider vinegar**
- ¼ **teaspoon ground mustard**
- 2 **cans (15¼ ounces each) lima beans, rinsed and drained**
- 2 **cans (15 ounces each) pork and beans**
- 1 **can (16 ounces) kidney beans, rinsed and drained**

1. Preheat oven to 350°. Meanwhile, in a Dutch oven, saute onions and bacon until the onions are tender. Add garlic; cook 1 minute longer. Add brown sugar, vinegar and mustard; bring to a boil. Reduce heat; simmer, uncovered, 20 minutes.
2. Stir beans into the sauce mixture. Transfer to a 3-qt. baking dish. Cover and bake 1 hour or until heated through.

SAUCY CALICO BEANS

CORDON BLEU
CASSEROLE

Vegetable Noodle Casserole

If you're looking for a filling side dish, look no further. This casserole combines nutritious vegetables and hearty noodles in a delectable cream sauce. Whenever I serve it, the pan is scraped clean.

—**JEANETTE HIOS** BROOKLYN, NY

PREP: 15 MIN. • **BAKE:** 45 MIN.
MAKES: 12-14 SERVINGS

- 1 can (10¾ ounces) condensed cream of chicken soup, undiluted
- 1 can (10¾ ounces) condensed cream of broccoli soup, undiluted
- 1½ cups 2% milk
- 1 cup grated Parmesan cheese, divided
- 3 garlic cloves, minced
- 2 tablespoons dried parsley flakes
- ½ teaspoon pepper
- ¼ teaspoon salt
- 1 package (16 ounces) wide egg noodles, cooked and drained
- 1 package (16 ounces) frozen California-blend vegetables, thawed
- 2 cup frozen corn, thawed

1. Preheat oven to 350°. In a large bowl, combine soups, milk, ¾ cup cheese, garlic, parsley, pepper and salt. Stir in noodles, vegetable blend and corn.
2. Pour into a greased 13x9-in. baking dish. Sprinkle with remaining cheese. Cover and bake 45-50 minutes or until heated through.

Cordon Bleu Casserole

I got this cherished recipe from a friend many years ago. I freeze several disposable pans to share with neighbors or to save for times when I'm scrambling to come up with an easy but good meal.

—**REA NEWELL** DECATUR, IL

PREP: 20 MIN. • **BAKE:** 40 MIN.
MAKES: 2 CASSEROLES (6 SERVINGS EACH)

- 2 packages (6 ounces each) reduced-sodium stuffing mix
- 1 can (10¾ ounces) condensed cream of chicken soup, undiluted
- 1 cup milk
- 8 cups cubed cooked chicken
- ½ teaspoon pepper
- ¾ pound sliced deli ham, cut into 1-inch strips
- 1 cup (4 ounces) shredded Swiss cheese
- 3 cups (12 ounces) shredded cheddar cheese

1. Preheat oven to 350°. Prepare stuffing mixes according to the package directions.
2. Meanwhile, in a large bowl, combine soup and milk; set aside.
3. Divide chicken between two greased 13x9-in. baking dishes. Sprinkle with pepper. Layer with ham, Swiss cheese, 1 cup cheddar cheese, the soup mixture and stuffing. Sprinkle with the remaining cheddar cheese.
4. Cover and bake 30 minutes. Uncover; bake 10-15 minutes longer or until cheese is melted.
FREEZE OPTION *Cover and freeze unbaked casseroles up to 3 months. To use, thaw in the refrigerator overnight. Remove from the refrigerator 30 minutes before baking. Preheat oven to 350°. Cover and bake 45 minutes. Uncover; bake 10-15 minutes longer or until heated through and cheese is melted.*

OVERNIGHT BRUNCH
CASSEROLE

Overnight Brunch Casserole

I love to cook for company and host brunches frequently. Here, scrambled eggs and a cheese sauce bake up into a creamy dish that stands out from other breakfast bakes.

—**CANDY HESCH** MOSINEE, WI

PREP: 30 MIN. + CHILLING • **BAKE:** 40 MIN. + STANDING
MAKES: 12 SERVINGS

- 3 **tablespoons butter, divided**
- 2 **tablespoons all-purpose flour**
- ½ **teaspoon salt**
- ⅛ **teaspoon pepper**
- 2 **cups fat-free milk**
- 5 **slices reduced-fat process American cheese product, chopped**
- 1½ **cups sliced fresh mushrooms**
- 2 **green onions, finely chopped**
- 1 **cup cubed fully cooked ham**
- 2 **cups egg substitute**
- 4 **eggs**

TOPPING

- 3 **slices whole wheat bread, cubed**
- 4 **teaspoons butter, melted**
- ⅛ **teaspoon paprika**

1. In a large saucepan, melt 2 tablespoons butter. Stir in flour, salt and pepper until smooth; gradually add milk. Bring to a boil; cook and stir 2 minutes or until slightly thickened. Stir in cheese until melted. Remove from heat.

2. In a large nonstick skillet, saute mushrooms and green onions in remaining butter until tender. Add ham; heat through. Whisk egg substitute and eggs; add to skillet. Cook and stir until almost set. Stir in the cheese sauce.

3. Transfer to a 13x9-in. baking dish coated with cooking spray. Toss bread cubes with butter. Arrange over egg mixture; sprinkle with paprika. Cover and refrigerate overnight.

4. Remove from refrigerator 30 minutes before baking. Preheat oven to 350°. Bake, uncovered, 40-45 minutes or until a knife inserted near the center comes out clean. Let stand 10 minutes before cutting.

CHEESY RIGATONI BAKE

FREEZE IT
Cheesy Rigatoni Bake

This is a family favorite. One of our four children always asks for it as a birthday dinner.

—NANCY URBINE LANCASTER, OH

PREP: 20 MIN. • **BAKE:** 30 MIN.
MAKES: 2 CASSEROLES (6 SERVINGS EACH)

- 1 package (16 ounces) rigatoni or large tube pasta
- 2 tablespoons butter
- ¼ cup all-purpose flour
- ½ teaspoon salt
- 2 cups milk
- ¼ cup water
- 4 eggs, lightly beaten
- 2 cans (8 ounces each) tomato sauce
- 2 cups (8 ounces) shredded part-skim mozzarella cheese, divided
- ¼ cup grated Parmesan cheese, divided

1. Preheat oven to 375°. Cook pasta according to package directions. Meanwhile, in a small saucepan, melt butter. Stir in flour and salt until smooth; gradually add milk and water. Bring to a boil; cook and stir for 2 minutes or until thickened.

2. Drain pasta; place in a large bowl. Add eggs. Spoon into two greased 8-in. square baking dishes. Layer each with one can of tomato sauce, half the mozzarella cheese and half the white sauce. Sprinkle each with half the Parmesan cheese.

3. Bake casseroles, uncovered, for 30-35 minutes or until a meat thermometer reads 160°.

FREEZE OPTION *Cover and freeze unbaked casseroles up to 3 months. To use, partially thaw in refrigerator overnight. Remove from refrigerator 30 minutes before baking. Preheat oven to 375°. Cover and bake 40 minutes. Uncover; bake 7-10 minutes longer or until a meat thermometer reads 165°.*

FREEZE IT
Cajun Chicken Pasta Bake

My family loves pasta, so I decided to get in the kitchen and come up with my own chicken pasta casserole. It tastes so good, everyone goes back for seconds.

—KIM WEISHUHN PENSACOLA, FL

PREP: 30 MIN. • **BAKE:** 20 MIN.
MAKES: 2 CASSEROLES (6 SERVINGS EACH)

- 2 packages (12 ounces each) bow tie pasta
- 2 pounds boneless skinless chicken breasts, cut into 1-inch strips
- 2 tablespoons olive oil, divided
- 2 bunches green onions, chopped
- 2 medium green peppers, chopped
- 2 medium sweet red peppers, chopped
- 1 can (14½ ounces) reduced-sodium chicken broth
- 2 cans (10¾ ounces each) condensed cream of chicken soup, undiluted
- 1 can (10¾ ounces) condensed cream of mushroom soup, undiluted
- ¾ cup 2% milk
- 2½ teaspoons Cajun seasoning
- 1½ teaspoons garlic powder
- 2 cups (8 ounces) shredded Colby-Monterey Jack cheese

1. Preheat oven to 350°. Cook pasta according to package directions to al dente.

2. Meanwhile, in a Dutch oven, saute chicken in 1 tablespoon oil until juices run clear. Remove with a slotted spoon and set aside. In same pan, saute onions and peppers in remaining oil until tender. Add broth, soups, milk, Cajun seasoning and garlic powder. Bring to a boil; remove from heat.

3. Drain pasta. Add pasta and chicken to soup mixture; toss to coat. Divide between two greased 13x9-in. baking dishes. Sprinkle with cheese. Cover and bake casseroles 20-25 minutes or until bubbly.

FREEZE OPTION *Cool unbaked casseroles; cover and freeze. To use, partially thaw in refrigerator overnight. Remove from refrigerator 30 minutes before baking. Preheat oven to 350°. Bake casseroles, as directed, increasing time as necessary to heat through and for a thermometer inserted in center to read 165°.*

Pizza Casserole

Friends and family love my new spin on pizza. I load this hearty pasta casserole with ground beef, pepperoni, mozzarella cheese, mushrooms and more.
—**NANCY FOUST** STONEBORO, PA

PREP: 20 MIN. • **BAKE:** 30 MIN.
MAKES: 2 CASSEROLES (8 SERVINGS EACH)

- 3 **cups uncooked spiral pasta**
- 2 **pounds ground beef**
- 1 **medium onion, chopped**
- 2 **cans (8 ounces each) mushroom stems and pieces, drained**
- 1 **can (15 ounces) tomato sauce**
- 1 **jar (14 ounces) pizza sauce**
- 1 **can (6 ounces) tomato paste**
- ½ **teaspoon sugar**
- ½ **teaspoon garlic powder**
- ½ **teaspoon onion powder**
- ½ **teaspoon dried oregano**
- 4 **cups (16 ounces) shredded part-skim mozzarella cheese, divided**
- 1 **package (3½ ounces) sliced pepperoni**
- ½ **cup grated Parmesan cheese**

1. Preheat oven to 350°. Cook pasta according to package directions.
2. Meanwhile, in a Dutch oven, cook beef and onion over medium heat until meat is no longer pink; drain. Stir in mushrooms, tomato sauce, pizza sauce, tomato paste, sugar and seasonings. Drain pasta; stir into meat sauce.
3. Divide half of the mixture between two greased 11x7-in. baking dishes; sprinkle each with 1 cup mozzarella cheese. Repeat layers. Top each with pepperoni and Parmesan cheese.
4. Cover and bake 20 minutes. Uncover; bake 10-15 minutes longer or until heated through.

FREEZE IT

Baked Two-Cheese & Bacon Grits

In the South, everyone loves three things; bacon, cheese and grits! After perfecting this recipe, I took it to my first family function as a newlywed and it was a hit. It was also popular at a church get-together and my husband's office party. Now I'm known as the "yummy food wife."
—**MELISSA ROGERS** TUSCALOOSA, AL

PREP: 25 MIN. • **BAKE:** 40 MIN. + STANDING • **MAKES:** 12 SERVINGS

- 6 **thick-sliced bacon strips, chopped**
- 3 **cups water**
- 3 **cups chicken stock**
- 1 **teaspoon garlic powder**
- ½ **teaspoon pepper**
- 2 **cups quick-cooking grits**
- 12 **ounces process cheese (Velveeta), cubed (about 2⅓ cups)**
- ½ **cup butter, cubed**
- ½ **cup 2% milk**
- 4 **eggs, lightly beaten**
- 2 **cups (8 ounces) shredded white cheddar cheese**

1. Preheat oven to 350°. In a large saucepan, cook bacon over medium heat until crisp, stirring occasionally. Remove pan from heat. Remove bacon with a slotted spoon; drain on paper towels.
2. Add water, stock, garlic powder and pepper to bacon drippings; bring to a boil. Slowly stir in grits. Reduce heat to medium-low; cook, covered, 5-7 minutes or until thickened, stirring occasionally. Remove from heat.
3. Add process cheese and butter; stir until melted. Stir in milk. Slowly stir in eggs until blended. Transfer to a greased 13x9-in. baking dish. Sprinkle with bacon and shredded cheese. Bake, uncovered, 40-45 minutes or until edges are golden brown and cheese is melted. Let stand 10 minutes before serving.
FREEZE OPTION *Cool unbaked casserole; cover and freeze. To use, partially thaw in refrigerator overnight. Remove casserole from refrigerator 30 minutes before baking. Preheat oven to 350°. Bake grits as directed, increasing time to 50-60 minutes or until heated through and a thermometer inserted in center reads 165°.*

BAKED TWO-CHEESE &
BACON GRITS

Seafood Lasagna

This rich, satisfying dish, adapted from a recipe given to me by a friend, is my husband's favorite. I usually serve it on his birthday. It's loaded with scallops and shrimp in a creamy sauce. I consider this the crown jewel in my repertoire of recipes.

—**ELENA HANSEN** RUIDOSO, NM

PREP: 35 MIN. • **BAKE:** 35 MIN. + STANDING
MAKES: 12 SERVINGS

- 1 **green onion, finely chopped**
- 2 **tablespoons canola oil**
- 2 **tablespoons plus ½ cup butter, divided**
- ½ **cup chicken broth**
- 1 **bottle (8 ounces) clam juice**
- 1 **pound bay scallops**
- 1 **pound uncooked small shrimp, peeled and deveined**
- 1 **package (8 ounces) imitation crabmeat, chopped**
- ¼ **teaspoon white pepper, divided**
- ½ **cup all-purpose flour**
- 1½ **cups 2% milk**
- ½ **teaspoon salt**
- 1 **cup heavy whipping cream**
- ½ **cup shredded Parmesan cheese, divided**
- 9 **lasagna noodles, cooked and drained**

1. In a large skillet, saute onion in oil and 2 tablespoons butter until tender. Stir in broth and clam juice; bring to a boil. Add scallops, shrimp, crab and ⅛ teaspoon pepper; return to a boil. Reduce heat; simmer, uncovered, for 4-5 minutes or until shrimp turn pink and scallops are firm and opaque, stirring gently. Drain, reserving cooking liquid; set seafood mixture aside.

SEAFOOD LASAGNA

2. In a large saucepan, melt the remaining butter; stir in flour until smooth. Combine milk and reserved cooking liquid; gradually add to the saucepan. Add salt and remaining pepper. Bring to a boil; cook and stir for 2 minutes or until thickened.

3. Remove from heat; stir in cream and ¼ cup cheese. Stir ¾ cup white sauce into the seafood mixture.

4. Preheat oven to 350°. Spread ½ cup white sauce in a greased 13x9-in. baking dish. Top with three noodles; spread with half of the seafood mixture and 1¼ cups sauce. Repeat layers. Top with remaining noodles, sauce and cheese.

5. Bake, uncovered, at for 35-40 minutes or until golden brown. Let stand for 15 minutes before cutting.

Mom's Tamale Pie

I don't recall my mom ever using a recipe for her tamale pie, but I came up with a version that tastes very much like hers did. The grits add a Southern accent.

—**WALDINE GUILLOTT** DEQUINCY, LA

PREP: 25 MIN. • **BAKE:** 20 MIN. • **MAKES:** 12 SERVINGS

- 2 **pounds ground beef**
- 1 **large onion, chopped**
- 1 **large green pepper, chopped**
- 1 **can (15¼ ounces) whole kernel corn, undrained**
- 1½ **cups chopped fresh tomatoes**
- 5 **tablespoons tomato paste**
- 1 **envelope chili seasoning**
- 1½ **teaspoons sugar**
- 1 **teaspoon garlic powder**
- 1 **teaspoon dried basil**
- 1 **teaspoon dried oregano**
- 6 **cups cooked grits (prepared with butter and salt)**
- 1½ **teaspoons chili powder, divided**
- 1½ **cups (6 ounces) shredded cheddar cheese**

1. Preheat oven to 325°. In a large skillet, cook beef, onion and green pepper over medium heat until meat is no longer pink; drain. Add corn, tomatoes, tomato paste, chili seasoning, sugar, garlic powder, basil and oregano. Cook and stir until heated through; keep warm.

2. Spread half of the grits in a greased 3-qt. baking dish. Sprinkle with 1 teaspoon chili powder. Top with beef mixture and cheese. Pipe remaining grits around edge of dish; sprinkle with remaining chili powder.

3. Bake, uncovered, 20-25 minutes or until cheese is melted. Let stand 5 minutes before serving.

SAUSAGE RICE CASSEROLE

Sausage Rice Casserole

I fiddled around with this dish, trying to adjust it to my family's tastes. When my pickiest child cleaned her plate, I knew I'd found the right flavor combination.
—**JENNIFER TROST** WEST LINN, OR

PREP: 30 MIN. • **BAKE:** 40 MIN.
MAKES: 2 CASSEROLES (6-8 SERVINGS EACH)

- 2 **packages (7.2 ounces each) rice pilaf**
- 2 **pounds bulk pork sausage**
- 6 **celery ribs, chopped**
- 4 **medium carrots, sliced**
- 1 **can (10¾ ounces) condensed cream of chicken soup, undiluted**
- 1 **can (10¾ ounces) condensed cream of mushroom soup, undiluted**
- 2 **teaspoons onion powder**
- ½ **teaspoon garlic powder**
- ¼ **teaspoon pepper**

1. Preheat oven to 350°. Prepare rice mixes according to package directions. Meanwhile, in a large skillet, cook the sausage, celery and carrots over medium heat until meat is no longer pink; drain.

2. In a large bowl, combine the sausage mixture, rice, soups, onion powder, garlic powder and pepper. Transfer to two greased 11x7-in. baking dishes.

3. Cover and bake 40-45 minutes or until vegetables are tender.

FREEZE OPTION *Cover and freeze unbaked casseroles up to 3 months. To use, partially thaw in refrigerator overnight. Remove from refrigerator 30 minutes before baking. Preheat oven to 350°. Bake as directed, increasing time as necessary to heat through and for a thermometer inserted in center to read 165°.*

TOP TIP

Freeze-It Meals Made Easy

Freezing meals for future use is a great idea for family cooks, particularly those who like to contribute to church suppers and charity potlucks but don't have much time to do so. Most casseroles can be frozen for up to 3 months, but always check the recipe for freezer guidelines. When freezing a casserole, consider using a disposable aluminum baking pan so your good casserole dishes aren't sitting in the freezer for months. Be sure to use heavy-duty foil to cover the pan, or use foil specifically meant to protect from freezer burn. Defrost casseroles in the refrigerator the day before baking.

Makeover Pecan Corn Pudding

Every bit as rich and creamy as the original recipe, this magical makeover has crunchy pecans, loads of cheese and a touch of jalapeno. It's destined to become a favorite!

—SHARON BESHOAR MONTROSE, CO

PREP: 20 MIN. • **BAKE:** 45 MIN.
MAKES: 12 SERVINGS

- 1 cup yellow cornmeal
- ¾ teaspoon baking soda
- 3 eggs
- 1¼ cups buttermilk
- ¾ cup reduced-fat butter, melted
- 2 cans (one 14¾ ounces, one 8¼ ounces) cream-style corn
- 2 cups frozen corn
- 2 medium onions, chopped
- 1½ cups (6 ounces) shredded sharp reduced-fat cheddar cheese
- 4 jalapeno peppers, seeded and chopped
- ½ cup chopped pecans, toasted

1. Preheat oven to 350°. In a large bowl, combine cornmeal and baking soda. In a small bowl, whisk eggs, buttermilk and butter. Add cream-style corn, corn and onions. Stir into dry ingredients just until moistened.

2. Pour half the mixture into a 13x9-in. baking dish coated with cooking spray. Sprinkle with cheese and jalapenos. Top with remaining batter; sprinkle with pecans.

3. Bake, uncovered, 45-50 minutes or until a thermometer reads 160°. Serve warm.

NOTE *This recipe was tested with Land O'Lakes light stick butter. We recommend wearing disposable gloves when cutting hot peppers. Avoid touching your face.*

CREAMY CHICKEN NOODLE BAKE

Creamy Chicken Noodle Bake

Talk about a potluck pleaser! This comforting casserole is bursting with flavor. Even the pickiest eater will enjoy this tasty bake.

—SHIRLEY UNGER BLUFFTON, OH

PREP: 25 MIN. • **BAKE:** 40 MIN. + STANDING
MAKES: 12 SERVINGS (1 CUP EACH)

- 4 cups uncooked egg noodles
- ½ cup butter, divided
- ¼ cup all-purpose flour
- ½ teaspoon salt
- ⅛ teaspoon white pepper
- 3½ cups 2% milk
- 4 cups cubed cooked chicken
- 2 jars (12 ounces each) chicken gravy
- 1 jar (2 ounces) diced pimientos, drained
- ½ cup cubed process cheese (Velveeta)
- ½ cup dry bread crumbs
- 4 teaspoons butter, melted

1. Cook noodles according to package directions.

2. Meanwhile, preheat oven to 350°. In a Dutch oven, melt 6 tablespoons butter. Stir in flour, salt and pepper until smooth. Gradually add milk. Bring to a boil; cook and stir 1-2 minutes or until thickened. Remove from heat. Stir in chicken, gravy and pimientos.

3. Drain noodles; toss with remaining butter. Stir into chicken mixture. Transfer to a greased 13x9-in. baking dish.

4. Cover and bake 30-35 minutes or until bubbly. Combine cheese, bread crumbs and melted butter. Sprinkle around edges of casserole. Bake, uncovered, 10 minutes longer or until golden brown. Let stand 10 minutes before serving.

Basil Corn & Tomato Bake

When sweet Jersey corn is in season, I often turn to this recipe. Combined with tomatoes, zucchini and basil, it's a zesty treat for brunch, lunch or dinner.

—ERIN CHILCOAT CENTRAL ISLIP, NY

PREP: 30 MIN. • **BAKE:** 45 MIN. + STANDING
MAKES: 10 SERVINGS

- 2 teaspoons olive oil
- 1 medium onion, chopped
- 2 eggs
- 1 can (10¾ ounces) reduced-fat reduced-sodium condensed cream of celery soup, undiluted
- 4 cups fresh or frozen corn
- 1 small zucchini, chopped
- 1 medium tomato, seeded and chopped
- ¾ cup soft whole wheat bread crumbs
- ⅓ cup minced fresh basil
- ½ teaspoon salt
- ½ cup shredded part-skim mozzarella cheese
- Additional minced fresh basil, optional

1. Preheat oven to 350°. In a small skillet, heat oil over medium heat. Add onion; cook and stir until tender. In a large bowl, whisk eggs and condensed soup until blended. Stir in vegetables, bread crumbs, basil, salt and onion. Transfer mixture to an 11x7-in. baking dish coated with cooking spray.
2. Bake, uncovered, 40-45 minutes or until bubbly. Sprinkle with cheese. Bake 5-10 minutes longer or until cheese is melted. Let stand 10 minutes before serving. If desired, sprinkle with additional basil.

NOTE *To make soft bread crumbs, tear bread into pieces and place in a food processor or blender. Cover and pulse until crumbs form. One slice of bread yields ½ to ¾ cup crumbs.*

Cabbage Roll Casserole

I layer cabbage with tomato sauce and beef to create a hearty dish that tastes like cabbage rolls, but without all the work!

—DOREEN MARTIN KITIMAT, BC

PREP: 20 MIN. • **BAKE:** 55 MIN.
MAKES: 12 SERVINGS

- 2 pounds ground beef
- 1 large onion, chopped
- 3 garlic cloves, minced
- 2 cans (15 ounces each) tomato sauce, divided
- 1 teaspoon dried thyme
- ½ teaspoon dill weed
- ½ teaspoon rubbed sage
- ¼ teaspoon salt
- ¼ teaspoon pepper
- ¼ teaspoon cayenne pepper
- 2 cups cooked rice
- 4 bacon strips, cooked and crumbled
- 1 medium head cabbage (2 pounds), shredded
- 1 cup (4 ounces) shredded part-skim mozzarella cheese

1. Preheat oven to 375°. In a large skillet, cook beef and onion over medium heat until meat is no longer pink. Add garlic; cook 1 minute longer. Drain. Stir in one can of the tomato sauce and seasonings. Bring to a boil. Reduce heat; cover and simmer 5 minutes. Stir in rice and bacon; heat through. Remove from heat.
2. Layer a third of the cabbage in a greased 13x9-in. baking dish. Top with half the meat mixture. Repeat layers; top with remaining cabbage. Pour remaining tomato sauce over top.
3. Cover and bake 45 minutes. Uncover; sprinkle with cheese. Bake 10 minutes longer or until cheese is melted. Let stand 5 minutes before serving.

BASIL CORN & TOMATO BAKE

Stuffing & Turkey Casserole

Here's a scrumptious way to recycle the leftovers from Thanksgiving. If you're in the mood for a taste of Thanksgiving at other times of the year, use chicken for the turkey and some quick-to-make stuffing for the leftover stuffing.
—**DEBBIE FABRE** FT MYERS, FL

PREP: 15 MIN. • **BAKE:** 45 MIN. + STANDING
MAKES: 12 SERVINGS

- 4 **cups leftover stuffing**
- 1 **cup dried cranberries**
- 1 **cup chopped pecans**
- ¾ **cup chicken broth**
- 1 **egg, lightly beaten**
- 2 **cups (8 ounces) shredded part-skim mozzarella cheese**
- 1 **cup whole-milk ricotta cheese**
- 4 **cups cubed cooked turkey, divided**
- 1 **cup (4 ounces) shredded cheddar cheese**

1. Preheat oven to 350°. Place stuffing, cranberries and pecans in a large bowl; stir in broth. In a small bowl, mix the egg and mozzarella and ricotta cheeses.
2. In a greased 13x9-in. baking dish, layer 2 cups turkey, 3 cups stuffing mixture and ricotta cheese mixture. Top with the remaining turkey and stuffing mixture. Sprinkle with cheddar cheese.
3. Bake, covered, 40-45 minutes or until heated through. Bake, uncovered, 5 minutes longer. Let stand 10 minutes before serving.

STUFFING & TURKEY CASSEROLE

Wild Rice Brunch Casserole

Wild rice is one of our state's prized foods. Paired with our garden specialty—fresh asparagus—this recipe can't miss at dinners with friends and family.

—MEREDITH BERG HUDSON, WI

PREP: 20 MIN. • **BAKE:** 40 MIN. • **MAKES:** 10 SERVINGS

- 1 package (4 ounces) wild rice
- 1½ pounds fresh asparagus, trimmed and cut into 1-inch pieces
- 2 cups cubed fully cooked ham
- 5 tablespoons butter, divided
- 12 eggs
- ½ cup milk
- 1 teaspoon salt
- ¼ teaspoon pepper

CHEESE SAUCE
- 2 tablespoons canola oil
- 3 tablespoons all-purpose flour
- 1 cup milk
- 2 cups (8 ounces) shredded Colby or Gouda cheese
- ½ teaspoon ground ginger
- Dash white pepper

1. Cook rice according to package directions. Spread in greased 13x9-in. baking dish; set aside.
2. Meanwhile, preheat oven to 325°. Place asparagus and ½ in. of water in a large saucepan; bring to a boil. Reduce heat; cover and simmer 3-5 minutes or until crisp-tender. Drain and set aside.
3. In a large skillet, saute ham in 2 tablespoons butter until lightly browned. Spoon over wild rice.
4. In a large bowl, whisk eggs, milk, salt and pepper. In the same skillet, heat remaining butter until hot. Add egg mixture; cook and stir over medium heat until eggs are completely set. Spoon over ham; top with the asparagus.
5. For sauce, heat oil in a saucepan. Stir in flour until smooth. Gradually stir in milk. Bring to a boil; cook and stir 2 minutes or until thickened. Reduce heat; add the cheese, ginger and pepper. Cook and stir 2 minutes longer or until cheese is melted.
6. Pour over casserole. Cover and bake 30 minutes. Uncover; bake 10-15 minutes longer or until a thermometer reads 160°.

Chicken Club Casseroles

Enjoy two casseroles with this warm and welcoming recipe. Every bite is fresh and delicious, even after it's been frozen.

—JANINE SMITH COLUMBIA, SC

PREP: 20 MIN. • **BAKE:** 35 MIN.
MAKES: 2 CASSEROLES (5 SERVINGS EACH)

- 4 cups uncooked spiral pasta
- 4 cups cubed cooked chicken
- 2 cans (10¾ ounces each) condensed cheddar cheese soup, undiluted
- 1 cup crumbled cooked bacon
- 1 cup 2% milk
- 1 cup mayonnaise
- 4 medium tomatoes, seeded and chopped
- 3 cups fresh baby spinach, chopped
- 2 cups (8 ounces) shredded Colby-Monterey Jack cheese

1. Preheat oven to 375°. Cook pasta according to package directions.
2. Meanwhile, in a large bowl, combine chicken, soup, bacon, milk and mayonnaise. Stir in tomatoes and spinach.
3. Drain pasta; stir into chicken mixture. Transfer to two greased 8-in. square baking dishes. Sprinkle with cheese.
4. Cover and bake 35-40 minutes or until bubbly and cheese is melted.

CHICKEN CLUB CASSEROLES

3. For topping, combine bread crumbs and melted butter; sprinkle over top. Bake 40-45 minutes or until a knife inserted near the center comes out clean.
FREEZE OPTION *Cool unbaked casserole. Sprinkle with topping; cover and freeze. To use, partially thaw in refrigerator overnight. Remove from refrigerator 30 minutes before baking. Preheat oven to 350°. Bake casserole as directed, increasing time as necessary for a knife inserted near the center to come out clean.*

Hamburger Noodle Casserole

I made a few substitutions to a classic casserole and ended up with a satisfying dish that's lighter but tastes just as rich and creamy as the original.
—**MARTHA HENSON** WINNSBORO, TX

PREP: 30 MIN. • **BAKE:** 35 MIN. • **MAKES:** 10 SERVINGS

- 5 cups uncooked egg noodles
- 1½ pounds lean ground beef (90% lean)
- 2 garlic cloves, minced
- 3 cans (8 ounces each) tomato sauce
- ½ teaspoon sugar
- ½ teaspoon salt
- ⅛ teaspoon pepper
- 1 package (8 ounces) reduced-fat cream cheese
- 1 cup reduced-fat ricotta cheese
- ¼ cup reduced-fat sour cream
- 3 green onions, thinly sliced, divided
- ⅔ cup shredded reduced-fat cheddar cheese

1. Preheat oven to 350°. Cook noodles according to package directions.
2. Meanwhile, in a large nonstick skillet over medium heat, cook beef until no longer pink. Add garlic; cook 1 minute longer. Drain. Stir in tomato sauce, sugar, salt and pepper; heat through. Drain noodles; stir into beef mixture.
3. In a small bowl, beat cream cheese, ricotta cheese and sour cream until blended. Stir in half of the onions.
4. Spoon half the noodle mixture into a 13x9-in. baking dish coated with cooking spray. Top with cheese mixture and remaining noodle mixture.
5. Cover and bake 30 minutes. Uncover; sprinkle with cheddar cheese. Bake 5-10 minutes longer or until heated through and cheese is melted. Sprinkle with remaining onions.

FREEZE IT

Harvest Squash Casserole

Flavored with cranberries and pecans, this nutritious recipe works very well as a comforting side dish with roasted turkey or chicken.
—**MARY ANN LEE** CLIFTON PARK, NY

PREP: 35 MIN. • **BAKE:** 40 MIN. • **MAKES:** 10 SERVINGS

- 1 large butternut squash (about 6 pounds), peeled, seeded and cubed
- 1 large onion, finely chopped
- 1 tablespoon butter
- 2 garlic cloves, minced
- 3 eggs, lightly beaten
- 2 tablespoons sugar
- 2 teaspoons salt
- ½ teaspoon pepper
- 1 cup chopped fresh or frozen cranberries
- ¾ cup chopped pecans

TOPPING
- 2 cups soft whole wheat bread crumbs
- 2 tablespoons butter, melted

1. Place squash in a Dutch oven; cover with water. Bring to a boil. Reduce heat; cover and cook 15-20 minutes or just until tender. Drain. In a large bowl, mash squash and set aside.
2. Preheat oven to 350°. In a large nonstick skillet, saute onion in butter until tender. Add garlic; cook 1 minute longer. Add to squash. Stir in eggs, sugar, salt and pepper. Gently fold in cranberries and pecans. Transfer mixture to a 13x9-in. baking dish coated with cooking spray.

HAMBURGER NOODLE
CASSEROLE

SHEPHERD'S PIE

FREEZE IT

Shepherd's Pie

When you need a real meat-and-potatoes fix, try this satisfying layered casserole. It combines creamy from-scratch mashed potatoes with a hearty meat filling. Your favorite barbecue sauce gives the dish an extra tang.

—CINDY KLISKEY PEPPERELL, MA

PREP: 25 MIN. • **BAKE:** 25 MIN.
MAKES: 2 CASSEROLES (8 SERVINGS EACH)

- 5 pounds potatoes (about 10 medium), peeled and cubed
- 2 pounds ground beef
- 2 large onions, chopped
- 2 garlic cloves, minced
- 2 cans (15½ ounces each) whole kernel corn, drained
- 1½ cups barbecue sauce
- 2 packages (8 ounces each) cream cheese, softened
- ¼ cup butter, cubed
- 1 teaspoon salt
- ¼ teaspoon pepper
- 2 cups (8 ounces) shredded cheddar cheese

1. Preheat oven to 350°. Place potatoes in a stockpot and cover with water. Bring to a boil. Reduce heat; cover and cook 10-15 minutes or until tender.
2. Meanwhile, cook beef, onions and garlic in a Dutch oven until meat is no longer pink; drain. Stir in corn and barbecue sauce.
3. Drain potatoes; mash with cream cheese, butter, salt and pepper. Spoon meat mixture into two greased 13x9-in. baking dishes. Spread mashed potatoes over tops; sprinkle with cheese.
4. Bake, uncovered, 25-30 minutes or until bubbly.

FREEZE OPTION *Cool unbaked casseroles; cover and freeze up to 3 months. To use, partially thaw in refrigerator overnight. Remove from refrigerator 30 minutes before baking. Preheat oven to 350°. Cover and bake 1¼ hours or until bubbly. Uncover; bake 5-10 minutes longer or until cheese is melted and a thermometer inserted in center reads 165°.*

Buffalo Chicken Lasagna

This recipe was inspired by my daughter's favorite food—Buffalo wings! It tastes just like it came from a restaurant, and it's perfect for potlucks.

—MELISSA MILLWOOD LYMAN, SC

PREP: 1 HOUR 40 MIN. • **BAKE:** 40 MIN. + STANDING
MAKES: 12 SERVINGS

- 1 tablespoon canola oil
- 1½ pounds ground chicken
- 1 small onion, chopped
- 1 celery rib, finely chopped
- 1 large carrot, grated
- 2 garlic cloves, minced
- 1 can (14½ ounces) diced tomatoes, drained
- 1 bottle (12 ounces) Buffalo wing sauce
- ½ cup water
- 1½ teaspoons Italian seasoning
- ½ teaspoon salt
- ¼ teaspoon pepper
- 9 lasagna noodles
- 1 carton (15 ounces) ricotta cheese
- 1¾ cups (7 ounces) crumbled blue cheese, divided
- ½ cup minced Italian flat leaf parsley
- 1 egg, lightly beaten
- 3 cups (12 ounces) shredded part-skim mozzarella cheese
- 2 cups (8 ounces) shredded white cheddar cheese

1. In a Dutch oven, heat oil over medium heat. Add chicken, onion, celery and carrot; cook and stir until meat is no longer pink and vegetables are tender. Add garlic; cook 2 minutes longer. Stir in tomatoes, wing sauce, water, Italian seasoning, salt and pepper; bring to a boil. Reduce heat; cover and simmer 1 hour.
2. Meanwhile, cook noodles according to package directions; drain. In a small bowl, mix the ricotta cheese, ¾ cup blue cheese, parsley and egg. Preheat oven to 350°.
3. Spread 1½ cups sauce into a greased 13x9-in. baking dish. Layer with three noodles, 1½ cups sauce, ⅔ cup ricotta mixture, 1 cup mozzarella cheese, ⅔ cup cheddar cheese and ⅓ cup blue cheese. Repeat layers twice.
4. Bake, covered, 20 minutes. Uncover; bake 20-25 minutes longer or until bubbly and cheese is melted. Let stand 10 minutes before serving.

FREEZE IT

Polish Casserole

When I first made this dish, my 2-year-old liked it so much that he wanted it for every meal! You can use any pasta that will hold the sauce.

—CRYSTAL BRUNS ILIFF, CO

PREP: 25 MIN. • **BAKE:** 45 MIN.
MAKES: 2 CASSEROLES (6 SERVINGS EACH)

- 4 cups uncooked penne pasta
- 1½ pounds smoked Polish sausage or kielbasa, cut into ½-inch slices
- 2 cans (10¾ ounces each) condensed cream of mushroom soup, undiluted
- 1 jar (16 ounces) sauerkraut, rinsed and well drained
- 3 cups (12 ounces) shredded Swiss cheese, divided
- 1⅓ cups 2% milk
- 4 green onions, chopped
- 2 tablespoons Dijon mustard
- 4 garlic cloves, minced

1. Preheat oven to 350°. Cook pasta according to package directions; drain and transfer to a large bowl. Stir in sausage, soup, sauerkraut, 2 cups cheese, milk, onions, mustard and garlic.
2. Spoon into two greased 8-in. square baking dishes; sprinkle with remaining cheese. Bake, uncovered, 45-50 minutes or until golden brown and bubbly.
FREEZE OPTION *Cover and freeze one casserole for up to 3 months. Thaw in the refrigerator overnight. Remove from the refrigerator 30 minutes before baking. Preheat oven to 350°. Bake casserole, uncovered, 50-55 minutes or until golden brown and bubbly.*

POLISH CASSEROLE

CHOCOLATE PECAN
PIE BARS, PAGE 180

ORANGE DREAM MINI
CUPCAKES, PAGE 194

CHOCOLATE PEAR
HAZELNUT TART, PAGE 192

DELIGHTFUL
DESSERTS

CHOCOLATE & PEANUT BUTTER
MOUSSE CHEESECAKE, PAGE 191

❝ He shall eat curds and
honey by the time he knows
how to refuse the evil and
choose the good. ❞
ISAIAH 7:15

Makeover Macaroon Cake

This is one of my husband's favorites. With it made over, he can really enjoy it—and even have seconds!
—**GAYE ANDREE** ROCHESTER, NY

PREP: 20 MIN. • **BAKE:** 65 MIN. + COOLING
MAKES: 16 SERVINGS

- 6 **egg whites**
- 4 **egg yolks**
- 2¼ **cups sugar**
- ½ **cup unsweetened applesauce**
- ¼ **cup canola oil**
- ¾ **cup fat-free milk**
- ½ **teaspoon almond extract**
- 1½ **cups cake flour**
- 1½ **cups all-purpose flour**
- 1 **cup flaked coconut**
- 3 **teaspoons baking powder**
- ¼ **teaspoon salt**
- ½ **teaspoon cream of tartar**
- 1 **teaspoon confectioners' sugar**

1. Let egg whites stand at room temperature for 30 minutes.
2. Move oven rack to lowest position. Preheat oven to 325°. In a large bowl, beat egg yolks, sugar, applesauce and oil until well blended; beat in milk and extract. Combine flours, coconut, baking powder and salt; gradually beat into egg yolk mixture until blended.
3. In another bowl, beat egg whites and cream of tartar until stiff peaks form; fold into batter.

**MAKEOVER
MACAROON CAKE**

4. Gently spoon into an ungreased 10-in. tube pan. Cut through batter with a knife to remove air pockets. Bake on the lowest oven rack 65-75 minutes or until cake springs back when lightly touched. Immediately invert pan; cool completely, about 1 hour.
5. Run a knife around side and center tube of pan. Remove cake to a serving plate. Sprinkle with confectioners' sugar.

Glazed Apple Pie Squares

Because they are glazed and a little bit sweeter, these bars are a bit of a change from apple pie. The dough is firm enough that you can eat them with your hands.
—**DIANE TURNER** BRUNSWICK, OH

PREP: 1 HOUR • **BAKE:** 45 MIN. + COOLING • **MAKES:** 2 DOZEN

- 2½ **cups all-purpose flour**
- 1 **teaspoon salt**
- 1 **cup cold butter, cubed**
- 1 **egg, separated**
- 3 **to 4 tablespoons 2% milk**
- 1 **cup crushed cornflakes**
- 9 **cups thinly sliced peeled tart apples (about 10 medium)**
- 1 **cup plus 2 tablespoons sugar, divided**
- 2 **teaspoons ground cinnamon, divided**
- ½ **teaspoon ground nutmeg**

GLAZE
- 1 **cup confectioners' sugar**
- ½ **teaspoon vanilla extract**
- 1 **to 2 tablespoons 2% milk**

1. In a large bowl, combine flour and salt; cut in butter until mixture resembles coarse crumbs. In a measuring cup, combine egg yolk and enough milk to measure ⅓ cup. Gradually add to the flour mixture, tossing with a fork until dough forms a ball.
2. Preheat oven to 350°. Divide dough in half. Roll one portion into a thin 15x10-in. rectangle. Transfer to the bottom of an ungreased 15x10x1-in. baking pan. Sprinkle with cornflakes.
3. In a large bowl, combine apples, 1 cup sugar, 1½ teaspoons cinnamon and nutmeg; toss to coat. Spoon over crust.
4. Roll remaining dough into a thin 15x10-in. rectangle; place over apple filling. Beat egg white; brush over pastry. Combine remaining sugar and cinnamon; sprinkle over the top. Bake 45-50 minutes or until golden brown.
5. For glaze, combine confectioners' sugar, vanilla and enough milk to achieve a drizzling consistency. Drizzle over warm pastry. Cool completely on a wire rack. Cut into squares.

Lemon-Blueberry Pound Cake

Pair a slice of this moist cake with a scoop of vanilla ice cream. Mmm!

—REBECCA LITTLE PARK RIDGE, IL

PREP: 25 MIN. • **BAKE:** 55 MIN. + COOLING • **MAKES:** 12 SERVINGS

- ⅓ **cup butter, softened**
- 4 **ounces cream cheese, softened**
- 2 **cups sugar**
- 3 **eggs**
- 1 **egg white**
- 1 **tablespoon grated lemon peel**
- 2 **teaspoons vanilla extract**
- 2 **cups fresh or frozen unsweetened blueberries**
- 3 **cups all-purpose flour, divided**
- 1 **teaspoon baking powder**
- ½ **teaspoon baking soda**
- ½ **teaspoon salt**
- 1 **cup (8 ounces) lemon yogurt**

GLAZE
- 1¼ **cups confectioners' sugar**
- 2 **tablespoons lemon juice**

1. Preheat oven to 350°. Grease and flour a 10-in. fluted tube pan. In a large bowl, cream the butter, cream cheese and sugar until blended. Add eggs and egg white, one at a time, beating well after each addition. Beat in lemon peel and vanilla.

2. Toss blueberries with 2 tablespoons flour. In another bowl, mix the remaining flour with baking powder, baking soda and salt; add to creamed mixture alternately with yogurt, beating after each addition just until combined. Fold in blueberry mixture.

3. Transfer batter to prepared pan. Bake 55-60 minutes or until a toothpick inserted in center comes out clean. Cool in pan 10 minutes before removing to wire rack; cool completely.

4. In a small bowl, mix confectioners' sugar and lemon juice until smooth. Drizzle over cake.

NOTE *For easier removal of cake, use solid shortening when greasing a fluted or plain tube pan.*

TOP TIP

Cooling Cakes

Cakes baked in tube pans should cool for 10-15 minutes before you move them to a wire rack to cool completely. Removing a cake too soon can cause it to crack, break or stick to the pan. Leaving it in too long, however, can cause moisture to form between the cake and the pan.

CARROT CAKE WITH PECAN FROSTING

Carrot Cake with Pecan Frosting

My husband constantly requests this homey, old-fashioned version of carrot cake. The frosting is still tasty even without the pecans.

—ADRIAN BADON DENHAM SPGS, LA

PREP: 35 MIN. • **BAKE:** 40 MIN. + COOLING
MAKES: 16 SERVINGS

- 1 cup shortening
- 2 cups sugar
- 4 eggs
- 1 can (8 ounces) unsweetened crushed pineapple, undrained
- 2½ cups all-purpose flour
- 2 teaspoons ground cinnamon
- 1 teaspoon baking powder
- 1 teaspoon baking soda
- ¾ teaspoon salt
- 3 cups shredded carrots (about 6 medium carrots)

FROSTING
- 1 package (8 ounces) reduced-fat cream cheese
- ½ cup butter, softened
- 1 teaspoon vanilla extract
- 3¾ cups confectioners' sugar
- 1 cup chopped pecans

1. Preheat oven to 325°. Line bottoms of two greased 9-in. round baking pans with parchment paper; grease the paper.

2. In a large bowl, cream shortening and sugar until fluffy. Add eggs, one at a time, beating well after each addition. Beat in pineapple. In another bowl, whisk flour, cinnamon, baking powder, baking soda and salt; gradually add to creamed mixture. Stir in carrots.

3. Transfer batter to prepared pans. Bake 40-45 minutes or until a toothpick inserted in center comes out clean. Cool in pans 10 minutes before removing to wire racks; remove paper. Cool completely.

4. In a large bowl, beat cream cheese, butter and vanilla until blended. Gradually beat in confectioners' sugar until smooth. Stir in pecans.

5. Spread frosting between layers and over top and sides of cake. Refrigerate until serving.

Chocolate & Vanilla Spritz

If you're looking for a gorgeous cookie, try my spritz. These tender treats are so cute and have a great buttery flavor. The dough is easy to work with and the cookies bake up beautifully every time.

—MARY BETH JUNG HENDERSONVILLE, NC

PREP: 40 MIN. • **BAKE:** 10 MIN./BATCH + COOLING
MAKES: 9 DOZEN

- 1½ cups butter, softened
- 1 cup sugar
- 1 egg
- 2 tablespoons 2% milk
- 1 teaspoon vanilla extract
- ½ teaspoon almond extract
- 3½ cups all-purpose flour
- 1 teaspoon baking powder
- 3 tablespoons baking cocoa
  Melted chocolate and chocolate jimmies, optional

1. Preheat oven to 375°. In a large bowl, cream butter and sugar until light and fluffy. Beat in egg, milk and extracts. Combine flour and baking powder; gradually add to creamed mixture and mix well.

2. Divide dough in half; add cocoa to one portion and mix well. Divide each portion into six pieces; shape each into a 5-in. log. Place a chocolate log and vanilla log together, pressing to form another log.

3. Using a cookie press fitted with the disk of your choice, press dough 2 in. apart onto ungreased baking sheets. Bake 9-11 minutes or until edges are lightly browned. Remove to wire racks to cool.

4. If desired, dip each cookie halfway into melted chocolate, allowing excess to drip off. Place on waxed paper; sprinkle with jimmies. Let stand until set.

Caramel Toffee Brownies

I love to make up recipes for foods that I'm craving, like chocolate, toffee and caramel. They came together in this brownie for one sensational treat. I frequently bake these to add to care packages for family and friends.
—**BRENDA CAUGHELL** DURHAM, NC

PREP: 30 MIN. • **BAKE:** 40 MIN. + COOLING • **MAKES:** 2 DOZEN

CARAMEL LAYER
- ½ cup butter, softened
- ⅓ cup sugar
- ⅓ cup packed brown sugar
- 1 egg
- ½ teaspoon vanilla extract
- 1 cup all-purpose flour
- ½ teaspoon baking soda
- ¼ teaspoon salt
- ½ cup caramel ice cream topping
- 2 tablespoons 2% milk
- 1 cup toffee bits

BROWNIE LAYER
- 1 cup butter, cubed
- 4 ounces unsweetened chocolate
- 4 eggs, lightly beaten
- 2 cups sugar
- 2 teaspoons vanilla extract
- 2 cups all-purpose flour

1. Preheat oven to 350°. In a large bowl, cream butter and sugars until light and fluffy; beat in egg and vanilla. Combine flour, baking soda and salt; gradually add to creamed mixture and mix well. In a small bowl, combine caramel topping and milk; add to batter and mix well. Fold in toffee bits; set aside.

CARAMEL TOFFEE BROWNIES

2. In a microwave, melt butter and chocolate. Beat in eggs, sugar and vanilla; gradually beat in flour.
3. Spread half of brownie batter into a greased 13x9-in. baking pan. Drop caramel batter by spoonfuls onto brownie batter; swirl to combine. Drop remaining brownie batter on top.
4. Bake 40-45 minutes or until a toothpick inserted in center comes out clean. Cool on a wire rack.

Raspberry Pie Squares

Making pie for a crowd may seem impossible, but not when you turn to this crowd-pleasing recipe! The sweet-tart raspberry filling pairs well with a flaky homemade pastry.
—***TASTE OF HOME* TEST KITCHEN**

PREP: 40 MIN. + CHILLING • **BAKE:** 40 MIN. + COOLING
MAKES: 24 SERVINGS

- 3¾ cups all-purpose flour
- 4 teaspoons sugar
- 1½ teaspoons salt
- 1½ cups cold butter
- ½ to 1 cup cold water

FILLING
- 2 cups sugar
- ⅔ cup all-purpose flour
- ¼ teaspoon salt
- 8 cups fresh or frozen unsweetened raspberries
- 1 tablespoon lemon juice
- 5 teaspoons heavy whipping cream
- 1 tablespoon coarse sugar

1. In a large bowl, combine flour, sugar and salt; cut in butter until crumbly. Gradually add water, tossing with a fork until dough forms a ball.
2. Divide dough in half so that one portion is slightly larger than the other; wrap each in plastic wrap. Refrigerate for 1¼ hours or until easy to handle. Preheat oven to 375°. Roll out larger portion of dough between two large sheets of waxed paper into a 17x12-in. rectangle. Transfer to an ungreased 15x10x1-in. baking pan. Press pastry onto the bottom and up the sides of pan; trim pastry even with edges.
3. For filling, in a large bowl, combine sugar, flour and salt. Add raspberries and lemon juice; toss to coat. Spoon over pastry.
4. Roll out remaining pastry; place over filling. Trim and seal edges. Cut slits in pastry. Brush top with cream and sprinkle with coarse sugar. Place pan on a baking sheet. Bake 40-45 minutes or until golden brown. Cool completely on a wire rack. Cut into squares.
NOTE *If using frozen raspberries, use without thawing to avoid discoloring the batter.*

Chocolate Pecan Pie Bars

These yummy pecan bars start with a homemade pastry crust and pile on lots of semisweet chocolate. They're perfect for a holiday bake sale or casual get-together.

—**HEATHER BIEDLER** MARTINSBURG, WV

PREP: 30 MIN. + CHILLING
BAKE: 50 MIN. + COOLING
MAKES: 3 DOZEN

1¾ cups all-purpose flour
¼ teaspoon salt
¾ cup cold butter
¼ to ½ cup ice water

FILLING

4 eggs
2 cups sugar
½ teaspoon salt
1 cup all-purpose flour
1 cup butter, melted and cooled
4 teaspoons vanilla extract
2⅔ cups (16 ounces) semisweet chocolate chips
1⅓ cups chopped pecans

1. In a small bowl, mix flour and salt; cut in butter until crumbly. Gradually add ice water, tossing with a fork until dough holds together when pressed. Shape into a disk; wrap in plastic wrap. Refrigerate 1 hour or overnight.
2. Preheat oven to 350°. On a lightly floured surface, roll dough to fit bottom of a 13x9-in. baking pan; press into pan. Refrigerate while preparing filling.
3. In a large bowl, beat eggs, sugar, and salt on high speed 2 minutes. Stir in flour, melted butter and vanilla. Fold in chocolate chips. Pour over pastry; sprinkle with pecans.
4. Cover loosely with foil. Place on a lower oven rack; bake 20 minutes. Bake, uncovered, 30 minutes longer or until top is golden brown and a knife inserted near the center comes out clean.
5. Cool in pan on a wire rack. Cut into bars. Refrigerate leftovers.

CHOCOLATE
PECAN PIE BARS

CHOCOLATE SPICE CAKE
WITH CARAMEL ICING

Chocolate Spice Cake with Caramel Icing

I found this recipe back in the late '80s and knew it was a special cake. The caramel icing can be a little tricky because you have to work quickly, but it's so worth it!

—MARIANN JAMES FERGUSON, MO

PREP: 30 MIN. • **BAKE:** 30 MIN. + COOLING • **MAKES:** 12 SERVINGS

- 3 ounces unsweetened chocolate, chopped
- ½ cup butter, softened
- 1 cup sugar
- 1 cup packed brown sugar
- 3 eggs
- 2 cups cake flour
- 3 teaspoons baking powder
- 1 teaspoon ground cinnamon
- ½ teaspoon salt
- ½ teaspoon ground allspice
- ⅛ teaspoon ground cloves
- 1⅓ cups 2% milk

ICING

- 1 cup plus 2 tablespoons packed brown sugar
- ¾ cup heavy whipping cream
- 6 tablespoons butter, cubed
- 1½ cups confectioners' sugar
- ¼ teaspoon vanilla extract
  Caramel popcorn with peanuts, optional

1. Preheat oven to 350°. Line bottoms of two well-greased 9-in. round baking pans with parchment paper; grease paper. In a microwave, melt chocolate; stir until smooth. Cool slightly.

2. In a large bowl, cream butter and sugars until light and fluffy. Add eggs, one at a time, beating well after each addition. Beat in chocolate. In another bowl,

whisk flour, baking powder, cinnamon, salt, allspice and cloves; add to creamed mixture alternately with milk, beating well after each addition.

3. Transfer batter to prepared pans. Bake 30-35 minutes or until a toothpick inserted in center comes out clean. Cool in pans 10 minutes before removing to wire racks; remove paper. Cool completely.

4. In a small saucepan, combine brown sugar, cream and butter. Bring to a boil over medium heat, stirring occasionally. Cook and stir 3 minutes. Remove from heat; gradually beat in confectioners' sugar and vanilla.

5. Place one cake layer on a serving plate; pour half of the warm icing over the cake. Top with remaining cake layer. Pour remaining icing over top of cake. If desired, top with caramel popcorn.

Lemon-Lime Bars

I baked these bars for a luncheon on a hot summer day. A gentleman made his way to the kitchen to compliment the cook who made them.

—HOLLY WILKINS LAKE ELMORE, VERMONT

PREP: 20 MIN. • **BAKE:** 20 MIN. + COOLING • **MAKES:** 4 DOZEN

- 1 cup butter, softened
- ½ cup confectioners' sugar
- 2 teaspoons grated lime peel
- 1¾ cups all-purpose flour
- ¼ teaspoon salt

FILLING

- 4 eggs
- 1½ cups sugar
- ¼ cup all-purpose flour
- ½ teaspoon baking powder
- ⅓ cup lemon juice
- 2 teaspoons grated lemon peel
  Confectioners' sugar

1. Preheat oven to 350°. In a large bowl, cream butter and confectioners' sugar until light and fluffy. Beat in lime peel. Combine flour and salt; gradually add to creamed mixture and mix well.

2. Press into a greased 13-in. x 9-in. baking dish. Bake 13-15 minutes or just until edges are lightly browned.

3. Meanwhile, in another large bowl, beat eggs and sugar. Combine flour and baking powder. Gradually add to egg mixture. Stir in lemon juice and peel; beat until frothy. Pour over hot crust.

4. Bake 20-25 minutes or until light golden brown. Cool on a wire rack. Dust with confectioners' sugar. Cut into squares. Store in the refrigerator.

RED VELVET
MARBLE CAKE

Red Velvet Marble Cake

I watched my grandma prepare this showstopper many
times for family get-togethers. The fluffy butter frosting
perfectly complements the flavor of this gorgeous cake.
—**JODI ANDERSON** OVERBROOK, KS

PREP: 20 MIN. • **BAKE:** 30 MIN. + COOLING
MAKES: 12 SERVINGS

- ¾ cup butter, softened
- 2¼ cups sugar
- 3 eggs
- 4½ teaspoons white vinegar
- 1½ teaspoons vanilla extract
- 3¾ cups cake flour
- 1½ teaspoons baking soda
- 1½ cups buttermilk
- 3 tablespoons baking cocoa
- 4½ teaspoons red food coloring

FROSTING

- 1 cup butter, softened
- 9 cups confectioners' sugar
- 3 teaspoons vanilla extract
- ⅔ to ¾ cup 2% milk

1. Preheat oven to 350°. Line bottoms of two greased
9-in. round baking pans with parchment paper; grease
paper.

2. In a large bowl, cream butter and sugar until light
and fluffy. Add eggs, one at a time, beating well after
each addition. Beat in vinegar and vanilla. In another
bowl, whisk flour and baking soda; add to creamed
mixture alternately with buttermilk, beating well
after each addition.

3. Transfer half of the batter to another bowl; stir in
cocoa and food coloring until blended. Alternately
drop plain and chocolate batters by ¼ cupfuls into
prepared pans, dividing batter evenly between pans.
To make batter level in pans, bang cake pans several
times on counter.

4. Bake 30-35 minutes or until a toothpick inserted in
center comes out clean. Cool 10 minutes before
removing from pans to wire racks to cool completely.

5. In a large bowl, beat butter, confectioners' sugar,
vanilla and enough milk to reach a spreading
consistency. Spread frosting between layers and over
top and sides of cake.

KEY LIME PIE CUPCAKES

Key Lime Pie Cupcakes

I bake over 200 of these cupcakes for our church suppers, and we always run out. If you can't find Key lime juice, use regular lime juice. Just add a tad more sugar.
—**JULIE LEMLER** ROCHESTER, MN

PREP: 45 MIN. • **BAKE:** 20 MIN. + COOLING • **MAKES:** 32 CUPCAKES

- 2 packages (14.1 ounces each) refrigerated pie pastry
- 1 cup butter, softened
- 2½ cups sugar
- 4 eggs
- ½ cup Key lime juice
- 2 cups all-purpose flour
- 1½ cups self-rising flour
- 1½ cups buttermilk

FROSTING
- 12 ounces cream cheese, softened
- 1½ cups butter, softened
- 1½ teaspoons vanilla extract
- 2¾ to 3 cups confectioners' sugar
- 6 tablespoons Key lime juice
  Fresh raspberries

1. Preheat oven to 350°. Line 32 muffin cups with foil liners. On a lightly floured work surface, unroll pastry sheets. Cut 32 circles with a floured 2¼-in. round cookie cutter (discard remaining pastry or save for another use). Press one pastry circle into each liner. Bake 10-12 minutes or until lightly browned. Cool on a wire rack.
2. In a large bowl, beat butter and sugar until crumbly. Add eggs, one at a time, beating well after each addition. Beat in lime juice. In another bowl, whisk flours; add to butter mixture alternately with buttermilk, beating well after each addition.
3. Pour batter into prepared cups. Bake 20-22 minutes or until a toothpick inserted in center comes out clean. Cool in pans 10 minutes before removing to wire racks to cool completely.
4. In a large bowl, beat cream cheese, butter and vanilla until blended. Beat in enough confectioners' sugar, alternately with lime juice, to reach desired consistency. Frost cupcakes; top with raspberries. Refrigerate leftovers.
NOTE *To substitute 1½ cups self-rising flour, increase all-purpose flour to 3 cups and add 2¼ teaspoons baking powder and ¾ teaspoon salt; whisk flour, baking powder and salt until blended before adding to butter mixture.*

Chocolate-Nut Caramel Tart

With just a few ingredients and in less time than you'd think, this sinfully rich tart is ready to go. It's a good recipe to have up your sleeve for any gathering.
—**KATHLEEN SPECHT** CLINTON, MT

PREP: 20 MIN. • **BAKE:** 15 MIN. + CHILLING • **MAKES:** 12 SERVINGS

- 1 sheet refrigerated pie pastry
- 1 jar (13 ounces) Nutella, divided
- 20 caramels
- ⅓ cup heavy whipping cream
- 1¾ cups chopped macadamia nuts, toasted
  Whipped cream, optional

1. Preheat oven to 450°. Unroll pastry into a 9-in. fluted tart pan with removable bottom. Press onto bottom and up sides of pan; trim pastry even with edge (discard or save trimmed pastry for another use). Generously prick bottom of crust with a fork. Bake 9-11 minutes or until golden brown. Cool completely on a wire rack.
2. Reserve 2 tablespoons Nutella for topping; spread remaining Nutella into cooled crust. In a small saucepan, combine caramels and cream; cook over medium-low heat until blended, stirring occasionally. Remove from heat; stir in macadamia nuts. Spread evenly over Nutella.
3. In a microwave, heat reserved Nutella until warmed; drizzle over filling. Refrigerate 1 hour or until firm. If desired, serve with whipped cream.
NOTE *To toast nuts, spread in a 15x10x1-in. baking pan. Bake at 350° for 5-10 minutes or until lightly browned, stirring occasionally. Or spread in a dry nonstick skillet and heat over low heat until lightly browned, stirring occasionally.*

FLAKY CREME-FILLED COOKIES

Flaky Creme-Filled Cookies

The light, incredibly flaky base of these delightful sandwich cookies is an easy-to-make form of French puff pastry. Mix and match the flavorings, and you'll have cookies for every taste.

—SUSAN FALK WARREN, MI

PREP: 55 MIN. + CHILLING • **BAKE:** 10 MIN./BATCH
MAKES: 6½ DOZEN

- 2 cups all-purpose flour
- ¼ teaspoon salt
- 1 cup cold butter, cubed
- 1 package (8 ounces) cream cheese, cubed
- ⅔ cup marshmallow creme
- ⅔ cup butter, softened
- 1⅓ cups confectioners' sugar
  Optional flavoring: 2 tablespoons baking cocoa, ½ teaspoon lemon extract or ½ teaspoon peppermint extract
  Optional filling: seedless raspberry preserves, blueberry preserves or crushed peppermint candies
  Confectioners' sugar

1. In a large bowl, combine flour and salt. Cut in cold butter and cream cheese until mixture resembles coarse crumbs. Shape into a disk; wrap in plastic wrap. Refrigerate 2 hours or until easy to handle.

2. Preheat oven to 350°. On a lightly floured surface, roll dough to ⅛-in. thickness. Cut out with a floured 1½-in. cookie cutter. Place 2 in. apart on parchment paper-lined baking sheets. Bake 7-10 minutes or until cookies are light golden brown. Remove to wire racks to cool completely.

3. Meanwhile, in a large bowl, beat marshmallow creme and softened butter until light and fluffy. Gradually beat in confectioners' sugar.

TO MAKE CHOCOLATE-RASPBERRY COOKIES
Beat cocoa into marshmallow creme mixture. Spread on the bottoms of half of the cookies. Spread raspberry preserves on the bottoms of remaining cookies; top with creme-topped cookies. Sprinkle with confectioners' sugar.

TO MAKE LEMON-BLUEBERRY COOKIES
Beat lemon extract into marshmallow creme mixture. Spread on the bottoms of half of the cookies. Spread blueberry preserves on the bottoms of remaining cookies; top with creme-topped cookies. Sprinkle with confectioners' sugar.

TO MAKE PEPPERMINT COOKIES
Beat peppermint extract into marshmallow creme mixture. (Tint with 1 drop red food coloring if desired.) Spread on the bottoms of half of the cookies; top with remaining cookies. Roll sides in peppermint candies if desired. Sprinkle with confectioners' sugar.

BLUEBERRY-RHUBARB CRUMBLE

Blueberry-Rhubarb Crumble

A dollop of whipped cream adds a nice finishing touch to this satisfying crumble. Sometimes I drizzle a little flavored coffee creamer on top instead of the whipped cream for a change of pace.

—**NANCY SOUSLEY** LAFAYETTE, IN

PREP: 15 MIN. • **BAKE:** 45 MIN. + COOLING • **MAKES:** 12 SERVINGS

- 6 cups fresh or frozen unsweetened blueberries
- 4 cups diced fresh or frozen rhubarb
- 1 cup sugar
- ¼ cup all-purpose flour

TOPPING

- 1 cup quick-cooking oats
- 1 cup packed brown sugar
- ½ cup all-purpose flour
- ½ teaspoon ground nutmeg
- ½ teaspoon ground cinnamon
- ½ cup cold butter
  Whipped cream, optional

1. Preheat oven to 350°. In a large bowl, combine blueberries, rhubarb, sugar and flour. Transfer to a greased 13x9-in. baking dish.
2. For topping, in a large bowl, combine oats, brown sugar, flour, nutmeg and cinnamon; cut in butter until crumbly. Sprinkle over fruit mixture.
3. Bake 45-55 minutes or until the fruit is bubbly and topping is golden brown. Let cool 10 minutes. Serve warm; dollop with whipped cream if desired.

NOTE *Cobbler may also be grilled. Place fruit mixture in a disposable foil pan; cover with foil. Grill, covered, over medium heat for 40 minutes or until bubbly. Carefully remove foil and sprinkle topping over fruit. Replace grill cover; grill 15-20 minutes longer or until topping is golden brown.*

Almond Pistachio Baklava

I discovered this traditional recipe at a Greek cultural event, and often get requests for it. The original version called for walnuts, but instead I decided to substitute almonds and pistachios.

—**JOAN LLOYD** BARRIE, ON

PREP: 1½ HOURS • **BAKE:** 35 MIN. + STANDING
MAKES: ABOUT 4 DOZEN

- 3¾ cups sugar, divided
- 2 cups water
- ¾ cup honey
- 2 tablespoons lemon juice
- 4 cups unsalted pistachios
- 3 cups unsalted unblanched almonds
- 1½ teaspoons ground cinnamon
- ½ teaspoon ground nutmeg
- 1¾ cups butter, melted
- 3 packages (16 ounces each, 14x9-inch sheet size) frozen phyllo dough, thawed

1. In a small saucepan, bring 2¾ cups sugar, water, honey and lemon juice to a boil. Reduce heat; simmer 5 minutes. Cool.
2. Preheat oven to 350°. In a food processor, combine pistachios and almonds; cover and process until finely chopped. Transfer to a large bowl. Stir in cinnamon, nutmeg and remaining sugar; set aside. Brush a 15x10x1-in. baking pan with some of the butter. Unroll one package of phyllo dough; cut stack into a 10½x9-in. rectangle. Repeat with remaining phyllo. Discard scraps.
3. Line bottom of prepared pan with two sheets of phyllo dough (sheets will overlap slightly). Brush with butter. Repeat layers 14 times. (Keep dough covered with plastic wrap and a damp towel until ready to use to prevent it from drying out.) Sprinkle with a third of the nut mixture.
4. Top with 15 layers of buttered phyllo dough and a third of the nut mixture; repeat layers. Top with remaining phyllo dough, buttering each layer.
5. Using a sharp knife, cut into 1½-in. diamond shapes. Bake 35-40 minutes or until golden brown. Place pan on a wire rack. Slowly pour cooled sugar syrup over baklava. Cover and let stand overnight.

Two-Chip Chocolate Chippers

When baking these cookies, I'm careful to use one stick of butter and one stick of margarine—the combination of fats gives them a terrific texture. And don't use a scoop, which compacts the dough too much.

—**LEE ANN MILLER** MILLERSBURG, OH

PREP: 20 MIN. • **BAKE:** 10 MIN./BATCH
MAKES: 5 DOZEN

- ½ cup butter, softened
- ½ cup stick margarine, softened
- ¾ cup packed brown sugar
- ¼ cup sugar
- 2 eggs
- 1½ teaspoons vanilla extract
- 2¼ cups all-purpose flour
- 1 package (3.4 ounces) instant vanilla pudding mix
- 1 teaspoon baking soda
- 1½ cups semisweet chocolate chips
- 1½ cups milk chocolate chips
- 1½ cups chopped pecans, optional

1. Preheat oven to 375°. In a large bowl, cream butter, margarine and sugars until light and fluffy. Beat in eggs and vanilla. Combine flour, pudding mix and baking soda; gradually add to creamed mixture and mix well. Stir in chocolate chips and pecans if desired.

2. Drop by rounded tablespoonfuls 1 in. apart onto ungreased baking sheets; flatten slightly with a glass. Bake 8-10 minutes or until lightly browned. Remove to wire racks.

Peach-Blueberry Crumble Tart

Fresh out of the oven or at room temperature with a scoop of vanilla ice cream, this easy-to-prepare tart is a family favorite in our home.

—**JAMES SCHEND**
PLEASANT PRAIRIE, WI

PREP: 30 MIN. + COOLING • **BAKE:** 35 MIN.
MAKES: 12 SERVINGS

- 1⅓ cups all-purpose flour
- ¼ cup sugar
- ¼ teaspoon ground cinnamon
- ½ cup butter, melted
- 2 cups frozen unsweetened blueberries, thawed
- 2 cups frozen unsweetened sliced peaches, thawed
- 1 tablespoon honey

CRUMB TOPPING
- ¼ cup all-purpose flour
- ¼ cup packed brown sugar
- ¼ cup old-fashioned oats
- ¼ cup chopped pecans
- ⅛ teaspoon ground cloves
- 2 tablespoons butter, melted

1. Preheat oven to 350°. In a small bowl, mix flour, sugar and cinnamon; stir in butter just until blended. Press onto the bottom and up the side of a 9-in. fluted tart pan with removable bottom. Bake 15-20 minutes or until lightly browned. Cool on a wire rack.

2. In a large bowl, combine blueberries, peaches and honey; toss to coat. In a small bowl, combine first five topping ingredients; stir in butter.

3. Spoon fruit mixture into crust; sprinkle with topping. Bake at 350° 35-40 minutes or until topping is golden brown and filling is bubbly. Cool on a wire rack at least 15 minutes before serving.

PEACH-BLUEBERRY CRUMBLE TART

Chunky Apple-Cinnamon Cake

Here's a nice change from apple pie that's tasty and worthy of a special get-together—plus, it's very easy to make. Add a scoop of ice cream if you like.

—ELLEN RUZINSKY
YORKTOWN HEIGHTS, NY

PREP: 25 MIN. • **BAKE:** 45 MIN. + COOLING
MAKES: 15 SERVINGS

- 2¾ **pounds McIntosh, Jonathan or Granny Smith apples, peeled and thinly sliced (11 cups)**
- ½ **cup packed brown sugar**
- 3 **teaspoons ground cinnamon, divided**
- 1 **cup plus 1 tablespoon sugar, divided**
- 1 **cup canola oil**
- 4 **eggs**
- 3 **tablespoons orange juice**
- 2 **teaspoons vanilla extract**
- 2½ **cups all-purpose flour**
- 2 **teaspoons baking powder**
- ½ **teaspoon kosher salt**

1. Preheat oven to 425°. In a large bowl, toss apples with brown sugar and 2 teaspoons cinnamon.

2. In a large bowl, beat 1 cup sugar, oil, eggs, orange juice and vanilla until well blended. In another bowl, whisk flour, baking powder and salt; gradually beat into sugar mixture.

3. Transfer half of the batter to an ungreased 13x9-in. baking pan. Top with apples. Spread remaining batter over apples. Mix remaining sugar and cinnamon; sprinkle over top. Bake 10 minutes.

4. Reduce oven setting to 375°. Bake 35-45 minutes or until golden brown and apples are tender. Cool on a wire rack.

Pecan Pie Thumbprints

A good buttery dough and nutty filling take time to make, but the results are so worth it. After munching on a few, I think you'll agree.

—PEGGY KEY GRANT, AL

PREP: 30 MIN. + CHILLING
BAKE: 10 MIN./BATCH
MAKES: 4½ DOZEN

- 1 **cup butter, softened**
- ½ **cup sugar**
- 2 **eggs, separated**
- ½ **cup dark corn syrup**
- 2½ **cups all-purpose flour**

FILLING

- ¼ **cup plus 2 tablespoons confectioners' sugar**
- 3 **tablespoons butter**
- 2 **tablespoons dark corn syrup**
- ¼ **cup plus 2 tablespoons finely chopped pecans**

1. In a large bowl, cream butter and sugar until light and fluffy. Beat in egg yolks and corn syrup.

Gradually beat in flour. Refrigerate, covered, 30 minutes or until firm enough to roll.

2. For filling, in a small saucepan, combine confectioners' sugar, butter and corn syrup. Bring to a boil over medium heat, stirring occasionally. Remove from heat; stir in pecans. Remove from pan; refrigerate 30 minutes or until cold.

3. Preheat oven to 375°. Shape dough into 1-in. balls; place 2 in. apart on parchment paper-lined baking sheets. In a small bowl, whisk egg whites; brush over tops.

4. Bake 5 minutes. Remove from oven. Gently press an indentation in center of each cookie with the end of a wooden spoon handle. Fill each with a scant ½ teaspoon pecan mixture. Bake 4-5 minutes longer or until edges are light brown.

5. Cool on pans 5 minutes. Remove to wire racks to cool.

Peanut Butter Cup Cookies

When I made my first batch of these tempting cookies, I got so many requests for the recipe that I knew I had a hit! My baking rewards are the smiles on the faces of my family and friends.

—**MARY HEPPERLE** TORONTO, ON

PREP: 20 MIN. + CHILLING • **BAKE:** 15 MIN./BATCH
MAKES: ABOUT 3 DOZEN

- 1 **cup butter, softened**
- ½ **cup creamy peanut butter**
- ¾ **cup packed brown sugar**
- ½ **cup sugar**
- 1 **egg**
- 1 **teaspoon vanilla extract**
- 2 **cups all-purpose flour**
- 1 **teaspoon baking soda**
- 1 **package (13 ounces) miniature peanut butter cups**

DRIZZLE

- 1 **cup (6 ounces) semisweet chocolate chips**
- 1 **tablespoon creamy peanut butter**
- 1 **teaspoon shortening**

1. Preheat oven to 350°. In a large bowl, cream butter, peanut butter and sugars until light and fluffy. Beat in egg and vanilla. Combine flour and baking soda; gradually add to creamed mixture and mix well. Cover and refrigerate 1 hour or until easy to handle.

2. Roll into 1¼-in. balls. Press a miniature peanut butter cup into each; reshape balls. Place 2 in. apart on ungreased baking sheets.

3. Bake 12-15 minutes or until edges are lightly browned. Cool 2 minutes before removing from pans to wire racks.

4. For drizzle, in a microwave, melt the chocolate chips, peanut butter and shortening; stir until smooth. Drizzle over cooled cookies.

NOTE *Reduced-fat peanut butter is not recommended for this recipe.*

Chocolate Orange Checkerboard Cookies

I use these for gifts during the holidays because I like the elegant flavor combination of chocolate and orange. The shortbread texture melts in your mouth, and the walnuts add a nice crunch.

—**SANDY PAIGE** LANDSTUHL, GERMANY

PREP: 30 MIN. + CHILLING • **BAKE:** 10 MIN./BATCH
MAKES: ABOUT 3½ DOZEN

- 1¼ **cups butter, softened**
- 1½ **cups confectioners' sugar**
- ¼ **teaspoon salt**
- 1 **egg**
- 1 **teaspoon vanilla extract**
- 3 **cups cake flour**
- 1½ **cups finely chopped pecans**
- ¼ **cup baking cocoa**
- 1 **teaspoon grated orange peel**
- ½ **teaspoon orange extract**

1. In a large bowl, cream butter, confectioners' sugar and salt until blended. Beat in egg and vanilla. Gradually beat in flour. Stir in pecans.

2. Divide dough in half. Mix baking cocoa into one half; mix orange peel and extract into remaining half.

3. Shape each portion into a 5½x2x2-in. block. Wrap each block in plastic wrap; refrigerate 30 minutes.

4. Unwrap dough; cut each block lengthwise into quarters, making four 5½x1x1-in. sticks. Switch two of the chocolate sticks with two of the orange sticks, forming two checkerboard blocks. Gently press sticks together to adhere. Rewrap in plastic wrap; refrigerate 2 hours or until firm.

5. Preheat oven to 350°. Unwrap and cut dough crosswise into ¼-in. slices. Place 1 in. apart on ungreased baking sheets. Bake 9-11 minutes or until set. Remove from pans to wire racks to cool.

CHOCOLATE ORANGE
CHECKERBOARD COOKIES

Glazed Ginger Bars

The ginger flavor in these bars is perfect for the holiday season. The light glaze adds a touch of sweetness.
—DARLENE BRENDEN SALEM, OR

PREP: 25 MIN. • **BAKE:** 20 MIN. + COOLING
MAKES: 32 BARS

- ⅔ cup butter, softened
- ¾ cup packed brown sugar
- ½ cup molasses
- 1 egg
- 2 cups all-purpose flour
- 2 teaspoons ground ginger
- ½ teaspoon baking soda
- ½ teaspoon baking powder
- ½ teaspoon ground cinnamon
- ¼ teaspoon salt
- ½ cup raisins

ORANGE GLAZE

- 1 cup confectioners' sugar
- 5 teaspoons orange juice
- 4 teaspoons butter, melted
- ¾ teaspoon vanilla extract
- ½ teaspoon grated orange peel

1. Preheat oven to 350°. In a large bowl, cream butter and brown sugar until light and fluffy. Beat in the molasses and egg. Combine flour, ginger, baking soda, baking powder, cinnamon and salt; add to creamed mixture and mix well. Stir in raisins.
2. Spread into a greased 13x9-in. baking pan. Bake 20-25 minutes or until a toothpick inserted in the center comes out clean.
3. Combine glaze ingredients until smooth; spread over warm bars. Cool completely on a wire rack before cutting into bars.

Summer Harvest Tart

One of my favorite bakeries makes a scrumptious tart that uses fall and summer fruit, so I created my own version. I like to serve it warm with whipped cream or ice cream and with a cup of coffee on a cool autumn night.
—SARAH KNOBLOCK HYDE PARK, IN

PREP: 45 MIN. • **BAKE:** 45 MIN. + COOLING
MAKES: 12 SERVINGS

- ⅔ cup butter, softened
- ¼ cup sugar
- Dash salt
- 2 tablespoons lightly beaten egg white
- ½ teaspoon vanilla extract
- 2 cups all-purpose flour

FILLING

- ⅔ cup sugar
- ⅓ cup all-purpose flour
- 1 teaspoon ground cinnamon
- ½ teaspoon ground nutmeg
- 1 cup each fresh blackberries, blueberries and raspberries
- 1 cup finely chopped peeled apple (about 1 medium)
- 1 cup sliced peaches (about 2 small)
- 2 teaspoons lemon juice

TOPPING

- ⅓ cup butter, softened
- ⅔ cup packed brown sugar
- ¾ teaspoon ground cinnamon
- ⅛ teaspoon ground nutmeg
- ⅛ teaspoon ground cloves
- ½ cup all-purpose flour
- ½ cup old-fashioned oats

1. Preheat oven to 350°. In a large bowl, cream butter, sugar and salt until light and fluffy. Beat in egg white and vanilla. Gradually beat in flour. Press onto bottom and up sides of an 11-in. fluted tart pan with removable bottom; place on a baking sheet.
2. Bake 25-30 minutes or until edges are light brown. Cool on a wire rack. Increase oven setting to 375°.
3. For filling, in a large bowl, mix sugar, flour, cinnamon and nutmeg. Add fruit and lemon juice; toss to combine.
4. For topping, in a small bowl, cream butter, brown sugar and spices until blended. Gradually beat in flour and oats.
5. Add the filling to crust; sprinkle with topping. Bake 45-50 minutes or until top is golden brown and filling is bubbly. Cool on a wire rack. Serve warm or at room temperature.

SUMMER HARVEST TART

**CHOCOLATE & PEANUT
BUTTER MOUSSE CHEESECAKE**

⅔ cup heavy whipping cream
1 teaspoon vanilla extract

1. In a small bowl, mix wafer crumbs and butter. Press onto bottom of a greased 9-in. springform pan.

2. In another bowl, beat cream until stiff peaks form. In a large bowl, beat peanut butter, cream cheese and butter until smooth. Beat in confectioners' sugar. Fold in half of the whipped cream. Spread evenly over crust. Refrigerate while preparing the next layer.

3. Place bittersweet and milk chocolates in a small bowl. In a small saucepan, combine sugar and milk; bring just to a boil, stirring constantly. Pour over chocolate; stir with a whisk until smooth. Stir in vanilla. Cool to room temperature, stirring occasionally. Fold in remaining whipped cream. Spread evenly over peanut butter layer. Freeze 2 hours or until firm.

4. For ganache, place chocolate in a small bowl. In a small saucepan, bring cream just to a boil. Pour over the chocolate; whisk until smooth. Stir in vanilla. Cool to room temperature or until the ganache thickens to a spreading consistency, stirring occasionally. Spread ganache over cheesecake. Refrigerate 1 hour or until set. Remove rim from pan.

FREEZE OPTION *Wrap individual portions of cheesecake in plastic wrap and place in a resealable plastic freezer bag. Seal bag and freeze for future use. To use, thaw completely in the refrigerator.*

FREEZE IT
Chocolate & Peanut Butter Mousse Cheesecake

It'll take a bit of time to make this no-bake cheesecake with chocolate, peanut butter mousse and a silky ganache, but it's worth it, because you won't have to heat up the kitchen.
—JANON FURRER PRESCOTT, AZ

PREP: 50 MIN. + CHILLING
MAKES: 16 SERVINGS

1½ cups chocolate wafer crumbs
   (about 24 wafers)
¼ cup butter, melted

MOUSSE LAYERS
1¼ cups heavy whipping cream
¾ cup creamy peanut butter
5 ounces cream cheese, softened
2 tablespoons butter, softened
1¼ cups confectioners' sugar
5 ounces bittersweet chocolate, chopped
1 milk chocolate candy bar (3½ ounces), chopped
⅓ cup sugar
¼ cup 2% milk
1 teaspoon vanilla extract

GANACHE
6 ounces bittersweet chocolate, chopped

Chocolate Pear Hazelnut Tart

While I was living in France as a high school foreign exchange student, my host family's grandmother taught me how to make this nutty, rustic tart. We formed a special bond, and she inspired my passion for baking.
—**LEXI MCKEOWN** LOS ANGELES, CA

PREP: 45 MIN. + CHILLING
BAKE: 30 MIN. + COOLING
MAKES: 12 SERVINGS

- 1¼ **cups all-purpose flour**
- ⅓ **cup ground hazelnuts**
- ¼ **cup packed brown sugar**
  Dash salt
- ½ **cup cold butter, cubed**
- 3 **to 5 tablespoons ice water**

FILLING

- 3 **eggs, separated**
- ⅓ **cup butter, softened**
- ⅓ **cup packed brown sugar**
- 2 **tablespoons amaretto or**
  ½ **teaspoon almond extract**
- 1 **cup ground hazelnuts**
- 2 **tablespoons baking cocoa**
- 6 **canned pear halves, drained, sliced and patted dry**
- 2 **tablespoons honey, warmed**
  Confectioners' sugar

1. In a small bowl, mix flour, hazelnuts, brown sugar and salt; cut in the butter until crumbly. Gradually add ice water, tossing with a fork until dough holds together when pressed. Shape into a disk; wrap dough in plastic wrap. Refrigerate for 30 minutes or overnight.

2. Place egg whites in a large bowl; let stand at room temperature for 30 minutes. Preheat oven to 400°. On a lightly floured surface, roll dough to a ⅛-in.-thick circle; transfer to a 9-in. fluted tart pan with removable bottom. Trim the pastry even with edge. Prick the bottom of the pastry with a fork. Refrigerate pastry while preparing filling.

3. In a large bowl, cream butter and brown sugar until blended. Beat in egg yolks and amaretto. Beat in hazelnuts and cocoa.

4. With clean beaters, beat egg whites on medium speed until stiff peaks form. Fold a third of the egg whites into hazelnut mixture, then fold in remaining whites. Spread onto bottom of pastry shell. Arrange pears over top.

5. Bake on a lower oven rack 30-35 minutes or until crust is golden brown. Brush pears with warm honey. Cool on a wire rack.

CHOCOLATE PEAR HAZELNUT TART

TOP TIP

Tart Pastry

A floured surface is essential to prevent sticking when rolling out tart or pie pastry. A pastry cloth and rolling pin cover are good investments—they will keep the pastry from sticking and minimize the amount of flour used. The less flour you add while rolling, the flakier and lighter the pastry will be.

Peppermint Patty Sandwich Cookies

These cookies are a hit with kids and adults at my annual holiday party. For extra flair, mix food coloring or crushed candy canes into the filling.

—AMY MARTIN VANCOUVER, WA

PREP: 30 MIN.
BAKE: 10 MIN./BATCH + COOLING
MAKES: 3 DOZEN

- 2 **packages devil's food cake mix (regular size)**
- 4 **eggs**
- ⅔ **cup canola oil**
  Granulated sugar
- 1 **package (8 ounces) cream cheese, softened**
- ½ **cup butter, softened**
- 1 **teaspoon peppermint extract**
- 4 **cups confectioners' sugar**

1. Preheat oven to 350°. In a large bowl, combine cake mixes, eggs and oil; beat until well blended. Shape into 1-in. balls; place 2 in. apart on greased baking sheets. Flatten with bottom of a glass dipped in granulated sugar.

2. Bake 7-9 minutes or until tops are cracked. Cool 2 minutes before removing to wire racks to cool completely.

3. In a large bowl, beat cream cheese, butter and extract until blended. Gradually beat in confectioners' sugar until smooth.

4. Spread filling on bottoms of half of the cookies; cover with remaining cookies. Refrigerate leftovers in an airtight container.

Fudge Nut Brownies

There's no brownie recipe or mix I've ever tried that's better than this! It's so easy besides—you can mix it in one bowl in just a few minutes. My husband's grandmother passed the recipe on; now our son makes these brownies for after-school snacks.

—BECKY ALBRIGHT NORWALK, OH

PREP: 15 MIN. • **BAKE:** 25 MIN.
MAKES: ABOUT 24 BROWNIES

- 1⅓ **cups all-purpose flour**
- 2 **cups sugar**
- ¾ **cup baking cocoa**
- 1 **teaspoon baking powder**
- ½ **teaspoon salt**
- ½ **cup chopped nuts**
- ⅔ **cup vegetable oil**
- 4 **eggs, lightly beaten**
- 2 **teaspoons vanilla extract**
- 1 **cup chopped nuts, optional**

1. Preheat oven to 350°. In a bowl, combine the first six ingredients. In another bowl, combine oil, eggs and vanilla; add to dry ingredients. Do not overmix.

2. Spread in a 13x9-in. baking pan. Sprinkle with nuts if desired. Bake 20-25 minutes or until toothpick inserted in center comes out clean. Cool in pan on a wire rack.

PEPPERMINT PATTY SANDWICH COOKIES

ORANGE DREAM
MINI CUPCAKES

Orange Dream Mini Cupcakes

The bright taste of these cute cupcakes reminds me and
my friends of orange-and-vanilla frozen treats.
—**JEN SHEPHERD** ST. PETERS, MO

PREP: 1 HOUR • **BAKE:** 15 MIN. + COOLING • **MAKES:** 4 DOZEN

- ½ cup butter, softened
- 1 cup sugar
- 2 eggs
- 1 tablespoon grated orange peel
- 1 tablespoon orange juice
- ½ teaspoon vanilla extract
- 1½ cups all-purpose flour
- 1½ teaspoons baking powder
- ¼ teaspoon salt
- ½ cup buttermilk

BUTTERCREAM
- ½ cup butter, softened
- ¼ teaspoon salt
- 2 cups confectioners' sugar
- 2 tablespoons 2% milk
- 1½ teaspoons vanilla extract
- ½ cup orange marmalade

1. Preheat oven to 325°. Line 48 mini-muffin cups
with paper liners. In a large bowl, cream butter and
sugar until light and fluffy. Add eggs, one at a time,
beating well after each addition. Beat in orange peel,
orange juice and vanilla. In another bowl, whisk flour,
baking powder and salt; add to creamed mixture
alternately with buttermilk, beating well after each
addition.

2. Fill prepared cups two-thirds full. Bake 11-13
minutes or until a toothpick inserted in center comes
out clean. Cool in pans 5 minutes before removing to
wire racks to cool completely.

3. For buttercream, in a large bowl, beat butter and
salt until creamy. Gradually beat in confectioners'
sugar, milk and vanilla until smooth.

4. Using a paring knife, cut a 1-in.-wide cone-shaped
piece from top of each cupcake; discard removed
portion. Fill cavity with marmalade. Pipe or spread
buttercream over tops.

**RASPBERRY & CHOCOLATE
SHORTBREAD BARS**

Raspberry & Chocolate Shortbread Bars

A very long time ago, when I was a child, I decided that chocolate and raspberries was a combination made in heaven, and that any treat made with these two delicious ingredients would be at the top of my holiday list. Any seedless jam or preserves may be used, but raspberry is our favorite.

—**LILY JULOW** LAWRENCEVILLE, GA

PREP: 25 MIN. • **BAKE:** 30 MIN. + COOLING
MAKES: 2 DOZEN

- 1 **cup unsalted butter, softened**
- 1 **cup sugar**
- 2 **egg yolks**
- ½ **teaspoon vanilla extract**
- 2 **cups all-purpose flour**
- 1 **teaspoon baking powder**
- ¼ **teaspoon salt**
- 1 **jar (10 ounces) seedless raspberry spreadable fruit**
- 4 **ounces bittersweet chocolate, finely chopped**
- ⅓ **cup heavy whipping cream**

1. Preheat oven to 350°. In a large bowl, cream butter and sugar until light and fluffy. Beat in egg yolks and vanilla. In a small bowl, mix flour, baking powder and salt; gradually add to creamed mixture, mixing well.

2. Press half of the dough onto bottom of a greased 11x7-in. baking dish. Top with spreadable fruit. Crumble remaining dough over fruit. Bake on lowest oven rack 30-40 minutes or until golden brown. Cool completely on a wire rack.

3. Place chocolate in a small bowl. In a small saucepan, bring cream just to a boil. Pour over chocolate; stir with a whisk until smooth. Drizzle over top; let stand until set. Cut into bars.

Vanilla Bean Cake with White Chocolate Ganache

When you make this dessert, you'll have a standout! Feel free to substitute your favorite jam to make it your own.
—**LISA BOGAR** COVENTRY, VERMONT

PREP: 1½ HOURS • **BAKE:** 35 MIN. + COOLING • **MAKES:** 16 SERVINGS

- 6 **eggs**
- 1 **cup unsalted butter, softened**
- 1¾ **cups sugar, divided**
- 2 **teaspoons vanilla extract**
- 1 **vanilla bean**
- 3 **cups cake flour**
- 3 **teaspoons baking powder**
- ½ **teaspoon salt**
- 1 **cup whole milk**

WHITE CHOCOLATE GANACHE

- 12 **ounces white baking chocolate, finely chopped**
- ½ **cup heavy whipping cream**

SWISS BUTTERCREAM

- 1 **cup sugar**
- ½ **teaspoon cream of tartar**
- 4 **egg whites**
- 1 **cup unsalted butter, softened**
- 7 **tablespoons shortening**
- 1 **teaspoon vanilla extract**

FILLING

- ⅓ **cup apricot preserves**
- 1 **cup sliced fresh strawberries**

GARNISH

   Additional sliced fresh strawberries

VANILLA BEAN CAKE WITH WHITE CHOCOLATE GANACH

1. Separate eggs; let eggs stand at room temperature for 30 minutes. Line two greased 9-in. round baking pans with parchment paper. Grease paper; set aside.

2. Preheat oven to 350°. In a large bowl, cream butter and 1 cup sugar until light and fluffy. Add egg yolks, one at a time, beating well after each addition. Beat in vanilla. Split vanilla bean and scrape seeds into creamed mixture; discard bean. Combine flour, baking powder and salt; add to the creamed mixture alternately with milk, beating well after each addition.

3. In a small bowl with clean beaters, beat egg whites on medium speed until soft peaks form. Gradually add remaining sugar, about 2 tablespoons at a time, beating on high until stiff peaks form. Fold a fourth of egg whites into the batter, then fold in remaining whites. Transfer to prepared baking pans.

4. Bake 35-40 minutes or until a toothpick inserted near the center comes out clean. Cool 10 minutes before removing from pans to wire racks to cool completely.

5. Place chocolate in a small bowl. In a small saucepan, bring cream just to a boil. Pour over chocolate; whisk until smooth. Cool, stirring occasionally, to room temperature, about 30 minutes. Beat with an electric mixer until ganache is double in volume, about 2 minutes.

6. For buttercream, in a small bowl, combine sugar and cream of tartar. Place egg whites in a double boiler or metal bowl over simmering water; stir in the sugar mixture.

7. Constantly whisk egg mixture until mixture reaches 120-130°. (Do not overheat.) Stirring gently, keep the egg white mixture at 120-130° for 2 minutes. Immediately transfer to a mixing bowl. With a whisk attachment, beat egg white mixture on high speed for 5 minutes. Reduce speed; beat 5 minutes longer or until cool and stiff. Transfer to a large bowl.

8. In the same mixing bowl with whisk attachment, beat butter, shortening and vanilla until light and fluffy. With a spatula, stir a fourth of the egg white mixture into creamed mixture until no white streaks remain. Fold in remaining egg white mixture until combined. If frosting is not completely smooth, attach paddle beater to mixer and beat on low speed for about 1 minute.

9. Cut each cake horizontally into two layers. Place bottom layer on a serving plate; spread with half of ganache. Top with another cake layer. Spread with apricot preserves; top with sliced strawberries. Place third cake layer on top; spread with remaining ganache. Top with remaining cake layer. Spread buttercream over top and sides of cake. Top with additional sliced strawberries.

RASPBERRY ALMONETTES

Raspberry Almonettes

I develop and prepare all my original recipes. Sometimes that "missing ingredient" comes to me in my sleep, and I have to get up and jot it down. These almonettes with their surprising filling—one of my creations—are fun to bake and even more fun to eat!

—ANGELA SHERIDAN OPDYKE, IL

PREP: 55 MIN. • **BAKE:** 10 MIN./BATCH + COOLING
MAKES: ABOUT 3½ DOZEN

- 1 **cup butter, softened**
- 2 **cups sugar**
- 2 **eggs**
- 1 **cup canola oil**
- 2 **tablespoons almond extract**
- 4½ **cups all-purpose flour**
- 1 **teaspoon salt**
- 1 **teaspoon baking powder**
- ¾ **cup sliced almonds, finely chopped**

FILLING

- 1 **package (8 ounces) cream cheese, softened**
- ½ **cup confectioners' sugar**
- 1 **tablespoon almond extract**
- ¼ **cup red raspberry preserves**

1. Preheat oven to 350°. In a large bowl, cream butter and sugar until light and fluffy. Add eggs, one at a time, beating well after each addition. Gradually beat in oil and extract. In another bowl, whisk flour, salt and baking powder; gradually beat into creamed mixture.

2. Shape dough into 1-in. balls; press one side into almonds. Place 2 in. apart on ungreased baking sheets, almond side up. Flatten to ¼-in. thickness with bottom of a glass.

3. Bake 8-10 minutes or until edges are light brown. Cool on pans 5 minutes; remove to wire racks to cool completely.

4. For filling, in a small bowl, beat cream cheese, confectioners' sugar and extract until smooth. Place rounded teaspoonfuls of filling on bottoms of half of the cookies. Make an indentation in center of each; fill with ¼ teaspoon preserves. Cover with remaining cookies. Store in an airtight container in the refrigerator.

Chewy Chocolate-Cherry Bars

Colorful dried cranberries and pistachios liven up this new take on seven-layer bars. To switch it up even more, try cinnamon or chocolate graham cracker crumbs instead of plain and substitute pecans or walnuts for the pistachios.
—**TASTE OF HOME TEST KITCHEN**

PREP: 10 MIN. • **BAKE:** 25 MIN. + COOLING
MAKES: 3 DOZEN

- 1½ cups graham cracker crumbs
- ½ cup butter, melted
- 1½ cups semisweet chocolate chips
- 1½ cups dried cherries
- 1 can (14 ounces) sweetened condensed milk
- 1 cup flaked coconut
- 1 cup pistachios, chopped

1. Preheat oven to 350°. In a small bowl, mix cracker crumbs and butter. Press into a greased 13x9-in. baking pan. In a large bowl, mix remaining ingredients until blended; carefully spread over crust.
2. Bake 25-28 minutes or until edges are golden brown. Cool in pan on a wire rack. Cut into bars.

Peaches 'n' Cream Bars

For a new spin on peach pie, try these easy-to-love bars. The mellow fruit flavor really comes through.
—**HUBERT SCOTT** COCKEYSVILLE, MD

PREP: 20 MIN.
BAKE: 25 MIN. + COOLING
MAKES: 2 DOZEN

- 1 tube (8 ounces) refrigerated seamless crescent dough sheet
- 1 package (8 ounces) cream cheese, softened
- ½ cup sugar
- ¼ teaspoon almond extract
- 1 can (21 ounces) peach pie filling
- ½ cup all-purpose flour
- ¼ cup packed brown sugar
- 3 tablespoons cold butter
- ½ cup sliced almonds

1. Preheat oven to 375°. Unroll crescent dough sheet into a rectangle. Press onto bottom and slightly up sides of a greased 13x9-in. baking pan. Bake 5 minutes. Cool completely on a wire rack.
2. In a large bowl, beat cream cheese, sugar and extract until smooth. Spread over crust. Spoon pie filling over cream cheese layer.
3. In a small bowl, whisk flour and brown sugar. Cut in butter until mixture resembles coarse crumbs. Stir in almonds; sprinkle over peach filling.
4. Bake 25-28 minutes or until edges are golden brown. Cool in pan on a wire rack. Cut into bars. Store in an airtight container in the refrigerator.

PEACHES 'N' CREAM BARS

CONFETTI CAKE WITH BROWN SUGAR BUTTERCREAM

Confetti Cake with Brown Sugar Buttercream

This moist, simple and appealing cake has been celebrated in my family for years. Dressed up with tinted frosting and confetti, it becomes pure party fun.
—**KAREN BERNER** MILWAUKEE, WI

PREP: 40 MIN.
BAKE: 20 MIN. + COOLING
MAKES: 16 SERVINGS

- 2¼ cups cake flour
- 1½ cups sugar
- 3½ teaspoons baking powder
- ½ teaspoon salt
- ½ cup unsalted butter, softened
- 4 egg whites
- ¾ cup whole milk
- 1 teaspoon clear vanilla extract
- ½ teaspoon almond extract
- ⅓ cup rainbow jimmies

BUTTERCREAM
- 4 egg whites
- 1 cup packed light brown sugar
- ¼ teaspoon salt
- 1½ cups unsalted butter, softened
- 1½ teaspoons clear vanilla extract

- ½ to ¾ teaspoon yellow food coloring
  Confetti sprinkles

1. Preheat oven to 350°. Line bottoms of two greased 9-in. round baking pans with parchment paper; grease paper.
2. In a large bowl, whisk flour, sugar, baking powder and salt. Beat in butter. Add egg whites, one at a time, beating well after each addition. Gradually beat in milk and extracts. Gently fold in jimmies.
3. Transfer batter to prepared pans. Bake 20-25 minutes or until a toothpick inserted in center comes out clean. Cool in pans 10 minutes before removing to wire racks; remove paper. Cool completely.
4. For buttercream, in a heatproof bowl of a stand mixer, whisk egg whites, brown sugar and salt until blended. Place over simmering water in a large saucepan over medium heat. Whisking constantly, heat mixture until a thermometer reads 160°, about 2-3 minutes.

5. Remove from heat. With whisk attachment of stand mixer, beat on high speed until stiff glossy peaks form, about 7 minutes.
6. Gradually beat in butter, a few tablespoons at a time, on medium speed until smooth. Beat in vanilla and enough food coloring to achieve desired color.
7. Immediately spread frosting between layers and over top and sides of cake. Decorate with sprinkles. Store in refrigerator.

Caramel Apple Crisp

When my children and I make this scrumptious layered dessert at home, we use a variety of apples to give it a nice combination of flavors.
—**MICHELLE BROOKS** CLARKSTON, MI

PREP: 20 MIN. • **BAKE:** 45 MIN.
MAKES: 12-14 SERVINGS

- 3 cups old-fashioned oats
- 2 cups all-purpose flour
- 1½ cups packed brown sugar
- 1 teaspoon ground cinnamon
- 1 cup cold butter, cubed
- 8 cups thinly sliced peeled tart apples
- 1 package (14 ounces) caramels, halved
- 1 cup apple cider, divided

1. Preheat oven to 350°. In a large bowl, combine oats, flour, brown sugar and cinnamon; cut in butter until crumbly. Press half the mixture into a greased 13x9-in. baking dish. Layer with half the apples, half the caramels and 1 cup oat mixture. Repeat layers. Pour ½ cup cider over top.
2. Bake, uncovered, 30 minutes. Drizzle with remaining cider; bake 15-20 minutes longer or until apples are tender.

Chocolate Truffle Cake

Chocolate lovers rejoice! With a ganache glaze and a fabulous bittersweet filling, this indulgence is worth it.

—JOANN KOERKENMEIER DAMIANSVILLE, IL

PREP: 35 MIN. + CHILLING • **BAKE:** 25 MIN. + COOLING
MAKES: 16 SERVINGS

- 2½ cups 2% milk
- 1 cup butter, cubed
- 8 ounces semisweet chocolate, chopped
- 3 eggs
- 2 teaspoons vanilla extract
- 2⅔ cups all-purpose flour
- 2 cups sugar
- 1 teaspoon baking soda
- ½ teaspoon salt

FILLING

- 6 tablespoons butter, cubed
- 4 ounces bittersweet chocolate, chopped
- 2½ cups confectioners' sugar
- ½ cup heavy whipping cream

GANACHE

- 10 ounces semisweet chocolate, chopped
- ⅔ cup heavy whipping cream

1. In a large saucepan, cook the milk, butter and chocolate over low heat until melted. Remove from the heat; let stand for 10 minutes. Preheat oven to 325°. In a large bowl, beat eggs and vanilla; stir in chocolate mixture until smooth. Combine the flour, sugar, baking soda and salt; gradually add to chocolate mixture and mix well (batter will be thin).

2. Transfer to three greased and floured 9-in. round baking pans. Bake 25-30 minutes or until a toothpick inserted in center comes out clean. Cool 10 minutes before removing from pans to wire racks to cool completely.

3. In a small saucepan, melt butter and chocolate. Stir in confectioners' sugar and cream until smooth.

4. For ganache, place chocolate in a small bowl. In a small saucepan, bring cream just to a boil. Pour over chocolate; whisk until smooth. Cool, stirring occasionally, until ganache reaches a spreading consistency.

5. Place one cake layer on a serving plate; spread with half of the filling. Repeat layers. Top with remaining cake layer. Spread ganache over top and sides of cake. Store in the refrigerator.

Blueberry-Apple Cobbler with Almond Topping

Combine the buttery richness of a cobbler with the crunch of a crumble for a wonderful dessert or brunch dish.

—CATHY RAU NEWPORT, OR

PREP: 25 MIN. • **BAKE:** 30 MIN. + COOLING • **MAKES:** 12 SERVINGS

- ⅔ cup sugar
- 3 tablespoons cornstarch
- ½ teaspoon ground cinnamon
- ⅛ teaspoon ground nutmeg
- 5 cups fresh or frozen unsweetened blueberries
- 1¼ cups shredded peeled apples (about 2 medium)
- 2 tablespoons lemon juice

BISCUIT TOPPING

- 1¾ cups all-purpose flour
- ¼ cup sugar
- 3 teaspoons baking powder
- ½ teaspoon salt
- ½ cup cold butter, cubed
- ½ cup half-and-half cream
- ½ cup plain yogurt
- 1 teaspoon vanilla extract

ALMOND CRUMBLE

- ½ cup sliced almonds, coarsely chopped
- ⅓ cup all-purpose flour
- ⅓ cup packed brown sugar
- 2 tablespoons cold butter

1. Preheat oven to 375°. In a large bowl, combine sugar, cornstarch, cinnamon and nutmeg. Add blueberries, apples and lemon juice; toss to coat. Transfer to a greased 13x9-in. baking dish.

2. For biscuit topping, in a small bowl, mix flour, sugar, baking powder and salt. Cut in butter until crumbly. Whisk cream, yogurt and vanilla; stir into flour mixture just until moistened. Drop by spoonfuls over fruit.

3. For almond crumble, in another bowl, combine almonds, flour and brown sugar. Cut in butter until crumbly. Sprinkle over top.

4. Bake 30-40 minutes or until filling is bubbly and topping is golden brown. Cool on a wire rack 30 minutes before serving.

CHOCOLATE TRUFFLE CAKE

RASPBERRY & WHITE CHOCOLATE CHEESECAKE

Raspberry & White Chocolate Cheesecake

My mom makes this cheesecake a lot because it's so good and really pretty. She calls it a "go-to recipe." Someday I'll try to make it myself.

—**PEGGY ROOS** MINNEAPOLIS, MN

PREP: 40 MIN. • **BAKE:** 1¾ HOURS + CHILLING
MAKES: 16 SERVINGS

- 1 package (10 ounces) frozen sweetened raspberries, thawed
- 1 tablespoon cornstarch

CRUST
- 1 cup all-purpose flour
- 2 tablespoons sugar
- ½ cup cold butter

FILLING
- 4 packages (8 ounces each) cream cheese, softened
- 1½ cups sugar
- 1¼ cups heavy whipping cream
- 2 teaspoons vanilla extract
- 2 eggs, lightly beaten
- 12 ounces white baking chocolate, melted and cooled

1. In a small saucepan, mix raspberries and cornstarch until blended. Bring to a boil; cook and stir 1-2 minutes or until thickened. Press through a fine-mesh strainer into a bowl; discard seeds. Cool completely.

2. Preheat oven to 350°. Place a greased 9x3-in.-deep springform pan on a double thickness of heavy-duty foil (about 18 in. square). Wrap foil securely around pan.

3. For crust, in a small bowl, mix flour and sugar. Cut in butter until crumbly. Press onto bottom of prepared pan. Place pan on a baking sheet. Bake 20-25 minutes or until golden brown. Cool on a wire rack. Reduce oven setting to 325°.

4. For filling, in a large bowl, beat cream cheese and sugar until smooth. Beat in cream and vanilla. Add eggs; beat on low speed just until blended. Stir in cooled chocolate. Pour half of the mixture over crust. Spread with half of the raspberry puree. Top with remaining batter. Drop remaining puree by tablespoonfuls over top. Cut through batter with a knife to swirl.

5. Place springform pan in a larger baking pan; add 1 in. of hot water to larger pan. Bake 1¾ to 2 hours or until edge of cheesecake is set and golden. (Center of cheesecake will jiggle when moved.) Remove springform pan from water bath. Cool cheesecake on a wire rack for 10 minutes. Loosen cheesecake from pan with a knife; remove foil. Cool 1 hour longer. Refrigerate overnight. Remove rim from pan.

**LIME DIVINE
TARTS, PAGE 226**

**SWEET POTATO
BAKE, PAGE 223**

**MAKE-AHEAD TURKEY
AND GRAVY, PAGE 224**

SEASONAL
FARE

STRAWBERRY ICE CREAM CHARLOTTE, PAGE 212

“ Why is one day more important than another, when all the daylight in the year is from the sun? By the Lord's wisdom they were distinguished, and he appointed the different seasons and festivals. ”

SIRACH 33:7-8

Tuscan-Style Roasted Asparagus

Here's a wonderful dish for spring celebrations because it can be served hot or cold. Double the recipe if needed.

—**JANNINE FISK** MALDEN, MA

PREP: 20 MIN. • **BAKE:** 15 MIN. • **MAKES:** 8 SERVINGS

- 1½ pounds fresh asparagus, trimmed
- 1½ cups grape tomatoes, halved
- 3 tablespoons pine nuts
- 3 tablespoons olive oil, divided
- 2 garlic cloves, minced
- 1 teaspoon kosher salt
- ½ teaspoon pepper
- 1 tablespoon lemon juice
- ⅓ cup grated Parmesan cheese
- 1 teaspoon grated lemon peel

1. Preheat oven to 400°. Place the asparagus, tomatoes and pine nuts on a foil-lined 15x10x1-in. baking pan. Mix 2 tablespoons oil, garlic, salt and pepper; add to asparagus and toss to coat.
2. Bake 15-20 minutes or just until asparagus is tender. Drizzle with remaining oil and lemon juice; sprinkle with cheese and lemon peel. Toss to combine.

FAST FIX
Elegant Spring Salad

Dried cranberries and grapes add fruity flavor to this lovely six-ingredient salad.

—**DANELLE MONTEVAGO** HANOVER, MD

START TO FINISH: 15 MIN. • **MAKES:** 12 SERVINGS

- 2 packages (5 ounces each) spring mix salad greens
- 3 cups green grapes, halved
- 1½ cups dried cranberries
- 1½ cups pistachios, roasted and salted
- 1¼ cups (5 ounces) crumbled Gorgonzola cheese
- ⅔ cup reduced-fat raspberry walnut vinaigrette

In a large bowl, combine the salad greens, grapes, cranberries, pistachios and cheese. Add vinaigrette; toss to coat.

Glazed Pineapple Ham

This is the recipe I used the first time I served a ham for a special dinner. I was so happy with how crispy and succulent it turned out to be.

—**CHRISSY CLARK** BOISE, ID

PREP: 15 MIN. • **BAKE:** 2¼ HOURS + STANDING
MAKES: 20 SERVINGS

- 1 fully cooked bone-in ham (7 to 9 pounds)
  Whole cloves
  GLAZE/SAUCE
- 2 tablespoons cornstarch
- ¼ cup cold water
- 2½ cups packed dark brown sugar, divided
- 1 can (20 ounces) unsweetened crushed pineapple, undrained
- ¼ cup lemon juice
- 2 tablespoons Dijon mustard
- ¼ teaspoon salt
- 1 cup packed light brown sugar

1. Preheat oven to 325°. Place ham on a rack in a shallow roasting pan. Using a sharp knife, score surface of ham with ¼-in.-deep cuts in a diamond pattern; insert a clove in each diamond. Cover and bake 2 to 2½ hours or until a thermometer reaches 130°.
2. Meanwhile, in a large saucepan, dissolve cornstarch in water; stir in 2 cups dark brown sugar, pineapple, lemon juice, mustard and salt. Bring to a boil; cook and stir 1-2 minutes or until slightly thickened. Reserve 2 cups for sauce; keep warm.
3. Remove ham from oven. Increase oven setting to 425°. Pour remaining pineapple mixture over ham. In a small bowl, mix light brown sugar and remaining dark brown sugar; spread over ham.
4. Bake ham, uncovered, 10-15 minutes longer or until a thermometer reads 140°. Serve with reserved sauce.

GLAZED PINEAPPLE HAM

Bunny Carrot Cakes & Cookies

These incredibly cute spring treats start with a cake mix that's doctored up with shredded carrots and cinnamon.
—TASTE OF HOME TEST KITCHEN

PREP: 45 MIN. • **BAKE:** 35 MIN. + COOLING
MAKES: 2 DOZEN CUPCAKES

- 1 tube (16½ ounces) refrigerated sugar cookie dough
- ⅔ cup all-purpose flour
- 3¾ to 4 cups confectioners' sugar
- 3 tablespoons meringue powder
- 5 to 6 tablespoons warm water
  Red, yellow and green paste food coloring
  Green colored sugar
- 1 package spice cake mix (regular size)
- 1½ cups shredded carrots
- 1 teaspoon ground cinnamon
- 12 ounces white baking chocolate, chopped
- 18 ounces cream cheese, softened
- 3 tablespoons butter, softened
- 4½ teaspoons lemon juice
  Brown and pink candy-coated sunflower kernels
- 1 tablespoon chocolate frosting

BUNNY CARROT CAKES & COOKIES

1. Preheat oven to 375°. In a large bowl, beat cookie dough and flour until combined. On a lightly floured surface, roll out dough to ¼-in. thickness. Cut out bunny ears with floured 3-in. cookie cutters. Reroll remaining dough; cut out 1½-in. carrots. Place 1 in. apart on ungreased baking sheets.

2. Bake 6-8 minutes or until firm. Let stand 2 minutes before removing to wire racks to cool.

3. In a large bowl, combine confectioners' sugar, meringue powder and warm water. Beat on high speed with a portable mixer 10-12 minutes or on low speed with a stand mixer for 7-10 minutes until peaks form. Tint 1 cup icing pink, ¼ cup orange and ¼ cup green. Cover frosting with damp paper towels or plastic wrap between uses.

4. Pipe white outlines on bunny ears; thin remaining white icing slightly with water. Fill ears with thinned icing; let stand 30 minutes. Pipe orange outlines on carrots; fill in centers. Let stand 30 minutes.

5. Pipe greens carrot tops, sprinkle with colored sugar. Pipe 3 orange lines on each carrot. Using pink icing, pipe inside of bunny ears. Let dry at room temperature for several hours or until firm.

6. Preheat oven to 350°. Prepare cake batter according to package directions. Fold in carrots and cinnamon.

7. Fill paper-lined muffin cups half full. Bake 18-23 minutes or until a toothpick inserted in the center comes out clean. Remove from pans to wire racks to cool completely.

8. In a microwave, melt baking chocolate; stir until smooth. Cool to room temperature.

9. In a large bowl, beat cream cheese and butter until light and fluffy. Beat in cooled baking chocolate and lemon juice until smooth.

10. Generously frost each cupcake with about ¼ cup cream cheese icing. Just before serving, add bunny ears, candy-coated sunflower kernels for eyes and nose. Pipe a smile with chocolate frosting.

NOTE *For a festive presentation, bake cupcakes using regular cupcake liners, then wrap the cooled cupcakes in a pretty paper liner. For bunny tails, attach ½-in. craft pompoms with a glue dot. You can also wrap the cupcake base in "edible grass," usually available in the grocery candy aisle at Easter time.*

**ROSEMARY
ROASTED LAMB**

Rosemary Roasted Lamb

Who knew so few ingredients could result in such an elegant and savory entree? One bite will make this no-fuss main dish memorable.

—**MATTHEW LAWRENCE** VASHON, WA

PREP: 10 MIN. + CHILLING • **BAKE:** 2 HOURS 5 MIN.
MAKES: 10 SERVINGS

- ½ cup olive oil
- 3 garlic cloves, minced
- 1 tablespoon kosher salt
- 1 tablespoon minced fresh rosemary
- 1 leg of lamb (7 to 9 pounds)

1. Preheat oven to 425°. In a small bowl, combine the oil, garlic, salt and rosemary; rub over lamb. Cover and refrigerate overnight. Place lamb, fat side up, on a rack in a shallow roasting pan.

2. Bake, uncovered, 20 minutes. Reduce heat to 350°; bake 1¾ to 2¼ hours longer or until meat reaches desired doneness (for medium-rare, a thermometer should read 145°; medium, 160°; well-done, 170°), basting occasionally with pan juices. Let stand 15 minutes before slicing.

TOP TIP

Church-Supper Servings

If you know you'll be preparing large cuts of meat for a church social, potluck or other fundraiser, watch for sales at grocery stores and stock up in advance. Freeze the meat until needed. Prepare the entree a day before the event, slicing it early on so it can be served easily at the function.

Red, White and Blue Cheesecake

I made this creamy cheesecake for a patriotic get-together with friends. Everyone raved about it, especially my friend's 9-year-old grandson. It looks so pretty and tastes delicious, and it really feeds a crowd!

—**CONNIE LAFOND** TROY, NY

PREP: 40 MIN. • **BAKE:** 1¼ HOURS + CHILLING
MAKES: 16 SERVINGS

- 1½ **cups all-purpose flour**
- ⅓ **cup sugar**
- 1 **teaspoon grated lemon peel**
- ¾ **cup cold butter, cubed**
- 2 **egg yolks**
- ½ **teaspoon vanilla extract**

FILLING

- 5 **packages (8 ounces each) cream cheese, softened**
- 1 **cup sugar**
- ¼ **cup half-and-half cream**
- 3 **tablespoons all-purpose flour**
- ½ **teaspoon grated lemon peel**
- ¼ **teaspoon salt**
- ¼ **teaspoon vanilla extract**
- 2 **eggs, lightly beaten**
- 1 **egg yolk**
- 1 **cup crushed strawberries**
- 1 **cup crushed blueberries**
  Fresh mixed berries, optional

1. Preheat oven to 400°. In a large bowl, combine flour, sugar and lemon peel. Cut in butter until crumbly. Whisk egg yolks and vanilla; add to flour mixture, tossing with a fork until dough forms a ball.

2. Press onto bottom and 3 in. up sides of a greased 9-in. springform pan. Place pan on a baking sheet. Bake 12-15 minutes or until golden brown. Cool on a wire rack.

3. For filling, in a large bowl, beat cream cheese and sugar until smooth. Beat in cream, flour, lemon peel, salt and vanilla. Add eggs and yolk; beat on low speed just until combined.

4. Divide batter in half. Fold crushed strawberries and crushed blueberries into half of the batter. Pour into crust. Top with remaining batter. Return pan to baking sheet.

5. Bake at 400° for 10 minutes. Reduce heat to 300° bake 60-70 minutes longer or until center is almost set. Cool on a wire rack 10 minutes. Carefully run a knife around edge of pan to loosen; cool 1 hour. Refrigerate overnight. Remove sides of pan.

6. Garnish with fresh mixed berries and currants, if desired.

Chicken & Summer Sausage Hobo Packets

Here's a tasty meal-in-one. Grill up several of the packets when you're hosting block parties or family reunions.

—**TONIA ANNE CARRIER** ELIZABETHTON, TN

PREP: 25 MIN. • **GRILL:** 20 MIN. • **MAKES:** 8 SERVINGS

- 1 **pound summer sausage, cut into 1-inch pieces**
- 4 **medium potatoes, peeled and cut into ½-inch cubes**
- 3 **cups shredded cabbage**
- 1 **large sweet onion, halved and sliced**
- 1 **medium green pepper, cut into strips**
- 1 **medium sweet red pepper, cut into strips**
- 1 **small zucchini, sliced**
- 1 **small yellow summer squash, sliced**
- 1 **pound chicken tenderloins, cut into 1-inch pieces**
- 2 **medium tomatoes, cut into wedges**
- ½ **cup butter, cut into eight cubes**
- ¼ **cup prepared Italian salad dressing**

1. In a bowl, combine the first eight ingredients. Gently stir in the chicken and tomatoes. Divide mixture among eight double thicknesses of heavy-duty foil (about 12 in. square). Top each with a butter cube.

2. Fold foil around mixture and seal tightly. Grill, covered, over medium heat for 20-25 minutes or until chicken is no longer pink and vegetables are tender. Carefully open foil to allow steam to escape; drizzle with dressing.

CHICKEN & SUMMER SAUSAGE
HOBO PACKETS

Flag Cake

Get ready to hear oohs and aahs! This stars-and-stripes cake is sure to light up the Fourth of July. Make it ahead to save some time.

—TASTE OF HOME TEST KITCHEN

PREP: 1½ HOURS + CHILLING
BAKE: 35 MIN. + COOLING
MAKES: 15 SERVINGS

- 1 **package French vanilla cake mix (regular size)**
- 1 **cup buttermilk**
- ⅓ **cup canola oil**
- 4 **eggs**

FILLING

- 1 **package (3 ounces) berry blue gelatin**
- 1½ **cups boiling water, divided**
- 1 **cup cold water, divided**
  Ice cubes
- 1 **package (3 ounces) strawberry gelatin**
- ⅔ **cup finely chopped fresh strawberries**
- ¼ **cup fresh blueberries**

FROSTING

- ¾ **cup butter, softened**
- 2 **cups confectioners' sugar**
- 1 **tablespoon 2% milk**
- 1 **jar (7 ounces) marshmallow creme**

1. Preheat oven to 350°. Line a 13x9-in. baking pan with waxed paper and grease the paper; set aside. In a large bowl, combine first four ingredients; beat on low speed 30 seconds. Beat on medium 2 minutes. Pour into prepared pan.

2. Bake 35-40 minutes or until a toothpick inserted in the center comes out clean. Cool 10 minutes before removing from pan to a wire rack to cool completely.

3. Transfer cake to a covered cake board. Using a small knife, cut out a 5x4-in. rectangle (½ in. deep) in the top left corner of cake, leaving a ½-in. border along edges of cake. For red stripes, cut out ½-in. wide rows (½ in. deep), leaving a ½-in. border. Using a fork, carefully remove cut-out cake pieces.

4. In a small bowl, dissolve berry blue gelatin in ¾ cup boiling water. Pour ½ cup cold water into a 2-cup measuring cup; add enough ice cubes to measure 1¼ cups. Stir into gelatin until slightly thickened. Scoop out and discard any remaining ice cubes. Repeat, making the strawberry gelatin.

5. In a small bowl, combine strawberries and 1 cup of the strawberry gelatin. In another bowl, combine blueberries and 1 cup blue gelatin. Refrigerate 20 minutes or just until soft-set. (Save remaining gelatin for another use.)

6. Stir gelatin mixtures. Slowly pour blueberry mixture into rectangle; spoon strawberry mixture into stripes.

7. In a large bowl, beat butter until fluffy; beat in the confectioners' sugar and milk until smooth. Add marshmallow creme; beat well until light and fluffy. Spread 1 cup over sides and top edge of cake. Refrigerate remaining frosting 20 minutes.

8. Cut a small hole in the corner of pastry or plastic bag; insert a large star tip. Fill the bag with remaining frosting. Pipe frosting in between rows of strawberry gelatin and around edges of cake.

TOP TIP

Kitchen Secret Shared

When making gelatin, stir the powder and hot liquid with a slotted spoon. This keeps clumps of powder from sticking to the sides of the dish or mold.

—JEANETTE S.
ERIE, PENNSYLVANIA

FLAG CAKE

PATRIOTIC GELATIN SALAD

Corn on the Cob with Lemon-Pepper Butter

Roasting fresh-picked corn is as old as the Ozark hills where I was raised. My Grandpa Mitchell always salted and peppered his butter on the edge of his plate before spreading it on his corn, and I did the same as a kid. Today I continue the tradition by serving lemon-pepper butter with roasted corn—it's a favorite!

—ALLENE BARY-COOPER

WICHITA FALLS, TX

PREP: 10 MIN. + SOAKING • **GRILL:** 25 MIN.
MAKES: 8 SERVINGS

- 8 **medium ears sweet corn**
- 1 **cup butter, softened**
- 2 **tablespoons lemon-pepper seasoning**

1. Carefully peel back corn husks to within 1 in. of bottoms; remove silk. Rewrap corn in husks; secure with kitchen string. Place in a stockpot; cover with cold water. Soak 20 minutes; drain.

2. Meanwhile, in a small bowl, mix butter and lemon pepper. Grill corn, covered, over medium heat 20-25 minutes or until tender, turning often.

3. Cut string and peel back husks. Serve corn with butter mixture.

Patriotic Gelatin Salad

Almost as spectacular as the fireworks, this lovely salad makes quite a bang at Fourth of July celebrations. It's a cool, fruity, creamy creation that makes the perfect ending to a summer feast.

—SUE GRONHOLZ BEAVER DAM, WI

PREP: 20 MIN. + CHILLING
MAKES: 16 SERVINGS

- 2 **packages (3 ounces each) berry blue gelatin**
- 2 **packages (3 ounces each) strawberry gelatin**
- 4 **cups boiling water, divided**
- 2½ **cups cold water, divided**
- 2 **envelopes unflavored gelatin**
- 2 **cups milk**
- 1 **cup sugar**
- 2 **cups (16 ounces) sour cream**
- 2 **teaspoons vanilla extract**

1. In four separate bowls, dissolve each package of gelatin in 1 cup boiling water. Add ½ cup cold water to each and stir. Pour one bowl of blue gelatin into a 10-in. fluted tube pan coated with cooking spray; chill until almost set, about 30 minutes.

2. Set other three bowls of gelatin aside at room temperature. Soften unflavored gelatin in remaining cold water; let stand 5 minutes.

3. Heat milk in a saucepan over medium heat just below boiling. Stir in softened gelatin and sugar until sugar is dissolved. Remove from heat; stir in sour cream and vanilla until smooth. When blue gelatin in pan in almost set, carefully spoon 1½ cups sour cream mixture over it. Chill until almost set, about 30 minutes.

4. Carefully spoon one bowl of strawberry gelatin over cream layer. Chill until almost set. Carefully spoon 1½ cups cream mixture over the strawberry layer. Chill until almost set. Repeat, adding layers of blue gelatin, cream mixture and strawberry gelatin, chilling in between each. Chill several hours or overnight.

NOTE *This recipe takes time to prepare since each layer must be set before the next layer is added.*

Strawberry Ice Cream Charlotte

My family loves ice cream cake, so they were delighted when I first served them this dessert. It's light, delicious and makes any occasion seem more festive.

—SCARLETT ELROD NEWNAN, GA

PREP: 35 MIN. + FREEZING
MAKES: 12 SLICES

- 2 packages (3 ounces each) soft ladyfingers, split
- 4 cups strawberry ice cream, softened if necessary
- 1¾ cups strawberry sorbet, softened if necessary
- 2 cups fresh strawberries, hulled
- 2 tablespoons confectioners' sugar
- ¾ cup marshmallow creme
- 1 cup heavy whipping cream

1. Line the sides and bottom of an ungreased 9-in. springform pan with ladyfingers, rounded sides out; trim to fit, if necessary. (Save remaining ladyfingers for another use.)
2. Quickly spread ice cream into prepared pan; freeze, covered, 30 minutes. Spread sorbet over ice cream; freeze 30 minutes longer.
3. Meanwhile, place strawberries and confectioners' sugar in a food processor; process until pureed. Reserve ¼ cup puree for swirling. Transfer remaining puree to a large bowl; whisk in marshmallow creme.

4. In a small bowl, beat cream until soft peaks form. Fold into marshmallow mixture. Spread evenly over sorbet; drizzle with reserved puree. Cut through puree with a knife to swirl. Freeze, covered, overnight.
5. Remove from freezer; carefully loosen sides from pan with a knife. Remove rim from pan. Serve immediately.

Three-Bean Salad

Fresh herbs and cayenne pepper provide the fantastic flavor in this marinated salad featuring fresh veggies and canned beans.

—CAROL TUCKER WOOSTER, OH

PREP: 20 MIN. + CHILLING
MAKES: 8 SERVINGS

- 1 can (15½ ounces) great northern beans, rinsed and drained
- 1 can (15 ounces) garbanzo beans or chickpeas, rinsed and drained
- 1 can (15 ounces) black beans, rinsed and drained
- 1 medium tomato, chopped
- 1 medium onion, chopped
- 1 celery rib, chopped
- ⅓ cup each chopped green, sweet red and yellow pepper
- ½ cup water
- 3 tablespoons minced fresh basil or 1 tablespoon dried basil
- 2 tablespoons minced fresh parsley
- 2 tablespoons lemon juice
- 2 tablespoons olive oil
- 1½ teaspoons minced fresh oregano or ½ teaspoon dried oregano
- ½ teaspoon salt
- ½ teaspoon pepper
- ¼ teaspoon cayenne pepper

In a large bowl, combine the beans, tomato, onion, celery and peppers. In a small bowl, whisk remaining ingredients; gently stir into bean mixture. Cover and refrigerate for 4 hours, stirring occasionally.

THREE-BEAN SALAD

EASY TEXAS BBQ BRISKET

Easy Texas BBQ Brisket

My mom tried my brisket and said it was even better than the version we used to have back in Texas. What a compliment!

—AUDRA RORICK WAKEENEY, KS

PREP: 15 MIN. + MARINATING
BAKE: 4 HOURS • **MAKES:** 10 SERVINGS

- 2 **tablespoons packed brown sugar**
- 1 **tablespoon salt**
- 1 **tablespoon onion powder**
- 1 **tablespoon garlic powder**
- 1 **tablespoon ground mustard**
- 1 **tablespoon smoked paprika**
- 1 **tablespoon pepper**
- 2 **fresh beef briskets (3½ pounds each)**
- 1 **bottle (10 ounces) Heinz 57 steak sauce**
- ½ **cup liquid smoke**
- ¼ **cup Worcestershire sauce**

1. In a small bowl, combine the first seven ingredients. With a fork or sharp knife, prick holes in briskets. Rub meat with seasoning mixture. Cover and refrigerate overnight.

2. Preheat oven to 325°. Place briskets, fat sides up, in a roasting pan. In a small bowl, combine steak sauce, liquid smoke and Worcestershire sauce; pour over meat.

3. Cover tightly with foil; bake 4 to 5 hours or until tender. Let stand in juices 15 minutes.

4. To serve, thinly slice across the grain. Skim fat from pan juices; spoon over meat.

NOTE *This is a fresh beef brisket, not corned beef.*

Jersey-Style Hot Dogs

I grew up in northern New Jersey, where this way of eating hot dogs was created. My husband never had them as a kid but has come to love them even more than I do. The combination of ingredients and flavors is simple but just right! What a great recipe when you're feeding a crowd of people.

—SUZANNE BANFIELD
BASKING RIDGE, NJ

PREP: 20 MIN. • **GRILL:** 40 MIN.
MAKES: 12 SERVINGS
(10 CUPS POTATO MIXTURE)

- 6 **medium Yukon Gold potatoes (about 3 pounds), halved and thinly sliced**
- 3 **large sweet red peppers, thinly sliced**
- 3 **large onions, peeled, halved and thinly sliced**
- ⅓ **cup olive oil**
- 6 **garlic cloves, minced**
- 3 **teaspoons salt**
- 1½ **teaspoons pepper**
- 12 **bun-length beef hot dogs**
- 12 **hot dog buns, split**

1. In a large bowl, combine potatoes, red peppers and onions. In a small bowl, mix oil, garlic, salt and pepper; add to potato mixture and toss to coat.

2. Transfer to two 13x9-in. disposable foil pans; cover with foil. Place pans on grill rack over medium heat; cook, covered, 30-35 minutes or until potatoes are tender. Remove from heat.

3. Grill hot dogs, covered, over medium heat 7-9 minutes or until heated through, turning occasionally. Place buns on grill, cut side down; grill until lightly toasted. Place hot dogs and potato mixture in buns. Serve with remaining potato mixture.

SOUTHWEST BURGERS

Southwest Burgers

I frequent a food stand that sells a burger with a Southwest flair. This is my version of its cheese-stuffed gourmet Southwest burger.
—**DEBORAH FORBES** FORT WORTH, TX

PREP: 25 MIN. + CHILLING • **GRILL:** 15 MIN. • **MAKES:** 8 SERVINGS

- 1 **can (15 ounces) black beans, rinsed and drained**
- 1 **small red onion, finely chopped**
- ½ **cup frozen corn, thawed**
- ¼ **cup dry bread crumbs**
- 1 **can (4 ounces) chopped green chilies**
- 2 **tablespoons Worcestershire sauce**
- 1 **teaspoon garlic powder**
- ½ **teaspoon ground cumin**
- ¼ **teaspoon pepper**
- ½ **pound lean ground beef (90% lean)**
- ½ **pound extra-lean ground turkey**
- ½ **cup fat-free mayonnaise**
- ¼ **cup salsa**
- 8 **slices pepper Jack cheese (½ ounce each)**
- 8 **whole wheat hamburger buns, split**

OPTIONAL TOPPINGS
Lettuce leaves, tomato slices and red onion rings

1. In a large bowl, coarsely mash beans. Stir in the onion, corn, bread crumbs, chilies, Worcestershire sauce and seasonings. Crumble beef and turkey over mixture and mix well. Shape into eight patties. Refrigerate for 1 hour. Combine mayonnaise and salsa; refrigerate until serving.
2. Using long-handled tongs, moisten a paper towel with cooking oil and lightly coat the grill rack. Grill burgers, covered, over medium heat or broil 4 in. from the heat for 5-7 minutes on each side or until a meat thermometer reads 165° and juices run clear.
3. Top with cheese; cover and grill 1-2 minutes longer or until cheese is melted. Serve on buns with toppings if desired.

SWEET CITRUS ICED TEA

Sweet Citrus Iced Tea

My family has been making iced tea this way since I was a child. It's great for potlucks and parties, and it's so refreshing everyone will want the recipe.
—**DIANE KIRKPATRICK** TERRE HILL, PA

PREP: 15 MIN. + CHILLING • **MAKES:** 1 GALLON

14½ cups water, divided
10 individual tea bags
1½ cups sugar
⅔ cup lemon juice
¼ cup thawed orange juice concentrate
    Ice cubes

1. In a large saucepan, bring 4 cups of water just to a boil. Remove from the heat. Add tea bags; let stand for 10 minutes. Discard tea bags.
2. Pour tea into a large container. Stir in the sugar, lemon juice, orange juice concentrate and remaining water. Refrigerate until chilled. Serve over ice.

Independence Day Ribs

I think our family recipe for ribs has evolved to near perfection. These country-style beauties are popular.
—**JOHN PURIFOY** BRISTOL, VA

PREP: 1 HOUR + CHILLING • **GRILL:** 1 HOUR 25 MIN.
MAKES: 12 SERVINGS

10 to 12 pounds pork baby back ribs (4 racks)
1⅓ cups packed brown sugar
2 teaspoons each garlic powder, onion powder, paprika, white pepper, chili powder, ground cumin and cayenne pepper

STEAM BATH

1 can (14½ ounces) beef broth
5 garlic cloves, crushed
1 tablespoon whole peppercorns
½ cup each fresh sage, parsley, rosemary and thyme sprigs
¼ cup sherry

SAUCE

¼ cup ketchup
2 tablespoons canola oil
2 tablespoons sherry
2 tablespoons honey
1 tablespoon brown sugar
1 tablespoon cider vinegar
2 teaspoons Worcestershire sauce
1 teaspoon salt
1 teaspoon ground mustard
½ teaspoon crushed red pepper flakes
¼ teaspoon paprika
¼ teaspoon cayenne pepper

1. Preheat oven to 350°. Sprinkle brown sugar over ribs and let stand 15 minutes. In a small bowl, mix seasonings; sprinkle over ribs.
2. In a large roasting pan, combine steam bath ingredients; place a wire rack on top, making sure rack is above liquid. Place ribs bone side down on rack, overlapping slightly as needed. Bake, covered, 3 to 3½ hours or until ribs are tender and meat starts to pull away from the bone; drain.
3. In a small bowl, mix sauce ingredients. Carefully remove ribs; cool slightly. Spread sauce over top of ribs; transfer to a large roasting pan. Refrigerate, covered, 8 hours or overnight.
4. Place ribs over direct heat. Grill, covered, over medium heat 15 to 20 minutes or until ribs are heated through and slightly charred, turning occasionally.

TOP TIP

What's a Steam Bath?

Steam baths tenderize meat and speed up cooking time. Many cooks add herbs or seasonings to the liquid in the bath to enhance the meat's flavor. Combine water or broth and seasonings in a roasting pan. Place meat on a wire rack over liquid mixture. Cover and cook until the meat is tender. Proceed with recipe's cooking instructions.

Pumpkin Soup with Sourdough Sage Croutons

We love soup in our house, and creamy ones are a big favorite. This Thanksgiving-inspired dish has all the aromas that fill the air during the holiday season. You can also make it with butternut squash if you prefer.

—JENNIFER TIDWELL FAIR OAKS, CA

PREP: 35 MIN. • **COOK:** 30 MIN.
MAKES: 10 SERVINGS (2½ QUARTS, 2 CUPS CROUTONS, ½ CUP SWEET CREAM).

- 1 **large onion, chopped**
- 2 **medium carrots, thinly sliced**
- 3 **tablespoons olive oil**
- 9 **cups cubed fresh pumpkin**
- 3 **cans (14½ ounces each) chicken broth**
- 2 **tablespoons minced fresh sage**
- 1½ **teaspoons garlic powder**
- ½ **teaspoon salt**
- ½ **teaspoon pepper**
- ⅛ **teaspoon ground nutmeg**

SWEET CREAM

- 1 **package (3 ounces) cream cheese, softened**
- ¼ **cup 2% milk**
- 2 **tablespoons confectioners' sugar**

CROUTONS

- 3 **slices sourdough bread, cubed**
- 2 **tablespoons olive oil**
- 2 **tablespoons butter, melted**
- 2 **tablespoons minced fresh sage**

1. In a Dutch oven, saute onion and carrots in oil for 5 minutes. Add pumpkin; cook 5-6 minutes longer. Stir in the broth, sage, garlic powder, salt, pepper and nutmeg; bring to a boil. Reduce heat; cover and simmer for 15-20 minutes or until pumpkin is tender.
2. Cool slightly. In a blender, process soup in batches until smooth. Return all to pan and heat through.
3. For sweet cream, combine ingredients until smooth. For croutons, place bread in a small bowl; drizzle with oil and butter. Sprinkle with sage and toss to coat. Transfer to a small skillet; cook and stir over medium heat for 4-6 minutes or until lightly toasted. Garnish servings with sweet cream and croutons.

Butternut Squash & Potato Mash

Some people like squash, some people like potatoes. Mash the two together and you've got true love. This is a great way to get kids to eat their veggies.

—JASMINE ROSE CRYSTAL LAKE, IL

PREP: 25 MIN. • **COOK:** 20 MIN.
MAKES: 10 SERVINGS (¾ CUP EACH)

- 8 **cups cubed peeled butternut squash (about 4 pounds)**
- 4 **cups cubed peeled potatoes (about 4 medium)**
- 16 **garlic cloves, peeled**
- 2 **tablespoons sesame seeds**
- 1 **teaspoon ground cumin**
- 1 **cup (4 ounces) shredded Colby-Monterey Jack cheese**
- 2 **tablespoons butter**
- 1½ **teaspoons salt**
- ½ **teaspoon pepper**

1. Place squash, potatoes and garlic in a Dutch oven; add water to cover. Bring to a boil. Reduce heat; cook, uncovered, 10-15 minutes or until tender.
2. Meanwhile, in a dry small skillet, toast sesame seeds and cumin over medium-low heat 3-4 minutes or until aromatic, stirring frequently. Remove from the heat.
3. Drain squash mixture. Mash vegetables, adding cheese, butter, salt and pepper. Sprinkle with sesame seed mixture.

PUMPKIN SOUP WITH
SOURDOUGH SAGE CROUTONS

Deluxe Pumpkin Cheesecake

Here's the ultimate pumpkin dessert, with a great gingersnap crust and rich, luscious swirls of pumpkin. If you want to contribute something special for the holidays, try this recipe!

—SHARON SKILDUM
MAPLE GROVE, MN

PREP: 35 MIN. • **BAKE:** 55 MIN. + CHILLING
MAKES: 12 SERVINGS

- 1 cup crushed gingersnap cookies (about 20 cookies)
- ⅓ cup finely chopped pecans
- ¼ cup butter, melted
- 4 packages (8 ounces each) cream cheese, softened, divided
- 1½ cups sugar, divided
- 2 tablespoons cornstarch
- 2 teaspoons vanilla extract
- 4 eggs
- 1 cup canned pumpkin
- 2 teaspoons ground cinnamon
- 1½ teaspoons ground nutmeg

GARNISH
- Chocolate syrup, caramel ice cream topping, whipped topping and additional crushed gingersnap cookies, optional

1. Preheat oven to 350°. Place a greased 9-in. springform pan on a double thickness of heavy-duty foil (about 18 in. square). Securely wrap foil around pan.

2. In a small bowl, combine cookie crumbs, pecans and butter. Press onto the bottom of prepared pan. Place on a baking sheet. Bake 8-10 minutes or until set. Cool on a wire rack.

3. For filling, in a large bowl, beat 1 package of cream cheese, ½ cup sugar and cornstarch until smooth, about 2 minutes. Beat in remaining cream cheese, one package at a time until smooth. Add remaining sugar and vanilla. Add eggs; beat on low speed just until combined.

4. Place 2 cups filling in a small bowl; stir in pumpkin, cinnamon and nutmeg. Remove ¾ cup pumpkin filling; set aside. Pour remaining pumpkin filling over crust; top with remaining plain filling. Cut through with a knife to swirl. Drop reserved pumpkin filling by spoonfuls over cheesecake; cut through with a knife to swirl.

5. Place springform pan in a large baking pan; add 1 in. of hot water to larger pan. Bake 55-65 minutes or until center is just set and top appears dull. Remove springform pan from water bath. Cool on a wire rack 10 minutes. Carefully run a knife around edge of pan to loosen; cool 1 hour longer. Refrigerate overnight.

6. Garnish with chocolate syrup, caramel sauce, whipped topping and additional crushed gingersnaps if desired.

TOP TIP

Is It Done Yet?

Judging the doneness of cheesecake can be tricky. Tap the side of the pan with a wooden spoon to measure the center of the cheesecake's jiggle. The area should be the size of a walnut. It's important to remember that cheesecakes do not set up completely until they are thoroughly chilled.

DELUXE PUMPKIN CHEESECAKE

APPLE, BLUE CHEESE
& BIBB SALAD

Pumpkin Patch Punch

Oranges are disguised as pumpkins in this fresh fall citrus-ade. Stir up a pitcher for your friends.
—*TASTE OF HOME* **TEST KITCHEN**

PREP: 15 MIN. + CHILLING
MAKES: 12 SERVINGS

- 4   **medium lemons**
- 4   **medium limes**
- 4   **medium oranges**
- 3   **quarts water**
- 1½ **to 2 cups sugar**
     Additional oranges and lime peel

1. Squeeze the juice from the lemons, limes and oranges; pour into a gallon container. Add water and sugar; mix well. Refrigerate until chilled.

2. To make pumpkins, cut the top and bottom thirds from desired amount of oranges. Using a paring knife, insert a small piece of lime peel for a pumpkin stem.

3. Just before serving, transfer punch to serving pitchers and add ice if desired. Top each serving with a pumpkin.

PUMPKIN
PATCH PUNCH

FAST FIX

Apple, Blue Cheese & Bibb Salad

Red or Golden Delicious apples add a burst of fall flavor to this simple salad. Blue cheese and toasted walnuts make it even more special.
—**REBEKAH BEYER** SABETHA, KS

START TO FINISH: 20 MIN.
MAKES: 9 SERVINGS

- 4   **cups torn Bibb or Boston lettuce**
- 3   **medium Red and/or Golden Delicious apples, chopped**
- ½   **cup olive oil**
- 1   **tablespoon white balsamic vinegar or white wine vinegar**
- 1   **tablespoon honey**
- 1   **tablespoon mayonnaise**
- ½   **teaspoon mustard seed, toasted**
- ½   **teaspoon stone-ground mustard (whole grain)**
- ¼   **teaspoon salt**
- ⅛   **teaspoon coarsely ground pepper**
- 1   **cup crumbled blue cheese**
- ¾   **cup walnut halves, toasted**
- ½   **cup golden raisins**

In a salad bowl, combine the lettuce and apples. In a small bowl, whisk the oil, vinegar, honey, mayonnaise, mustard seed, mustard, salt and pepper. Drizzle over salad and toss to coat. Sprinkle with cheese, walnuts and raisins. Serve immediately.

Pumpkin Hot Pockets

The combination of simple ingredients in these hand-held sandwiches is sure to please kids and adults alike.
—*TASTE OF HOME* TEST KITCHEN

PREP: 30 MIN. • **BAKE:** 15 MIN. • **MAKES:** 8 SERVINGS

- 1 package (15 ounces) refrigerated pie pastry
- 3 tablespoons honey mustard
- ½ pound fully cooked ham, thinly sliced
- 3 tablespoons thinly sliced green onions
- ½ cup shredded Swiss cheese
- ½ cup shredded Monterey Jack cheese
- 2 egg yolks
- 4 to 6 drops red food coloring
- 1 egg white
- 2 to 3 drops green food coloring

1. Preheat oven to 400°. On a lightly floured surface, roll one sheet of pastry into a 15-in. circle. Using a floured 5x4-in. pumpkin cookie cutter, cut out eight pumpkins. Repeat with remaining pastry. Spread mustard over eight pumpkins. Layer with ham, onions and cheeses to within ¾ in. of edges.

2. In a small bowl, beat yolks with enough red food coloring to achieve an orange color. In another small bowl, beat egg white with green food coloring. Brush orange mixture over edges of pastry. Top with remaining pumpkins. Press edges to seal; trim edges with a fluted pastry wheel. Brush stems with green mixture and pumpkins with orange.

3. Transfer to greased baking sheets. Bake 15 minutes or until browned.

Smashed Root Vegetables with Crispy Shallots

It's funny how simple things can trigger random thoughts. This dish is special to me because the roasted potatoes remind me of Sunday suppers at my grandma's house—delicious and comforting!
—KATHI JONES-DELMONTE ROCHESTER, NY

PREP: 35 MIN. • **BAKE:** 40 MIN. • **MAKES:** 8 SERVINGS

- 3 medium potatoes, peeled and cubed
- 2 large sweet potatoes, peeled and cubed
- 1 large rutabaga, peeled and cubed
- 2 medium carrots, sliced
- 1 medium turnip, peeled and cubed
- 1 medium parsnip, peeled and cubed
- 5 tablespoons olive oil, divided
- 1½ teaspoons dried thyme
- 1 teaspoon salt
- 1 teaspoon coarsely ground pepper
- 1 teaspoon paprika
- 5 shallots, peeled and thinly sliced
- ½ teaspoon sugar
- ½ teaspoon balsamic vinegar
- ¼ cup butter, cubed
- ¼ cup 2% milk
- ⅛ teaspoon ground nutmeg

1. Preheat oven to 400°. In a large bowl, combine the first six ingredients. Drizzle with 3 tablespoons oil. Combine thyme, salt, pepper and paprika. Sprinkle over vegetables; toss to coat. Divide between two 15x10x1-in. baking pans.

2. Bake, uncovered, 40-45 minutes or until tender and golden brown, stirring occasionally.

3. Meanwhile, in a small skillet, saute shallots in remaining oil until golden brown and crispy. Stir in sugar and vinegar; cook 1 minute longer. Drain; set aside.

4. Transfer vegetables to a large bowl. Coarsely mash with butter, milk and nutmeg. Sprinkle with shallots; serve immediately.

PUMPKIN HOT POCKETS

MONSTER
OWICHES

Silly Monster Sandwiches

Why serve chicken salad on ordinary rolls when you can make these deliciously creepy sandwiches?
—*TASTE OF HOME* **TEST KITCHEN**

PREP: 35 MIN. • **MAKES:** 1 DOZEN

- 2 **cups cubed cooked chicken breast**
- ½ **cup dried cranberries, optional**
- ½ **cup mayonnaise**
- ¼ **cup finely chopped onion**
- ¼ **cup chopped celery**
- ¼ **teaspoon salt**
- ¼ **teaspoon pepper**
- 12 **dinner rolls, split and toasted**
- 1 **jar (15 ounces) process cheese sauce**
- 24 **pimiento-stuffed olives**
- 12 **pimiento strips**
- 6 **whole baby dill pickles, cut in half lengthwise**

1. In a large bowl, combine the chicken, cranberries if desired, mayonnaise, onion, celery, salt and pepper. Fill rolls with the chicken mixture.

2. Heat cheese sauce to soften; drizzle or pipe over top of each sandwich.

3. For each monster sandwich, attach olives for eyes, pimiento strips for noses and sliced pickles for fangs.

TOP TIP

Get Creative!

Feel free to mix things up when you assemble Silly Monster Sandwiches. For instance, replace the pickles with strips of red pepper to resemble a snake's tongue. These make great classroom bites when learning about reptiles.

Dancing Mummies

Use a gingerbread boy cookie cutter to make these adorable Halloween mummy cookies.

—DORE' MERRICK GRABSKI

UTICA, NY

PREP: 15 MIN. + CHILLING
BAKE: 10 MIN./BATCH • **MAKES:** 3 DOZEN

- ⅔ cup shortening
- ½ cup sugar
- ½ cup molasses
- 1 egg
- 3 cups all-purpose flour
- 1 teaspoon baking soda
- 1 teaspoon each ground cinnamon, ginger and cloves
- ½ teaspoon salt
- ½ teaspoon ground nutmeg
- 1 can (16 ounces) vanilla frosting Candy buttons and black decorating gel

1. In a large bowl, cream shortening and sugar until light and fluffy. Beat in egg. Beat in molasses. Combine the flour, baking soda, cinnamon, ginger, cloves, salt and nutmeg; gradually add to creamed mixture and mix well. Divide dough in half. Refrigerate for at least 1 hour.
2. Preheat oven to 350°. On a lightly floured surface, roll out each portion of dough to ⅛-in. thickness. Cut with a floured 3-in. dancing gingerbread boy-shaped cookie cutter. Place 2 in. apart on greased baking sheets. Bake 8-10 minutes or until edges are firm. Cool on wire racks.
3. For mummy bandages, pipe frosting using basket weave pastry tip #47. Add candy buttons and decorating gel for eyes.

Maple-Walnut Spritz Cookies

I love the combination of maple syrup, walnuts and spritz cookies, so I use all of these elements to create these perfectly delicious bites. I just love the aroma in the house as these delightful little treats are baking.

—PAULA MARCHESI

LENHARTSVILLE, PA

PREP: 30 MIN. • **BAKE:** 10 MIN./BATCH
MAKES: 6½ DOZEN

- ½ cup butter, softened
- ⅓ cup packed brown sugar
- 1 egg
- ¼ cup maple syrup
- 1 teaspoon vanilla extract
- 1½ cups all-purpose flour
- ⅔ cup ground walnuts
- ½ teaspoon baking powder
- ¼ teaspoon salt
  Coarse sugar
- ⅔ cup walnut pieces

1. Preheat oven to 350°. In a bowl, cream butter and brown sugar until light and fluffy. Beat in egg, maple syrup and vanilla. In another bowl, whisk flour, ground walnuts, baking powder and salt; gradually beat into creamed mixture (dough will be soft).
2. Using a cookie press fitted with a flower or star disk, press dough 1 in. apart onto ungreased baking sheets. Sprinkle with coarse sugar. Top with walnuts.
3. Bake 10-12 minutes or until bottoms are light brown. Cool on pans 2 minutes. Remove to wire racks to cool.

MAPLE-WALNUT SPRITZ COOKIES

SWEET POTATO BAKE

Sweet Potato Bake

Easy to prepare, these sweet potatoes make a perfect addition to a special meal. The topping is slightly sweet and has a nice contrast of textures.

—PAM HOLLOWAY MARION, LA

PREP: 35 MIN. • **BAKE:** 20 MIN. + STANDING
MAKES: 10-12 SERVINGS

- **7** large sweet potatoes (about 6 pounds), peeled and cubed
- **¼** cup butter, cubed
- **½** cup orange marmalade
- **¼** cup orange juice
- **¼** cup packed brown sugar
- **2** teaspoons salt
- **1** teaspoon ground ginger

TOPPING

- **12** oatmeal cookies, crumbled
- **6** tablespoons butter, softened

1. Preheat oven to 400°. Place sweet potatoes in a Dutch oven and cover with water. Bring to a boil. Reduce heat; cover and cook just 10-15 minutes or until tender. Drain.
2. Mash potatoes with butter. Add marmalade, orange juice, brown sugar, salt and ginger. Transfer to a greased 13x9-in. baking dish. Toss cookie crumbs with butter; sprinkle over the top.
3. Bake, uncovered, 20 minutes or until browned. Let stand 15 minutes before serving.

Boo Berry Ghosts

Ghoulish treats cause quite a fright, but these cakes are so yummy they won't haunt you for long!

—TASTE OF HOME TEST KITCHEN!

PREP: 1 HOUR • **BAKE:** 25 MIN. + COOLING
MAKES: 1 DOZEN

- **12** egg whites
- **1¼** cups confectioners' sugar
- **1** cup all-purpose flour
- **1½** teaspoons cream of tartar
- **1** teaspoon vanilla extract
- **¼** teaspoon salt
- **1** cup sugar
- **½** cup strawberry preserves

DECORATING

- **1** can (16 ounces) vanilla frosting
- **24** miniature semisweet chocolate chips
- **12** brown M&M's minis

1. Line two ungreased 18x13-in. baking pans with parchment paper. Place egg whites in a large bowl; let stand at room temperature 30 minutes. Sift confectioners' sugar and flour together three times; set aside.
2. Preheat oven to 350°. Add cream of tartar, vanilla and salt to egg whites; beat on medium speed until soft peaks form. Gradually add sugar, 1 tablespoon at a time, beating on high until stiff peaks form. Gradually fold in flour mixture, about ¼ cup at a time.
3. Gently spoon into prepared pans. Cut through batter with a knife to remove air pockets. Bake 25-35 minutes or until golden brown on top. Cool completely, about 1 hour.
4. Cut with a 4-in. ghost-shaped cookie cutter. Spread half of the cakes with preserves; top with remaining cakes. Place on wire racks over waxed paper.
5. Transfer frosting to a microwave-safe bowl. Microwave on high 20-30 seconds or until melted; stir until smooth. Spoon over cakes. Add chocolate chips for eyes and M&M's for mouths. Let stand until set.

Chestnut Stuffing

It wouldn't be Thanksgiving without a serving of my longtime favorite stuffing. It's a savory side dish that feeds many people at one time.
—**LEE BREMSON** KANSAS CITY, MO

PREP: 40 MIN. • **BAKE:** 35 MIN. • **MAKES:** 21 SERVINGS

- 1 large onion, chopped
- ½ cup chopped fennel bulb
- 1½ cups butter, cubed, divided
- 2 garlic cloves, minced
- 2 cups peeled cooked chestnuts, coarsely chopped
- 1 large pear, chopped
- 1 cup chicken broth
- ½ cup mixed dried fruit, coarsely chopped
- 2 teaspoons poultry seasoning
- 2 teaspoons minced fresh rosemary
- 2 teaspoons minced fresh thyme
- ½ teaspoon salt
- ½ teaspoon pepper
- 2 loaves day-old white bread (1 pound each), cubed
- 3 eggs
- ¼ cup 2% milk

1. Preheat oven to 350°. In a large skillet, saute onion and fennel in ½ cup butter until tender. Stir in garlic; cook 2 minutes longer. Stir in chestnuts, pear, broth, dried fruit, seasonings and remaining butter; cook until butter is melted. Bring to a boil. Reduce heat; simmer, uncovered, 3-4 minutes or until dried fruit is softened.
2. Place in a large bowl. Stir in bread cubes. Whisk eggs and milk; drizzle over stuffing and toss to coat.
3. Transfer to a greased 13x9-in. and a greased 8-in.-square baking dish. Bake, uncovered, at 25 minutes. Uncover; bake 10-15 minutes longer or until lightly browned.

Make-Ahead Turkey and Gravy

This turkey is cooked, sliced and ready to serve when you need it. It's a great way to bring turkey to a potluck.
—**MARIE PARKER** MILWAUKEE, WI

PREP: 4¼ HOURS + FREEZING • **BAKE:** 50 MIN.
MAKES: 16 SERVINGS (2½ CUPS GRAVY)

TURKEY
- 1 turkey (14 to 16 pounds)
- 2 teaspoons poultry seasoning
- 1 teaspoon pepper
- 3 cups reduced-sodium chicken broth
- ½ cup minced fresh parsley
- ¼ cup lemon juice
- 1 tablespoon minced fresh thyme or 1 teaspoon dried thyme
- 1 tablespoon minced fresh rosemary or 1 teaspoon dried rosemary, crushed
- 2 teaspoons grated lemon peel
- 2 garlic cloves, minced

FOR SERVING
- 1½ cups reduced-sodium chicken broth
- 1 tablespoon butter
- 1 tablespoon all-purpose flour

1. Preheat oven to 325°. Sprinkle turkey with poultry seasoning and pepper. Tuck wings under turkey; tie drumsticks together. Place on a rack in a shallow roasting pan, breast side up.
2. Roast, uncovered, 30 minutes. In a 4-cup measuring cup, mix remaining turkey ingredients; carefully pour over turkey. Roast, uncovered, 3 to 3½ hours longer or until a thermometer inserted in thigh reads 180°, basting occasionally with broth mixture. Cover loosely with foil if turkey browns too quickly.
3. Remove turkey from pan; let stand at least 20 minutes before carving. Skim fat from cooking juices.
4. Carve turkey; place in shallow freezer containers. Pour strained juices over turkey; cool completely. Freeze, covered, up to 3 months.
TO SERVE *Partially thaw turkey in refrigerator overnight. Preheat oven to 350°. Transfer turkey and cooking juices to a baking dish; pour broth over turkey. Bake, covered, 50-60 minutes or until a thermometer reads 165°.*
5. Remove turkey from baking dish, reserving cooking liquid; keep warm. In a small saucepan, melt butter; stir in flour until smooth. Gradually whisk in reserved cooking liquid. Bring to a boil, stirring constantly; cook and stir 2 minutes or until thickened. Serve with turkey.
NOTE *It's best not to use a prebasted turkey for this recipe.*

MAKE-AHEAD
TURKEY AND GRAVY

LIME DIVINE TARTS

Lime Divine Tarts

Winter is prime time for limes, so why not showcase them at a seasonal get-together? These cute cups are impressive but easy to make.

—ANN YRI LEWISVILLE, TX

PREP: 30 MIN. + CHILLING • **BAKE:** 15 MIN. + COOLING
MAKES: 2 DOZEN

- 2 **eggs**
- 1 **egg yolk**
- ½ **cup sugar**
- ¼ **cup lime juice**
- 1 **teaspoon grated lime peel**
- ¼ **cup unsalted butter, cubed**

TART SHELLS
- ½ **cup unsalted butter, softened**
- 1 **package (3 ounces) cream cheese, softened**
- 1 **cup all-purpose flour**
  White chocolate curls and lime peel strips

1. In a small heavy saucepan over medium heat, whisk eggs, egg yolk, sugar, lime juice and peel until blended. Add butter; cook, whisking constantly, until mixture is thickened and coats the back of a spoon. Transfer to a small bowl; cool. Cover and refrigerate until chilled.

2. In a small bowl, cream butter and cream cheese until smooth. Gradually add flour; mix well. Cover and refrigerate 1 hour or until easy to handle.

3. Preheat oven to 375°. Shape dough into 1-in. balls; press onto bottom and up sides of 36 ungreased miniature muffin cups. Prick bottoms with a fork. Bake 15-17 minutes or until golden brown. Cool 5 minutes before removing from pans to wire racks to cool completely.

4. Fill shells with lime mixture. Garnish with chocolate curls and lime peel. Refrigerate leftovers.

Spiced Cider Punch

I've shared this beverage with many friends. It never wears out its welcome and is so easy to make! Serve it warm to take the chill off in winter.

—CHARLES PIATT LITTLE ROCK, AR

PREP: 15 MIN. + CHILLING • **MAKES:** 13 SERVINGS (ABOUT 3 QUARTS)

- 1 **cup sugar**
- 2 **quarts apple cider or juice, divided**
- 1 **teaspoon ground cinnamon**
- 1 **teaspoon ground allspice**
- 1 **can (12 ounces) frozen orange juice concentrate, thawed**
- 1 **quart ginger ale, chilled**

1. In a Dutch oven, combine the sugar, 1 cup cider, cinnamon and allspice. Cook and stir over medium heat until sugar is dissolved. Remove from the heat; add orange juice concentrate and remaining cider. Cool. Cover and refrigerate until chilled.

2. Just before serving, transfer to a punch bowl; stir in ginger ale.

Honey-Orange Winter Vegetable Medley

This combo of vegetables with a sweet-savory sauce makes a lovely addition to a holiday buffet.
—**JENNIFER CODUTO** KENT, OH

PREP: 30 MIN. • **BAKE:** 1 HOUR
MAKES: 9 SERVINGS

- 3 **cups fresh baby carrots**
- 2 **cups cubed red potatoes**
- 2 **cups pearl onions, peeled**
- 2 **cups cubed peeled sweet potatoes**
- ¾ **cup reduced-sodium chicken broth**
- ½ **cup orange marmalade**
- ¼ **cup honey**
- 2 **tablespoons lemon juice**
- 1½ **teaspoons poultry seasoning**
- ¾ **teaspoon salt**
- ¾ **teaspoon pepper**
- 3 **tablespoons butter, cubed**

1. Preheat oven to 375°. Place the vegetables in a greased shallow 3-qt. baking dish. In a small bowl, combine broth, marmalade, honey, lemon juice and seasonings. Pour over vegetables and toss to coat. Dot with butter.

2. Cover and bake 30 minutes. Uncover and bake 30-40 minutes longer or until the vegetables are tender.

TOP TIP

Getting Out of a Sticky Situation

If your honey has crystallized, place the jar in warm water and stir until the crystals dissolve. Or set the honey in a microwave-safe container and microwave on high, stirring every 30 seconds, until the crystals dissolve.

HONEY-ORANGE WINTER VEGETABLE MEDLEY

ROASTED GARLIC &
HERB PRIME RIB

Roasted Garlic & Herb Prime Rib

An herb rub creates a flavorful crust over this impressive rib roast. The creamy horseradish sauce adds a bit of zest.
—**MICHELE SOLOMON** CRESTVIEW, FL

PREP: 1 HOUR • **BAKE:** 2½ HOURS + STANDING
MAKES: 12 SERVINGS

- 1 **whole garlic bulb**
- ¼ **teaspoon plus 2 tablespoons olive oil, divided**
- 3 **green onions, finely chopped**
- 1 **tablespoon dried rosemary, crushed**
- 1 **teaspoon dried thyme**
- 1 **teaspoon dill weed**
- 1 **teaspoon onion powder**
- ½ **teaspoon salt**
- ¼ **teaspoon pepper**
- ½ **cup dry red wine or beef broth**
- 1 **bone-in beef rib roast (6 to 8 pounds)**
- 2 **cups beef broth**

SAUCE
- 1 **cup (8 ounces) sour cream**
- 1 **tablespoon prepared horseradish**
- 1½ **teaspoons dill weed**

1. Preheat oven to 425°. Remove papery outer skin from garlic (do not peel or separate cloves). Cut top off of garlic bulb. Brush with ¼ teaspoon oil. Wrap garlic bulb in heavy-duty foil. Bake 30-35 minutes or until softened. Cool 10-15 minutes.
2. Preheat oven to 450°. Squeeze softened garlic into a small bowl; stir in onions, herbs, onion powder, salt and pepper. Add wine and remaining oil. Place roast fat side up in a shallow roasting pan. Cut slits into roast; spoon garlic mixture into slits. Rub remaining garlic mixture over roast. Pour beef broth into bottom of pan.
3. Bake, uncovered, 15 minutes. Reduce heat to 325°; bake 2¼ to 2¾ hours longer or until meat reaches desired doneness (for medium-rare, a thermometer should read 145°; medium, 160°; well-done, 170°).
4. Meanwhile, in a small bowl, combine sauce ingredients. Cover and chill until serving. Remove roast to a serving platter and keep warm; let stand 15 minutes before slicing. Serve with sauce.

FAST FIX
Holiday Eggnog Mix

Prepare this easy mix when you need to feed a holiday crowd. It's delightful!
—*TASTE OF HOME* TEST KITCHEN

START TO FINISH: 10 MIN.
MAKES: 18 SERVINGS (6 CUPS EGGNOG MIX)

- 6⅔ **cups nonfat dry milk powder**
- 2 **packages (3.4 ounces each) instant vanilla pudding mix**
- 1 **cup buttermilk blend powder**
- 1 **tablespoon ground nutmeg**

ADDITIONAL INGREDIENT (FOR EACH BATCH)
- ¾ **cup cold whole milk**

In a food processor, combine the first four ingredients; cover and pulse until blended. Store in airtight containers in a cool dry place for up to 6 months.
TO PREPARE EGGNOG *Place ⅓ cup mix in a glass. Stir in ¾ cup milk until blended.*

Green Beans in Yellow Pepper Butter

Colorful, crunchy and buttery beans will be all the rage at your holiday gathering. For a variation, sprinkle pine nuts over the top before serving.

—JUDIE WHITE FLORIEN, LA

START TO FINISH: 30 MIN. • **MAKES:** 8 SERVINGS

- 2 medium sweet yellow peppers, divided
- 7 tablespoons butter, softened, divided
- ¼ cup pine nuts
- 1 tablespoon lemon juice
- ¼ teaspoon salt
- ⅛ teaspoon pepper
- 1½ pounds fresh green beans, trimmed

1. Finely chop one yellow pepper. In a small skillet, saute pepper in 1 tablespoon butter until tender. Set aside.

2. Place the pine nuts, lemon juice, salt, pepper and remaining butter in a food processor; cover and process until blended. Add cooked pepper; cover and process until blended. Set butter mixture aside.

3. Place beans in a large saucepan and cover with water. Cut remaining pepper into thin strips; add to beans. Bring to a boil. Cover and cook for 5-7 minutes or until crisp-tender; drain. Place vegetables in a large bowl; add butter mixture and toss to coat.

Chunky Garlic Mashed Potatoes

I like to dress up these mashed spuds with a whole bulb of roasted garlic. It may seem like overkill, but once cooked, any harshness mellows out and you're left with sweet and delicate garlic flavor.

—JACKIE GREGSTON HALLSVILLE, TX

START TO FINISH: 30 MIN. **MAKES:** 9 SERVINGS

- 3 pounds Yukon Gold potatoes, cut into quarters
- 1 whole garlic bulb, cloves separated and peeled
- ½ cup butter, cubed
- ½ cup half-and-half cream
- 2 tablespoons prepared horseradish
- ¾ teaspoon salt
- ¾ teaspoon pepper
  Fresh thyme leaves, optional

1. Place potatoes and garlic cloves in a large saucepan; cover with water. Bring to a boil. Reduce heat; cover and cook for 15-20 minutes or until potatoes are tender.

2. Meanwhile, in a small saucepan, heat butter and cream; keep warm. Drain potatoes and garlic; return to pan. Add the horseradish, salt, pepper and butter mixture; mash to reach desired consistency. Garnish with thyme if desired.

GREEN BEANS IN YELLOW PEPPER BUTTER

CHUNKY GARLIC MASHED POTATOES

Christmas Cauliflower

Here, my Swiss cheese sauce gives this vegetable casserole an extra-special flavor.

—**BETTY CLAYCOMB** ALVERTON, PA

PREP: 25 MIN. • **BAKE:** 25 MIN.
MAKES: 8-10 SERVINGS

- 1 large head cauliflower, broken into florets
- ¼ cup chopped green pepper
- 1 jar (7.3 ounces) sliced mushrooms, drained
- ¼ cup butter, cubed
- ⅓ cup all-purpose flour
- 2 cups 2% milk
- 1 cup (4 ounces) shredded Swiss cheese
- 2 tablespoons diced pimientos
- 1 teaspoon salt
  Paprika, optional

1. Place 1 in. of water in a large saucepan; add cauliflower. Bring to a boil. Reduce heat; cover and cook for 6-8 minutes or until crisp-tender. Drain and pat dry.
2. Meanwhile, in a large saucepan, saute green pepper and mushrooms in butter for 2 minutes or until crisp-tender. Add flour; gradually stir in milk. Bring to a boil; cook and stir for 2 minutes or until thickened. Remove from the heat; stir in cheese until melted. Add pimientos and salt.
3. Place half of the cauliflower in a greased 2-qt. baking dish; top with half of the sauce. Repeat layers. Bake, uncovered, at 325° for 25 minutes or until bubbly. Sprinkle with paprika if desired.

FLAVORFUL FRENCH ONION SOUP

Flavorful French Onion Soup

This soup complements any dinner. What a delightful change-of-pace contribution to a church supper!

—*TASTE OF HOME* TEST KITCHEN

PREP: 20 MIN. • **COOK:** 1¾ HOURS
MAKES: 11 SERVINGS (ABOUT 2½ QUARTS)

- ¼ cup butter, cubed
- 2½ pounds onions, thinly sliced
- 3 tablespoons brown sugar
- 1 teaspoon pepper
- 3 tablespoons all-purpose flour
- 8 cups beef broth
- 1 cup dry red wine or additional beef broth
- ¼ cup A.1. steak sauce

HOMEMADE CROUTONS

- 3 cups cubed French bread
- 2 tablespoons olive oil
- 2 tablespoons butter, melted
- ½ teaspoon dried oregano
- ½ teaspoon dried basil
- ¼ teaspoon salt
- ¼ teaspoon pepper
- ¾ cup shredded Swiss cheese

1. In a Dutch oven, melt butter. Add the onions, brown sugar and pepper; cook over low heat until onion are lightly browned, about 1 hour.
2. Sprinkle onions with flour; stir to blend. Gradually stir in broth. Add wine and steak sauce. Bring to a boil. Reduce heat; cover and simmer for 45 minutes.
3. Meanwhile, preheat oven to 375°. In a large bowl, toss bread cubes with oil and butter.
4. Combine oregano, basil, salt and pepper; sprinkle over bread and toss to coat.
5. Transfer to an ungreased 15x10x1-in. baking pan. Bake 10-12 minutes or until golden brown.
6. Garnish soup with croutons and cheese.

Cranberry-Eggnog Gelatin Salad

Refreshing and bursting with flavor, this festive salad is a great choice for a holiday potluck. The sweet pineapple-eggnog layer contrasts nicely with the cool and tangy gelatin on top. Since it has to chill overnight, it's a good pick for those dishes you want to prepare a day ahead.
—**NANCY FOUST** STONEBORO, PA

PREP: 30 MIN. • **COOK:** 5 MIN. + CHILLING
MAKES: 16 SERVINGS

- 2 packages (3 ounces each) raspberry gelatin
- 2 cups boiling water
- 1 cup cold water
- 1 can (14 ounces) whole-berry cranberry sauce
- 1 medium navel orange, peeled and chopped
- 1 tablespoon grated orange peel
- 1 can (20 ounces) unsweetened crushed pineapple, undrained
- 2 envelopes unflavored gelatin
- 1½ cups eggnog
- 3 tablespoons lime juice

1. In a large bowl, dissolve raspberry gelatin in boiling water. Stir in cold water, then cranberry sauce, orange and orange peel.

Pour into a 10-in. fluted tube pan or 12-cup ring mold coated with cooking spray; refrigerate for 40 minutes or until firm.

2. Meanwhile, drain pineapple; pour juice into a saucepan. Sprinkle unflavored gelatin over juice and let stand for 1 minute. Cook and stir over low heat until gelatin is completely dissolved.

3. In a large bowl, combine eggnog and lime juice. Gradually stir in gelatin mixture. Chill until soft-set. Fold in pineapple. Spoon over raspberry layer. Refrigerate overnight. Unmold onto a serving platter.

NOTE *This recipe was tested with commercially prepared eggnog.*

Nanny's Fruitcake Cookies

My grandmother always made a holiday fruitcake. I took her recipe and made it a cookie that's perfect any time with a cup of tea.
—**AMANDA DIGGES**
SOUTH WINDSOR, CT

PREP: 35 MIN. + CHILLING
BAKE: 15 MIN./BATCH
MAKES: ABOUT 4 DOZEN

- 1⅔ cups chopped pecans or walnuts
- 1⅓ cups golden raisins

- 1 cup pitted dried plums, chopped
- ⅔ cup dried apricots, finely chopped
- ½ cup dried cranberries
- ¼ cup Triple Sec
- 1 cup butter, softened
- ½ cup sugar
- ⅓ cup packed light brown sugar
- ½ teaspoon ground nutmeg
- 1 egg
- 2⅔ cups all-purpose flour

1. Place the first five ingredients in a large bowl. Drizzle with Triple Sec and toss to combine. Let stand, covered, overnight.

2. In a large bowl, cream butter, sugars and nutmeg until light and fluffy. Beat in egg. Gradually beat in flour. Stir in fruit mixture.

3. Divide dough in half; shape each into a 12x3x1-in. rectangular log. Wrap in plastic wrap; refrigerate overnight or until firm.

4. Preheat oven to 350°. Unwrap and cut dough crosswise into ½-in. slices. Place 2 in. apart on ungreased baking sheets. Bake 13-16 minutes or until edges are light brown. Remove from pans to wire racks to cool.

CRANBERRY-EGGNOG GELATIN SALAD

Chocolate Gingerbread Yule Log

If you've tasted a traditional Yule Log cake, you'll love this version with fresh ginger and holiday spices.

—**LAUREN KNOELKE** MILWAUKEE, WI

PREP: 1¼ HOURS • **BAKE:** 10 MIN. + COOLING • **MAKES:** 16 SERVINGS

- 5 **eggs, separated**
- ¾ **cup cake flour**
- 1 **to 1½ teaspoons each ground ginger and cinnamon**
- ¼ **teaspoon each ground nutmeg and pepper**
- ¼ **teaspoon salt**
- ⅓ **cup packed dark brown sugar**
- ¼ **cup molasses**
- 2 **tablespoons canola oil**
- 1 **tablespoon grated fresh gingerroot**
- ⅛ **teaspoon cream of tartar**
- ¼ **cup sugar**
  Baking cocoa

FILLING

- 1 **carton (8 ounces) mascarpone cheese**
- ⅓ **cup confectioners' sugar**
- 2 **tablespoons heavy whipping cream**
- ⅛ **teaspoon salt**
- ⅓ **cup crystallized ginger, dried cranberries or miniature semisweet chocolate chips**

CHOCOLATE BARK

- 4 **to 6 ounces high-quality bittersweet chocolate, melted**

BUTTERCREAM

- 2 **egg whites**
- ½ **cup sugar**
- ⅛ **teaspoon salt**
- ¾ **cup unsalted butter, softened**
- 4 **ounces high-quality milk chocolate, melted and cooled**

CHOCOLATE GINGERBREAD YULE LOG

1. Place egg whites in a large bowl; let stand at room temperature 30 minutes. Preheat oven to 350°. Line bottom of a greased 15x10x1-in. baking pan with parchment paper; grease paper. Sift flour, spices and salt together twice.

2. In a large bowl, beat egg yolks until slightly thickened. Gradually add brown sugar, beating on high speed until thick. Beat in molasses, oil and fresh ginger. Fold in flour mixture (batter will be thick).

3. Add cream of tartar to egg whites; with clean beaters, beat on medium until soft peaks form. Gradually add sugar, 1 tablespoon at a time, beating after each addition until sugar is dissolved. Beat on high until stiff, glossy peaks form. Using a large whisk, fold a fourth of the whites into batter, then fold in remaining whites. Transfer to prepared pan, spreading evenly.

4. Bake 10-12 minutes or until top springs back when lightly touched. Cool 5 minutes. Invert onto a tea towel dusted with cocoa. Gently peel off paper. Roll up cake in towel jelly-roll style. Cool completely on a wire rack.

5. For filling, in a small bowl, mix mascarpone cheese, confectioners' sugar, cream and salt just until blended; stir in ginger. Refrigerate, covered, while preparing bark and buttercream.

6. For bark, line the underside of a 15x10x1-in. baking pan with parchment paper. Using an offset spatula, spread melted chocolate in a thin, even layer on parchment. Refrigerate until set, about 30 minutes.

7. For buttercream, place egg whites, sugar and salt in a heatproof bowl; whisk until blended. Place bowl over simmering water in a large saucepan over medium heat. Whisking constantly, heat mixture until a thermometer reads 160°, about 1-2 minutes.

8. Remove from heat. With the whisk attachment of a hand mixer, beat on high speed until stiff glossy peaks form and mixture has cooled, about 5 minutes. Gradually beat in butter, a few tablespoons at a time, on medium speed until smooth. Beat in cooled chocolate.

9. To assemble, unroll cake; spread filling over cake to within ¼ in. of edges. Roll up again, without towel; trim ends. Transfer to a platter. Spread buttercream over cake.

10. To decorate cake, lift chilled chocolate with fingers and break carefully into shards; arrange over buttercream, overlapping slightly. If chocolate becomes too soft, return to refrigerator as necessary.

11. Refrigerate cake, loosely covered, until serving. Using a serrated knife, cut cake into slices.

PEPPERMINT CHEESECAKE

Peppermint Cheesecake

People are thrilled when they see me coming with this rich, smooth cheesecake..it's always a crowd-pleaser. Not only does it look sensational, it's scrumptious, too!

—CARRIE PRICE OTTAWA, IL

PREP: 40 MIN. • **BAKE:** 1¼ HOURS + CHILLING
MAKES: 16 SERVINGS

- 2½ cups cream-filled chocolate sandwich cookie crumbs
- ⅓ cup butter, melted
- 5 packages (8 ounces each) cream cheese, softened
- 1 cup sugar
- 1 cup (8 ounces) sour cream
- 3 tablespoons all-purpose flour
- 3 teaspoons vanilla extract
- 1 teaspoon peppermint extract
- 3 eggs, lightly beaten
- 1 package (10 ounces) Andes creme de menthe baking chips or 2 packages (4.67 ounces each) mint Andes candies, chopped

TOPPING

- 1 package (8 ounces) cream cheese, softened
- ⅓ cup sugar
- 1 carton (12 ounces) frozen whipped topping, thawed
  Miniature candy canes, optional

1. Preheat oven to 325°. Place a greased 9-in. springform pan on a double thickness of heavy-duty foil (about 18 in. square). Securely wrap foil around the pan.

2. In a small bowl, combine cookie crumbs and butter. Press onto the bottom and 1 in. up the sides of prepared pan. Place pan on a baking sheet. Bake 12-14 minutes or until set. Cool on a wire rack.

3. In a large bowl, beat cream cheese and sugar until smooth. Beat in the sour cream, flour and extracts. Add eggs; beat on low speed just until combined. Fold in the chips. Pour into crust. (Pan will be full.) Place springform pan in a large baking pan; add 1 in. of hot water to larger pan.

4. Bake at 325° 1¼ to 1½ hours or until center is just set and top appears dull. Remove springform pan from water bath. Cool on a wire rack 10 minutes. Carefully run a knife around edge of pan to loosen; cool 1 hour longer. Refrigerate overnight. Remove sides of pan.

5. For topping, in a large bowl, beat cream cheese and sugar until smooth. Stir one-fourth whipped topping into mixture; fold in remaining whipped topping. Spread or pipe onto cheesecake. Garnish with miniature candy canes if desired.

Almond-Filled Stollen

I've been making this during the holiday season for nearly 50 years. When we flew to Alaska one year to spend Christmas with our daughter's family, I even carried this stollen on the plane!

—**RACHEL SEEL** ABBOTSFORD, BC

PREP: 1 HOUR + RISING
BAKE: 30 MIN. + COOLING
MAKES: 3 LOAVES (12 SLICES EACH)

- 1¾ cups chopped mixed candied fruit
- ½ cup plus 2 tablespoons rum, divided
- 2 packages (¼ ounce each) active dry yeast
- ½ cup warm water (110° to 115°)
- 1½ cups warm 2% milk (110° to 115°)
- 1¼ cups butter, softened
- ⅔ cup sugar
- 2½ teaspoons salt
- 2 teaspoons grated lemon peel
- 1 teaspoon almond extract
- 7 to 8 cups all-purpose flour
- 4 eggs
- ⅓ cup slivered almonds
- 1 can (8 ounces) almond paste
- 1 egg yolk
- 2 teaspoons water
- 2 to 2¼ cups confectioners' sugar

1. In a small bowl, combine candied fruits and ½ cup rum; let stand, covered, 1 hour.

2. In a small bowl, dissolve yeast in warm water. In a large bowl, combine milk, butter, sugar, salt, lemon peel, almond extract, remaining rum, yeast mixture and 4 cups flour; beat on medium speed until smooth. Cover with plastic wrap and let stand in a warm place, about 30 minutes.

3. Beat in eggs. Stir in enough remaining flour to form a soft dough (dough will be sticky). Drain candied fruit, reserving rum for glaze. Reserve ½ cup candied fruit for topping. Stir almonds and remaining candied fruit into dough.

4. Turn dough onto a floured surface; knead until smooth and elastic, about 6-8 minutes. Place in a greased bowl, turning once to grease the top. Cover with plastic wrap and let rise in a warm place until doubled, about 1 hour.

5. Punch down dough; divide into three portions. On a greased baking sheet, roll each portion into a 12-in. circle. Crumble one-third of the almond paste over one-half of each circle. Fold dough partially in half, covering filling and placing top layer within 1 in. of bottom edge. Cover with kitchen towels and let rise in a warm place until doubled in size, about 1 hour. Preheat oven to 375°.

6. In a small bowl, whisk egg yolk and water; brush over loaves. Bake 30-35 minutes or until golden brown. Cover loosely with foil if tops brown too quickly. Remove from pans to wire racks to cool completely.

7. In a small bowl, mix reserved rum with enough confectioner's sugar to make a thin glaze. Drizzle over stollen. Sprinkle with reserved candied fruit.

ALMOND-FILLED STOLLEN

PEPPERMINT MELTAWAYS

Peppermint Meltaways

These minty little bites are so pretty and festive-looking on a cookie platter. I often cover a plate with red or green plastic wrap and a bright bow in one corner. And yes, they really do melt in your mouth!
—DENISE WHEELER NEWAYGO, MI

PREP: 30 MIN.
BAKE: 10 MIN./BATCH + COOLING
MAKES: 3½ DOZEN

- 1 **cup butter, softened**
- ½ **cup confectioners' sugar**
- ½ **teaspoon peppermint extract**
- 1¼ **cups all-purpose flour**
- ½ **cup cornstarch**

FROSTING
- 2 **tablespoons butter, softened**
- 1½ **cups confectioners' sugar**
- 2 **tablespoons 2% milk**
- ¼ **teaspoon peppermint extract**
- 2 **to 3 drops red food coloring, optional**
- ½ **cup crushed peppermint candies**

1. Preheat oven to 350°. In a small bowl, cream butter and confectioners' sugar until light and fluffy. Beat in extract. Combine flour and cornstarch; gradually add to creamed mixture and mix well.

2. Shape into 1-in. balls. Place 2 in. apart on ungreased baking sheets. Bake 10-12 minutes or until bottoms are lightly browned. Remove to wire racks to cool.

3. In a small bowl, beat butter until fluffy. Add confectioners' sugar, milk, extract and, if desired, food coloring; beat until smooth. Spread over cooled cookies; sprinkle with crushed candies. Store in an airtight container.

Iced Holiday Ornament Cookies

It wouldn't be Christmas without these sugar cookies. You can bake and decorate them a week before by storing them in a plastic container. Just make sure the icing is dry before you stack and store them. You can use the recipe and seasonal cookie cutters for cute sugar cookies all year long!
—LEA REITER THOUSAND OAKS, CA

PREP: 1 HOUR + CHILLING
BAKE: 10 MIN./BATCH + STANDING
MAKES: 4 DOZEN

- ½ **cup butter, softened**
- ⅔ **cup sugar**
- 1 **egg**
- 3 **tablespoons orange liqueur or orange juice**
- 2¼ **cups all-purpose flour**
- 1 **teaspoon baking powder**
- ½ **teaspoon salt**

ICING
- 3¾ **cups confectioners' sugar**
- ¼ **cup water**
- ¼ **cup orange liqueur or additional water**
- 4 **teaspoons meringue powder**
   Food coloring of your choice
   Ribbon, optional

1. In a large bowl, cream butter and sugar until light and fluffy. Beat in egg and liqueur. Combine the flour, baking powder and salt; gradually add to creamed mixture and mix well. Shape dough into a ball, then flatten into a disk. Wrap in plastic wrap and refrigerate for 1 hour.

2. Preheat oven to 350°. On a lightly floured surface, roll dough to ⅛-in. thickness. Cut with floured 2½-in. ornament-shaped cookie cutters. Place 2 in. apart on greased baking sheets. If hanging cookies, make a hole with a plastic straw about ½ in. from the top of each cookie.

3. Bake 6-8 minutes or until lightly browned. Remove to wire racks to cool completely. Use plastic straw to reopen holes in cookies.

4. For icing, in a bowl, combine the confectioners' sugar, water, liqueur and meringue powder; beat on low speed just until combined. Beat on high 4-5 minutes or until stiff peaks form. Tint with food coloring as desired. (Keep unused icing covered with a damp cloth. Beat again on high speed to restore texture.)

5. Using pastry bags and small round tips, decorate cookies as desired. Let dry at room temperature for several hours or until firm. Thread ribbon through holes if desired. Store in an airtight container.

LEMON CHEESECAKE PIES, PAGE 240

CHICKEN SALAD FOR 50, PAGE 241

BROADWAY BROWNIE BARS, PAGE 242

FEEDING A
CROWD

LARGE-BATCH SLOPPY
JOES, PAGE 249

“ On this mountain the
Lord of hosts will make
for all peoples a feast of rich
food, a feast of well-aged
wines, of rich food filled
with marrow, of well-aged
wines strained clear. ”

ISAIAH 25:6

MAC 'N' CHEESE
FOR A BUNCH

Mac 'n' Cheese for a Bunch

You'll delight lots of people with this rich and comforting dish. Tender macaroni is covered in a creamy, homemade cheese sauce, and then topped with golden bread crumbs. At 36 servings, it's a true crowd-pleaser!
—**DIXIE TERRY** GOREVILLE, IL

PREP: 30 MIN. • **BAKE:** 35 MIN. • **MAKES:** 36 SERVINGS (1 CUP EACH)

- 3 packages (two 16 ounces, one 7 ounces) elbow macaroni
- 1¼ cups butter, divided
- ¾ cup all-purpose flour
- 2 teaspoons salt
- 3 quarts milk
- 3 pounds sharp cheddar cheese, shredded
- 1½ cups dry bread crumbs

1. Cook macaroni according to package directions until almost tender.

2. Preheat oven to 350°. In a large stock pot, melt 1 cup butter. Stir in flour and salt until smooth. Gradually stir in milk. Bring to a boil; cook and stir 2 minutes or until thickened. Reduce heat. Add cheese, stirring until melted. Drain macaroni; stir into sauce.

3. Transfer to three greased 13x9-in. baking dishes. Melt remaining butter; toss with bread crumbs. Sprinkle over casseroles.

4. Bake, uncovered, 35-40 minutes or until golden brown.

Stroganoff for a Crowd

This big-batch dish is perfect for a winter charity event or potluck. Don't expect to have any leftovers of this one!
—**ADA LOWER** MINOT, ND

PREP: 45 MIN. • **COOK:** 30 MIN.
MAKES: 70 SERVINGS (1 CUP EACH)

- 20 pounds ground beef
- 5 large onions, chopped
- 7 cans (26 ounces each) condensed cream of mushroom soup, undiluted
- 3 quarts milk
- ½ cup Worcestershire sauce
- 3 tablespoons garlic powder
- 2 tablespoons salt
- 1 tablespoon pepper
- 1 teaspoon paprika
- 5 pints sour cream
  Hot cooked noodles

1. In several large stockpots, cook beef and onions over medium heat until meat is no longer pink; drain. In several large bowls, combine the soup, milk, Worcestershire sauce, garlic powder, salt, pepper and paprika; add to beef mixture. Bring to a boil. Reduce heat and keep warm.

2. Just before serving, stir in sour cream; heat through but do not boil. Serve with noodles.

CLAM CHOWDER FOR A CROWD

Church Supper Clam Chowder

This chowder is a very popular dish at church camp and family reunions. It has a slightly thinner broth than most chowders but it's still very flavorful.

—**LYNN RICHARDSON** BAUXITE, AR

PREP: 40 MIN. • **COOK:** 30 MIN.
MAKES: 60-65 SERVINGS (1 CUP EACH)

- 10 **quarts water**
- 3 **tablespoons salt**
- 8 **pounds red potatoes, peeled and cubed**
- 6 **large onions, chopped**
- 1 **cup butter, cubed**
- 4 **large carrots, grated**
- 16 **cans (6½ ounces each) chopped clams**
- 3 **cans (12 ounces each) evaporated milk**
- ½ **cup minced fresh parsley**
- 1 **to 2 tablespoons pepper**
- 2 **pounds bacon strips, cooked and crumbled**

1. In two stockpots, bring water and salt to a boil. Carefully add potatoes; cook until tender (do not drain). In another large pan, saute onions in butter until tender. Add onions and carrots to potato mixture; heat through.

2. Drain clams if desired. Add the clams, milk, parsley and pepper to vegetable mixture; heat through. Just before serving, stir in bacon.

TOP TIP

Clamoring for Clam Chowder

Instead of a chili cook-off or spaghetti dinner, consider raising funds with a clam chowder night. Use the recipe above and round out the menu with corn on the cob and biscuits. Ask patrons to contribute a few desserts.

Lemon Cheesecake Pies

I've been making these scrumptious pies for at least 50 years. There's little cleanup, and everyone seems to love the fluffy lemon filling.

—**LORRAINE FOSS** PUYALLUP, WA

PREP: 30 MIN. + CHILLING
MAKES: 4 PIES (8 SLICES EACH)

- 1 can (12 ounces) evaporated milk
- 2 packages (3 ounces each) lemon gelatin
- 2 cups boiling water
- 1 package (8 ounces) cream cheese, cubed
- 1 tablespoon lemon juice
- 1 cup sugar
- 4 graham cracker crusts (9 inches)

TOPPING
- 1 cup graham cracker crumbs
- ¼ cup butter, melted
- 2 tablespoons sugar

1. Pour milk into a large metal bowl; cover and refrigerate for at least 2 hours.
2. In a large bowl, dissolve gelatin in boiling water. Cool for 10 minutes. Add cream cheese and lemon juice; beat until blended. Set aside.
3. Beat chilled milk until soft peaks form. Gradually add sugar. Beat in gelatin mixture. Pour into crusts.
4. Combine topping ingredients; sprinkle over pies. Refrigerate for 4 hours or until set.

Stew for a Crowd

Need a no-fuss feast to feed a crowd? With lots of meat and vegetables, this big-batch stew is sure to satisfy.

—**MIKE MARRATZO** FLORENCE, AL

PREP: 1 HOUR • **COOK:** 3 HOURS
MAKES: 120 (1-CUP) SERVINGS

- 25 pounds beef stew meat
- 5 pounds onions, diced (about 16 cups)
- 2 bunches celery, cut into 1-in. pieces (about 14 cups)
  About 5 quarts water
- ½ cup browning sauce, optional
- ¼ cup salt
- 3 tablespoons garlic powder
- 3 tablespoons dried thyme
- 3 tablespoons seasoned salt
- 2 tablespoons pepper
- 12 bay leaves
- 15 pounds red potatoes, cut into 1-in. cubes (about 16 cups)
- 10 pounds carrots, cut into 1-in. pieces (about 24 cups)
- 10 cups frozen peas
- 10 cups frozen corn
- 4 cups all-purpose flour
- 3 to 4 cups milk

1. Divide stew meat, onions and celery among several large Dutch ovens or stockpots. Add water to fill pans half full. Add browning sauce if desired and seasonings.
2. Bring to a boil. Reduce heat; cover and simmer 1½ hours or until the meat is tender. Add the potatoes and carrots; bring to a boil. Reduce heat; cover and simmer 30 minutes or until the vegetables are tender.
3. Add the peas and corn; bring to a boil. Reduce heat; simmer, uncovered, 15 minutes or until heated through.
4. Combine flour and enough milk to achieve a creamy, smooth paste; gradually add to the stew. Bring to a boil. Cook and stir 2 minutes or until thickened. Discard bay leaves.

STEW FOR
A CROWD

CHICKEN SALAD FOR 50

Chicken Salad for 50

When I brought my chicken salad to a women's luncheon, there were lots of recipe requests. I think the creamy dressing, grapes and cashews make it extra special.

—FLORENCE VOLD STORY CITY, IA

PREP: 40 MIN. + CHILLING
MAKES: 50 SERVINGS (1 CUP EACH)

- 9 **cups cubed cooked chicken**
- 9 **cups cooked small pasta shells**
- 8 **cups chopped celery**
- 8 **cups seedless green grapes halves**
- 18 **hard-cooked eggs, chopped**
- 2 **cans (20 ounces each) pineapple tidbits, drained**

DRESSING
- 4 **cups mayonnaise**
- 2 **cups (16 ounces) sour cream**
- 2 **cups whipped topping**
- ¼ **cup lemon juice**
- ¼ **cup sugar**
- 1½ **teaspoons salt**
- 2 **cups cashew halves**

In two large bowls, combine the first six ingredients. In another large bowl, whisk the first six dressing ingredients. Pour over the chicken mixture; toss to coat. Cover and refrigerate for at least 1 hour. Stir in the cashews just before serving.

Cheese Rye Appetizers

I enjoy serving this hors d'oeuvre at family gatherings. It can be mixed ahead of time, refrigerated and then spread on bread and baked at the last minute. Even kids like it!

—JOYCE DYKSTRA LANSING, IL

PREP: 20 MIN. • **BAKE:** 10 MIN./BATCH
MAKES: 2½ DOZEN

- 2 **cups (8 ounces) shredded Swiss cheese**
- 1 **cup mayonnaise**
- 1 **can (4¼ ounces) chopped ripe olives**
- 4 **bacon strips, cooked and crumbled**
- ¼ **cup chopped green onions**
- 1½ **teaspoons minced fresh parsley or ½ teaspoon dried parsley flakes**
- 30 **slices snack rye bread**

Preheat oven to 450°. In a small bowl, combine the first six ingredients. Spread a rounded tablespoonful over each slice of bread. Place on an ungreased baking sheet. Bake 6-8 minutes or until cheese is melted.

Crowd-Pleasing Potato Salad

With creamy chunks of potato and crunchy bits of veggies, this classic potato salad will gain rave reviews from your gang. It's perfect for the last big gathering of summer.

—DIXIE TERRY GOREVILLE, IL

PREP: 1¾ HOURS + CHILLING
MAKES: 50 SERVINGS (¾ CUP EACH)

- 15 **pounds potatoes, peeled and cubed**
- 4 **cups mayonnaise**
- 1 **cup sweet pickle relish**
- ¼ **cup prepared mustard**
- 1 **jar (4 ounces) diced pimientos, drained**
- 2 **tablespoons salt**
- 1 **tablespoon sugar**
- 2 **teaspoons pepper**
- 6 **celery ribs, chopped**
- 8 **hard-cooked eggs, chopped**
- 1 **small onion, chopped**
  Paprika and green pepper rings, optional

1. Place potatoes in two stockpots and cover with water. Bring to a boil. Reduce heat; cover and simmer for 10-15 minutes or until tender. Drain and cool to room temperature.

2. In a large bowl, combine the mayonnaise, relish, mustard, pimientos, salt, sugar and pepper.

3. Divide the potatoes, celery, eggs and onion between two very large bowls; add mayonnaise mixture. Stir to combine.

4. Cover and refrigerate for at least 1 hour. Garnish with paprika and green pepper rings if desired.

BROADWAY BROWNIE BARS

Broadway Brownie Bars

I named these brownies after Broadway because they're a hit every time I serve them! I especially like to make these for the holidays or for hostess gifts.

—ANNE FREDERICK NEW HARTFORD, NY

PREP: 20 MIN. + CHILLING • **BAKE:** 30 MIN. • **MAKES:** 2½ DOZEN

FILLING
- 6 **ounces cream cheese, softened**
- ½ **cup sugar**
- ¼ **cup butter, softened**
- 2 **tablespoons all-purpose flour**
- 1 **egg, lightly beaten**
- ½ **teaspoon vanilla extract**

BROWNIE
- ½ **cup butter, cubed**
- 1 **ounce unsweetened chocolate**
- 2 **eggs, lightly beaten**
- 1 **teaspoon vanilla extract**
- 1 **cup sugar**
- 1 **cup all-purpose flour**
- 1 **teaspoon baking powder**
- 1 **cup chopped walnuts**

TOPPING
- 1 **cup (6 ounces) semisweet chocolate chips**
- ¼ **cup chopped walnuts**
- 2 **cups miniature marshmallows**

FROSTING
- ¼ **cup butter**
- ¼ **cup milk**
- 2 **ounces cream cheese**
- 1 **ounce unsweetened chocolate**
- 3 **cups confectioners' sugar**
- 1 **teaspoon vanilla extract**

1. Preheat oven to 350°. In small bowl, combine first six ingredients until smooth; set aside.

2. In a large saucepan over medium heat, melt butter and chocolate. Remove from heat and cool. Stir in eggs and vanilla. Add sugar, flour, baking powder and nuts, stirring until blended.

3. Spread batter in a 13x9-in. baking pan coated with cooking spray. Spread filling over batter. For topping, in small bowl, combine chocolate chips and nuts; sprinkle over filling.

4. Bake 28 minutes or until almost set. Sprinkle with marshmallows; bake 2 minutes longer.

5. For frosting, in a large saucepan, heat butter, milk, cream cheese and chocolate until melted; stirring until smooth. Remove from heat; stir in confectioners' sugar and vanilla. Immediately drizzle over marshmallows. Chill well; cut into bars.

Hot Turkey Sandwiches

If you're looking for a deliciously different potluck entree, try these turkey sandwiches. This version features tender shredded turkey in a basil cream sauce. It's a nice change of pace from turkey in traditional gravy.

—**JANICE BILEK** HOLLAND, MI

PREP: 15 MIN. • **BAKE:** 2 HOURS + STANDING • **MAKES:** 50 SERVINGS

- **3 bone-in turkey breasts (6 to 7 pounds each)**
- **3 cups sliced fresh mushrooms**
- **3 cups thinly sliced green onions**
- **1½ cups butter, cubed**
- **¾ cup all-purpose flour**
- **3 to 4 tablespoons dried basil**
- **3 teaspoons salt**
- **1 teaspoon pepper**
- **6 cups chicken broth**
- **3 cups heavy whipping cream**
- **50 sandwich rolls, split**

1. Preheat oven to 325°. Place turkey on racks in roasting pans. Bake, uncovered, 2 hours or until a meat thermometer reads 170°, basting several times with pan drippings. Cover and let stand 10 minutes. Shred the turkey.

2. In several Dutch ovens or large pans, saute mushrooms and onion in butter until tender. Stir in flour, basil, salt and pepper until blended. Gradually stir in broth. Bring to a boil; cook and stir 2 minutes or until thickened and bubbly. Add the turkey and heat through. Stir in cream; cook until heated through. Spoon ½ cup onto each roll.

FREEZE IT

French Canadian Tourtieres

Each fall, my sister and I make 20 of these savory pies to use at Christmas or to freeze for unexpected company.

—**PAT MENEE** CARBERRY, MB

PREP: 45 MIN. • **BAKE:** 40 MIN. • **MAKES:** 4 PIES (8 SERVINGS EACH)

- **4 celery ribs**
- **4 medium carrots**
- **2 large onions**
- **2 garlic cloves, peeled**
- **4 pounds ground pork**
- **2 pounds ground veal**
- **2 pounds bulk pork sausage**
- **1 can (14½ ounces) chicken broth**
- **½ cup minced fresh parsley**
- **1 tablespoon salt**
- **1 teaspoon pepper**
- **1 teaspoon dried basil**
- **1 teaspoon dried rosemary, crushed**
- **1 teaspoon cayenne pepper**
- **1 teaspoon ground mace**
- **1 teaspoon ground cloves**
- **1 cup dry bread crumbs**
- **Pastry for four double-crust pies (9 inches)**

1. Coarsely chop the celery, carrots and onions; place in a food processor with garlic. Cover and process until finely chopped; set aside.

2. In a stockpot or two Dutch ovens, cook vegetables, pork, veal and sausage until meat is no longer pink; drain. Stir in broth, parsley and seasonings. Reduce heat; cover and cook on low 20 minutes. Stir in bread crumbs.

3. Preheat oven to 400°. Line four 9-in. pie plates with bottom crusts; trim pastry even with edges. Fill each with about 4 cups filling. Roll out remaining pastry to fit tops of pies; place over filling. Trim, seal and flute edges. Cut slits in pastry.

4. Cover edges of remaining pies loosely with foil. Bake for 25 minutes. Reduce heat to 350°; remove foil and bake 15-20 minutes longer or until crusts are golden brown.

FREEZE OPTION *Cover and freeze unbaked pies. To use, remove from freezer 30 minutes before baking (do not thaw). Preheat oven to 400°. Place pie on a baking sheet; cover edge loosely with foil. Bake 25 minutes. Reduce heat to 350°; remove foil and bake 50-60 minutes longer or until crusts are golden brown and a thermometer inserted in center reads 165°.*

FRENCH CANADIAN TOURTIERES

Danish Coffee Cakes

I think that as long as I'm in the kitchen baking, I might as well make enough to share. This traditional recipe gives me three cheese-filled coffee cakes drizzled with a sweet vanilla icing.

—SHERI KRATCHA AVOCA, WI

PREP: 45 MIN. + CHILLING • **BAKE:** 20 MIN. + COOLING
MAKES: 3 COFFEE CAKES (10 SLICES EACH)

- 1   package (¼ ounce) active dry yeast
- ¼   cup warm water (110° to 115°)
- 4   cups all-purpose flour
- ¼   cup sugar
- 1   teaspoon salt
- 1   cup shortening
- 1   cup warm 2% milk (110° to 115°)
- 2   eggs, lightly beaten

FILLING
- 1   package (8 ounces) cream cheese, softened
- ¾   cup sugar
- 2   tablespoons all-purpose flour
- 1   egg, lightly beaten
- 1   teaspoon poppy seeds
- 1   teaspoon vanilla extract
- ½   teaspoon lemon extract

ICING
- 1   cup confectioners' sugar
- 2   tablespoons milk
- ⅛   teaspoon vanilla extract

1. In a small bowl, dissolve yeast in warm water. In a large bowl, combine the flour, sugar and salt; cut in shortening until crumbly. Add the yeast mixture, milk and eggs; beat until smooth (dough will be soft). Do not knead. Cover and refrigerate overnight.
2. In a small bowl, beat the cream cheese, sugar and flour until smooth. Add egg, poppy seeds and extracts; mix until blended.
3. Punch dough down. Turn onto a well-floured surface; divide into thirds. Return two portions to the refrigerator. Roll remaining portion into a 14x8-in. rectangle; place on a parchment-lined baking sheet. Spread a third of the filling down center of rectangle.
4. On each long side, cut ¾-in.-wide strips about 2¼ in. into the center. Starting at one end, fold alternating strips at an angle across filling. Pinch ends to seal. Repeat with remaining dough and filling. Cover and let rise in a warm place until doubled, about 45 minutes.
5. Preheat oven to 350°. Bake 20-25 minutes or until golden brown. Cool on pans on wire racks. Combine icing ingredients; drizzle over coffee cakes.

Old-Fashioned Brown Bread

Here's a chewy, old-fashioned favorite with a slightly sweet flavor. It'll take you back to a simpler time.

—PATRICIA DONNELLY KINGS LANDING, NB

PREP: 20 MIN. + RISING • **BAKE:** 35 MIN. + COOLING
MAKES: 2 LOAVES (16 SLICES EACH)

- 2⅓   cups boiling water
- 1   cup old-fashioned oats
- ½   cup butter, cubed
- ⅓   cup molasses
- 5½ to 6½ cups all-purpose flour
- 5   teaspoons active dry yeast
- 2   teaspoons salt

1. In a large bowl, pour boiling water over oats. Stir in butter and molasses. Let stand until mixture cools to 120°-130°, stirring occasionally.
2. In another bowl, combine 3½ cups flour, yeast and salt. Beat in oat mixture until blended. Stir in enough remaining flour to form a soft dough.
3. Turn onto a floured surface; knead until smooth and elastic, about 6-8 minutes. Place in a greased bowl, turning once to grease the top. Cover and let rise in a warm place until doubled, about 1 hour.
4. Punch dough down. Turn onto a lightly floured surface; divide in half. Shape into loaves. Place in two greased 9x5-in. loaf pans. Cover and let rise until doubled, about 30 minutes.
5. Meanwhile, preheat oven to 375°. Bake 35-40 minutes or until golden brown. Remove from pans to wire racks to cool.

DANISH COFFEE CAKES

Crab Salad Tea Sandwiches

I make these delightful sandwiches for special occasions. I received the recipe from a friend who served them at her daughter's wedding.

—**EDIE DESPAIN** LOGAN, UT

PREP: 1 HOUR • **MAKES:** 4 DOZEN

- 4 **celery ribs, finely chopped**
- 2 **cups reduced-fat mayonnaise**
- 4 **green onions, chopped**
- ¼ **cup lime juice**
- ¼ **cup chili sauce**
- ½ **teaspoon seasoned salt**
- 8 **cups cooked fresh or canned crabmeat**
- 6 **hard-cooked eggs, chopped**
- 48 **slices whole wheat bread**
- ½ **cup butter, softened**
- 48 **lettuce leaves**
- ½ **teaspoon paprika**
  Green onions, cut into thin strips, optional

1. In a large bowl, combine the first six ingredients; gently stir in crab and eggs. Refrigerate.

2. With a 3-in. round cookie cutter, cut a circle from each slice of bread. Spread each with ½ teaspoon butter. Top with lettuce and 2 rounded tablespoonfuls of crab salad; sprinkle with paprika. Garnish with onion strips if desired.

Smoked Sausage Appetizers

A savory-sweet sauce with a touch of currant jelly glazes these yummy little sausages. They make a great appetizer, and both kids and adults seem to love them.

—**KATHRYN BAINBRIDGE**
PENNSYLVANIA FURNACE, PA

START TO FINISH: 25 MIN.
MAKES: 8 DOZEN

- ¾ **cup red currant jelly**
- ¾ **cup barbecue sauce**
- 3 **tablespoons prepared mustard**
- 2 **packages (1 pound each) miniature smoked sausages, drained**

1. In a large saucepan, combine the jelly, barbecue sauce and mustard. Cook, uncovered, over medium heat, for 15-20 minutes or until jelly is melted and mixture is smooth, stirring occasionally.

2. Add sausages; stir to coat. Cover and cook 5-6 minutes longer or until heated through, stirring occasionally. Serve with toothpicks.

Pepperoni Pizza Spread

Loaded with popular pizza flavors, this cheesy concoction comes together in minutes.

—**CONNIE MILINOVICH** CUDAHY, WI

PREP: 10 MIN. • **BAKE:** 25 MIN.
MAKES: 6 CUPS

- 2 **cups (8 ounces) shredded part-skim mozzarella cheese**
- 2 **cups (8 ounces) shredded cheddar cheese**
- 1 **cup mayonnaise**
- 1 **cup chopped pimiento-stuffed olives**
- 1 **cup chopped pepperoni**
- 1 **can (6 ounces) ripe olives, drained and chopped**
- 1 **can (4 ounces) mushroom stems and pieces, drained and chopped**
- ½ **cup chopped onion**
- ½ **cup chopped green pepper**
  Crackers, breadsticks and/or French bread

Preheat oven to 350°. In a large bowl, combine the first nine ingredients. Transfer to an 11x7-in. baking dish. Bake, uncovered, 25-30 minutes or until edges are bubbly and lightly browned. Serve with crackers, breadsticks and/or French bread.

SMOKED SAUSAGE APPETIZERS

MEAT LOAF FOR A MOB

Meat Loaf for a Mob

Our small synagogue has two teams that alternate with churches of various denominations and civic organizations to provide meals at a homeless shelter. This tasty satisfying meat loaf is always well received.

—NIKI REESE ESCHEN
SANTA MARIS, CA

PREP: 20 MIN. • **BAKE:** 1 HOUR
MAKES: 4 MEAT LOAVES

- 8 **eggs, lightly beaten**
- 1 **can (46 ounces) V8 juice**
- 2 **large onions, finely chopped**
- 4 **celery ribs, finely chopped**
- 4¼ **cups seasoned bread crumbs**
- 2 **envelopes onion soup mix**
- 2 **teaspoons pepper**
- 8 **pounds ground beef**
- ¾ **cup ketchup**
- ⅓ **cup packed brown sugar**
- ¼ **cup prepared mustard**

1. Preheat oven to 350°. In a very large bowl, combine the eggs, V8 juice, onions, celery, bread crumbs, soup mix and pepper. Crumble beef over mixture and mix well,

2. Shape into four loaves; place each loaf in a greased 13x9-in. baking dish. Bake, uncovered, 45 minutes.
3. Meanwhile, combine ketchup, brown sugar and mustard. Spread over loaves. Bake 15 minutes longer until no pink remains and a meat thermometer reads 160°.

Hearty Beef Soup

This quick-to-fix soup feeds a lot of hungry people. The tender sirloin pieces and diced veggies make a satisfying meal.

—MARCIA SEVERSON HALLOCK, MN

PREP: 1 HOUR • **COOK:** 40 MIN.
MAKES: 32 SERVINGS (8 QUARTS)

- 4 **pounds beef top sirloin steak, cut into ½-inch cubes**
- 4 **cups chopped onions**
- ¼ **cup butter**
- 4 **quarts hot water**
- 4 **cups sliced carrots**
- 4 **cups cubed peeled potatoes**
- 2 **cups chopped cabbage**
- 1 **cup chopped celery**
- 1 **large green pepper, chopped**
- 8 **teaspoons beef bouillon granules**
- 1 **tablespoon seasoned salt**
- 1 **teaspoon dried basil**
- 1 **teaspoon pepper**
- 4 **bay leaves**
- 6 **cups tomato juice**

1. In two Dutch ovens, brown beef and onions in butter in batches; drain. Add the water, vegetables and seasonings; bring to a boil. Reduce heat; cover and simmer for 20 minutes.
2. Add tomato juice; cover and simmer 10 minutes longer or until the beef and vegetables are tender. Discard bay leaves.

8-Pie Pecan Pie

Honey gives these pies a uniquely delicious flavor. I sometimes add chocolate for a special twist.

—LOUISE COVINGTON
BENNETTSVILLE, SC

PREP: 15 MIN. • **BAKE:** 40 MIN. + COOLING
MAKES: 8 PIES (8 SERVINGS EACH)

- 12 **eggs, lightly beaten**
- 1 **cup dark brown sugar**
- 5 **cups sugar**
- 2 **cups dark corn syrup**
- 1⅓ **cups honey**
- 1 **cup butter, melted**
- 3 **tablespoons vanilla extract**
- 12 to 15 **cups chopped pecans**
- 8 **unbaked pastry shells (9 inches)**

1. Preheat oven to 300°. In large bowls, combine the first seven ingredients. Add pecans. Pour 2¼ cups filling into each pastry shell.
2. Bake 40-50 minutes or until set (cover edges with foil during the last 15 minutes to prevent overbrowning if necessary). Cool on a wire rack. Refrigerate leftovers.
NOTE *To make chocolate pecan pies, melt 3 cups semisweet chocolate chips and add to the batter before adding pecans.*

COFFEE-GLAZED DOUGHNUTS

Coffee-Glazed Doughnuts

No one will guess that you included potatoes in this big-batch recipe. The doughnuts are ideal for coffee socials and charity breakfasts.

—**PAT SIEBENALER** RANDOM LAKE, WI

PREP: 25 MIN. + RISING • **COOK:** 5 MIN./BATCH
MAKES: ABOUT 4 DOZEN

- 2 packages (¼ ounce each) active dry yeast
- ¼ cup warm water (110° to 115°)
- 2 cups warm 2% milk (110° to 115°)
- ½ cup butter, softened
- 1 cup hot mashed potatoes (without added milk and butter)
- 3 eggs
- ½ teaspoon lemon extract, optional
- 1 cup sugar
- 1½ teaspoons salt
- ½ teaspoon ground cinnamon
- 9¼ to 9¾ cups all-purpose flour

COFFEE GLAZE

- 6 to 8 tablespoons cold 2% milk
- 1 tablespoon instant coffee granules
- 2 teaspoons vanilla extract
- ¾ cup butter, softened
- 6 cups confectioners' sugar
- ½ teaspoon ground cinnamon
  Dash salt
  Oil for deep-fat frying

1. In a large bowl, dissolve yeast in warm water. Add milk, butter, potatoes, eggs and, if desired, extract. Add sugar, salt, cinnamon and 3 cups flour. Beat until smooth. Stir in enough remaining flour to form a soft dough. Cover and let rise in a warm place until doubled, about 1 hour.

2. Stir down dough. On a well-floured surface, roll out to ½-in. thickness. Cut with a floured 2½-in. doughnut cutter. Place on greased baking sheets; cover and let rise for 45 minutes.

3. Meanwhile, for glaze, combine 6 tablespoons milk, coffee and vanilla; stir to dissolve coffee. In a large bowl, beat butter, sugar, cinnamon and salt. Gradually add milk mixture; beat until smooth, adding additional milk to make a dipping consistency.

4. In an electric skillet or deep-fat fryer, heat oil to 375°. Fry doughnuts, a few at a time, about 1½ minutes per side or until golden. Drain on paper towels. Dip tops in glaze while warm.

100-Cup Bean Soup

When I was a cook in the service, I learned all I could from the cooks alongside me. This soup was a favorite, and it yields enough to serve an extremely large crowd.

—**JENE CAIN** NORTHRIDGE, CA

PREP: 10 MIN. • **COOK:** 2 HOURS 40 MIN.
MAKES: 100 SERVINGS (6¼ GALLONS)

- 6 cans (15 ounces each) white kidney or cannellini beans, rinsed and drained
- 8 meaty ham bones
- 7 gallons ham or chicken stock
- 4½ cups finely chopped onions (about 2 pounds)
- 2¾ cups shredded carrots (about 1 pound)
- 2 teaspoons pepper
- 2 cups all-purpose flour
- 3 cups cold water

1. Place the beans and ham bones in a large stockpot; add ham stock. Bring to a boil. Reduce heat; cover and simmer for 1 to 1½ hours or until the beans are tender.

2. Stir in the onions, carrots and pepper; cover and simmer for 30 minutes or until vegetables are tender. Combine flour and water until smooth; gradually stir into soup. Cook for 10 minutes or until thickened, stirring occasionally. If too thick, add additional water.

LARGE-BATCH SLOPPY JOES

Large-Batch Sloppy Joes

My husband and I raised 3 boys, and they had great appetites. I always cooked and baked huge amounts of everything!

—WANIETA PENNER MCPHERSON, KS

PREP: 20 MIN. • **COOK:** 1½ HOURS • **MAKES:** 96 SERVINGS

- 15 **pounds ground beef**
- 6 **medium onions, chopped**
- 1 **gallon ketchup**
- ¾ **cup Worcestershire sauce**
- ½ **cup packed brown sugar**
- ½ **cup prepared yellow mustard**
- ¼ **cup white vinegar**
- 1 **tablespoon chili powder**
- 96 **hamburger buns, split**

1. In two stockpots over medium heat, cook and stir beef and onions until meat is no longer pink; drain.

2. Stir in the ketchup, Worcestershire sauce, brown sugar, mustard, vinegar and chili powder. Bring to a boil. Reduce heat; simmer, uncovered, for 1 hour to allow flavors to blend. Spoon ⅓ cup onto each bun.

Melon and Grape Salad

Fruit salad is a nice way to round out a potluck. This one—with an easy-to-prepare refreshing citrus dressing—makes a nice addition to any get-together with lots of hungry folks.

—MARY ETTA BURAN OLMSTED TOWNSHIP, OH

PREP: 20 MIN. + CHILLING
MAKES: 50-54 SERVINGS (ABOUT 1 CUP EACH)

- 1 **medium-large watermelon, cut into cubes or balls**
- 3 **honeydew melons, cut into cubes orballs**
- 3 **cantaloupe melons, cut into cubes or balls**
- 1½ **pounds seedless green grapes**
- 1½ **pounds seedless red grapes**
- 3 **cups sugar**
- ⅓ **cup lemon juice**
- ⅓ **cup lime juice**
- ⅓ **cup orange juice**

Combine melons and grapes. Combine sugar and juices; our over fruit and toss to coat. Cover and chill for 1 hour. Serve with a slotted spoon.